Norman S. Grabo
English Department
Texas A & M University
College Station, TX 1982

REFERENCE GUIDES IN LITERATURE
NUMBER 6
Joseph Katz, *Consulting Editor*

Washington Irving:
A Reference Guide

Haskell Springer

G. K. HALL & CO., 70 LINCOLN STREET, BOSTON, MASS.

Copyright © 1976 by Haskell Springer

Library of Congress Cataloging in Publication Data

Springer, Haskell S
   Washington Irving : a reference guide.

   (Reference guides in literature ; no. 6)
   Includes index.
   1. Irving, Washington, 1783–1859—Bibliography.
Z8439.7.S65 [PS2081]   016.818'2'09   76–2489
ISBN 0–8161–1101–4

Contents

Preface... vii

Chronological List of Works.. xi

Writings About Washington Irving, 1807–1974......................... 1

Author/Title Index.. 161

Preface

This bibliographical reference guide annotates scholarship, criticism, reviews, and miscellaneous commentary on Washington Irving and his works, published between 1807 and 1974.* Though it includes entries which appear in no other bibliographical lists, it does not intend to be definitive. Some of Irving's books were so popular that when they first appeared virtually every British and American journal and newspaper which gave some attention to belles lettres reviewed them or at least noted their publication. Innumerable items of "literary intelligence" concerning Irving's travels, his reported composition of new works, and various details of his personal and public life, are to be found in American, British, and Continental periodicals. In addition, interest in Irving's books stimulated interest in his home, his relatives, and all sorts of other, tangential matters. Obviously, inclusion of these brief notes and popular effusions would needlessly clutter a reference guide. Consequently, hundreds of items examined were excluded because of brevity, triviality, or marginal significance. And, no doubt, some few items do not appear here because I have overlooked or inadvertently excluded them.

Other standards of inclusion and exclusion are as follows: Books and articles on other subjects, other writers, are annotated here only if the references in them to Irving are substantial. Not only is Irving briefly mentioned in uncounted books on other authors, but he is also included in the great number of books which, during the last one hundred years, have appeared under titles such as Our Literary Heritage, New World Authors, Fiction in America, etc. Most of these general commentaries, directed to a mass audience, are, for obvious reasons, not included, nor are M. A. theses, encyclopedia entries, or comments in the modern, standard literary histories. Primary works by Irving are cited when they are accompanied by significant editorial apparatus or criticism. Such items are cited as "Shorter Writings," since the secondary material alone is of concern here. (As a procedural matter, items included under "A. Books" are limited to long studies; brief pamphlets, though separately

---

*The annotations were completed in February 1975, before the appearance of the MLA International Bibliography for 1973.

bound, are listed under "B. Shorter Writings.") Reprinted books and
articles are also often noted, not only to give a valid picture of
interest in Irving over the years, but because the original appear-
ances are often difficult to locate and examine. Because this is not
intended as a bibliography, however, not all reappearances of an item
are cited for the record. The reader's access to information, rather
than bibliographical definitiveness, has been the key consideration
in compiling this book. Consequently, for example, where several authors are treated under one general heading in an omnibus article, my
entry specifies the pagination for the Irving material itself, there-
by preventing the reader from being misled into thinking that the
comment on Irving is much longer than it is.

For the sake of accuracy and usefulness, every item in this reference guide has been examined, except for those preceded by an as-
terisk. In those cases, searches proved futile or impractical, or,
occasionally, the original citation was so fragmentary that not
enough information was available on which to base an adequate search.
Such unlocatable items sometimes conclude with the note "[incomplete
data]," informing the reader that he is being given all the information available. Some few items, for various reasons, remained fugi-
tive, although bibliographically complete. These are marked "Unobtainable." In any case, I give the sources of my citation in all
such instances. Also for the sake of accuracy I distinguish between
an item on which the author's name appears, and an unsigned item
which is credited to a particular writer by my source. In this lat-
ter case I cite the author's name in square brackets.

So much for the mechanics of the entries themselves. The long
and detailed index to this volume makes the entries as accessible as
possible. All substantial writings (but not mere brief mentions) on
Irving's works are cited under Irving's titles, including his most
significant short stories and sketches. Several of his books appeared
under more than one title, and they are listed here under the one
judged most commonly used today. See the list on p. xi.

Selected subject headings in the index point to matters of particular interest over the years. Discussions of Irving's sources,
his influence on literature and culture, his use of folklore, his
treatment of Indians, women, Blacks, his reception abroad, his home
(Sunnyside), and many key people in his life, can be pursued through
the index, as can, of course, such traditional areas of scholarship
as biography, bibliography, and textual study. "Irving, Washington,
Poetry" cites treatments of the scattered poems he wrote, and "Short
Story" includes only those secondary works which specifically con-
sider Irving as a writer in that genre, not critical or scholarly
treatments of works which happen to be short stories.

To look at the number of items listed under "Biographical Contributions," "Biography, brief," and "Biography, full-length," is to
realize that Irving the man has been, for many observers, even more

PREFACE

interesting than Irving the writer. He was deeply admired, even loved, by his contemporaries; testimonials to the "sweetness" of his personality are everywhere. That, perhaps, does not impress us as much as it should, though we do treat with respect the fact that during his lifetime, if one was literate, one had read Irving. And though "Irving" is not now among the greatest names in American literature, it is still one of the best known; it continues to attract scholars and critics. Loved in his day, respected in ours--Irving will no doubt continue to command attention in the foreseeable future.

I would like to acknowledge the research help I received from Sandra Eiges, Jan Moore, and especially G. Edward Veith who helped me see the manuscript through its final stages. I am also indebted to the University of Kansas General Research Fund and Graduate Research Fund for financial assistance.

Chronological List of Works

Salmagundi, 1807-08
A History of New York, 1809
Life of Thomas Campbell, 1810
Biography of James Lawrence, 1813
The Sketch Book, 1819-20
Bracebridge Hall, 1822
Tales of a Traveller, 1824
Letters of Jonathan Oldstyle, 1824
The Life and Voyages of Christopher Columbus, 1828
A Chronicle of the Conquest of Granada, 1829
Voyages and Discoveries of the Companions of Columbus, 1831
The Alhambra, 1832
The Crayon Miscellany, 1835
    1. A Tour on the Prairies
    2. Abbotsford and Newstead Abbey
    3. Legends of the Conquest of Spain
Astoria, 1836
Adventures of Captain Bonneville, 1837
Biography & Poetical Remains of the Late Margaret M. Davidson, 1841
The Life of Oliver Goldsmith, 1849
A Book of the Hudson, 1849
Mahomet and His Successors, 1850
Life of George Washington, 1855-59
Wolfert's Roost, 1855
Spanish Papers and Other Miscellanies, 1866
Abu Hassan, 1924
The Wild Huntsman, 1924
An Unwritten Drama of Lord Byron, 1925 (1836)

[Plus other miscellaneous pieces]

Writings About Washington Irving, 1807 - 1974

1807 A   BOOKS - NONE

1807 B   SHORTER WRITINGS

   1   ANON. "Satirical." Port Folio, III (16 May 1807), 307-308.
Praise of the wit and taste of Salmagundi. Reprints one
of the Mustapha letters and says that it successfully emu-
lates the style of Goldsmith's Citizen of the World.

   2   ANON. Review of Salmagundi. Monthly Register, Magazine and
Review of the United States, III (August 1807), 149-56.
Salmagundi is brilliant satire, "on the same height of ex-
cellence with the effusions of Rabelais, of Swift, of Addison, and Voltaire." Wit, though, is by nature superficial. The authors exhibit "far higher powers," and it would
be well to see them in a more serious mood. Their grammat-
ical inaccuracies and occasional profanity are objectionable.

1810 A   BOOKS - NONE

1810 B   SHORTER WRITINGS

   1   ANON. Review of A History of New York. Monthly Anthology
and Boston Review, VIII (February 1810), 123-28.
The wittiest book ever produced in America. It combines
witty history with good-natured satire on contemporary
faults and follies.

1811 A   BOOKS - NONE

1811 B   SHORTER WRITINGS

   1   ANON. Review of Salmagundi. Monthly Review, LXV (August
1811), 418-24.
"The broad humor of a Smollett is here heightened into
absolute caricature, in too many instances. . . . This
overshooting of the mark is a true test of the young and
inexperienced archer. Yet some good hits are discover-
able. . . ." The work is interesting as an example of

1811

(ANON.)
American literature. It is marred by provincialisms and
some errors. TThe authors should take Addison and Johnson
as their models.

2   LAMBERT, JOHN. "Introduction," Salmagundi. London: J. M.
Richardson, 1811, pp. v-liv.
Favorably evaluates the state of American literature and
culture in general, and praises Salmagundi's style, subjects, and wit in detail.

1812 A   BOOKS - NONE

1812 B   SHORTER WRITINGS

1   Σ. "Knickerbocker's Newyork [sic]." Port Folio, 3rd Ser.,
VIII (October 1812), 344-45.
Tongue-in-cheek commentary on Diedrich Knickerbocker as
an author, which, in effect, is high praise of A History
of New York for its style, humor, and originality.

1819 A   BOOKS - NONE

1819 B   SHORTER WRITINGS

1   ANON. Review of The Sketch Book. Analectic Magazine, XIV
(July 1819), 78-79.
Glowing description of the first number of The Sketch Book.

2   ANON. "Specimens of American Literature." Edinburgh Magazine
and Literary Miscellany, V (September 1819), 206-11.
The Sketch Book (No. I) has traces of affectation, but is
nevertheless written with feeling and elegance. It sup-
ports a belief in the rising glories of American literature. "The Author's Account of Himself" and "The Voyage"
are reprinted here.

3   BENSON, EGBERT. Brief Remarks on The Wife of Washington
Irving. New York: Grattan and Banks, 1819.
An 18-page pamphlet, primarily attacking Irving's style
in "The Wife."

4   [DANA, R. H.] Review of The Sketch Book. North American Review, IX (September 1819), 322-56.
Treats only parts I and II. This work adds a great deal
to America's "literary character," but it is inferior to
Irving's earlier writings primarily because its style is
"feminine, dressy, elegant and languid." Most of the sketches,
though, contain fine touches, and as a whole they are

([DANA, R. H.])
    works of genius. Irving is justifiably America's most pop-
ular author. Discussion of Salmagundi and A History of New
York, mainly in terms of style and wit.

5   VERPLANCK, G. C. The State Triumvirate, A Political Tale:
and the Epistles of Brevet Major Pindar Puff. New York:
Printed for the Author, 1819.
    A mild satire on Irving on pp. 196-99. There is nothing
in The Sketch Book to recommend him to the serious student
of the natural sciences.

1820 A BOOKS - NONE

1820 B SHORTER WRITINGS

1   ANON. "The Sketch Book." New Monthly Magazine, XIII (March
1820), 303-308.
    A review, praising it for "its originality, its social
and conciliating spirit, the poetic feeling which pervades
its imagery and descriptions, and the chastity of its
style." "The Art of Book Making" is reprinted whole.

2   ANON. Review of The Sketch Book. Literary Chronicle and
Weekly Review, II (18 March 1820), 177-80.
    A favorable review with extensive quotation. "The Broken
Heart" is reprinted. Favorable mention of A History of New
York.

3   ANON. Review of The Sketch Book, Vol. I. Literary Gazette
(London), IV (8 April 1820), 228-29.
    Praises the style and subjects, and the mind of the au-
thor. Takes exception only to "English Writers on America."

4   ANON. "American Literature and Intelligence." Investigator,
I (May 1820), 156-63.
    Finds The Sketch Book elegant and interesting. High
praise for the judiciousness of "English Writers on America." Approves of "Mr. Irvine."

5   ANON. Review of The Sketch Book, Vol. I. British Critic,
XIII (June 1820), 645-54.
    Praises the humor and morality, but finds the book as a
whole insubstantial.

6   ANON. "Some Remarks on the Genius and Writings of Washington
Irving, Esq." New York Literary Journal, III (15 June
1820), 118-22.
    Americans have unfortunately neglected their own native
writers in favor of Europeans. Irving, though, has been
appreciated. Salmagundi and A History of New York are

3

1820

(ANON.)
imaginative, bold, and forceful, but undisciplined. The
highest quality of The Sketch Book is its moral tone, which
enhances its other excellences. Irving is "at once an ac-
complished scholar, and universal philanthropist." Reprinted from Poulson's American Daily Advertiser.

7   ANON. Review of The Sketch Book, Vol. II. Literary Chronicle
and Weekly Review, II (26 August 1820), 546-49.
Volume II is as good as the first. Irving is intimately
acquainted with things British. Reprints "Little Britain."

8   ANON. Review of The Sketch Book. Edinburgh Monthly Review,
IV (September 1820), 303-334.
Although the book suffers from several failures of taste,
it has great descriptive power, humor and fancy. Comparison to Tatler and Spectator. Extensive quotation from
several sketches.

9   ANON. Review of The Sketch Book. Gold's London Magazine,
and Theatrical Inquisitor, II (September 1820), 281-84.
The Sketch Book "affords the most unquestionable proof
of first rate abilities." Applauds Irving for modelling
his writing on the old authors instead of contemporary
ones. Reprints "The Broken Heart."

10 ANON. Review of The Sketch Book. Monthly Review, 2nd Ser.,
XCIII (October 1820), 198-207.
Recognition of Irving as an aspiring young imitator of
English models. Expresses regret at English animosity to
everything American, and credits Irving with trying to
foster friendly national relations. Mild criticism of his
romanticism and "gaudy" style.

11 ANON. Review of A History of New York. Literary Chronicle
and Weekly Review, II (7 October 1820), 641-44; (14 October), 659-61; (21 October), 678-81.
Expresses "unqualified approbation" for the work, but
makes no other critical comment. Almost exclusively quotation. Suggests that Irving would make a good novelist.

12 ANON. Review of A History of New York. Literary Gazette, IV
(21 October 1820), 674-76; (28 October), 695-96; (4 November), 707-709.
Irving's burlesque humor and knowledge of human nature
are fine, but the work is too long. Mostly quotation.

13 ANON. "Critical Notices of Books of the Month." Monthly
Magazine or, British Register, L (November 1820), 362-63.
Favorable review of The Sketch Book, Vol. II, on general
grounds. Comparison to Sterne.

4

14   ANON. Review of <u>The Sketch Book</u>, Vol. II. <u>British Critic</u>,
      XIV (November 1820), 514-25.
         ". . . in spite of a good deal of mistaken taste and mis-
      directed talent," the author's delicate humor and tone of
      mind render the book enjoyable. Sees Irving as imitating
      Mackenzie's "Man of Feeling."

15   ANON. Review of <u>The Sketch Book</u>. <u>Monthly Magazine or, Brit-</u>
      <u>ish Register</u>, L (1 November 1820), 304.
         The book is valuable to Americans as a "work of taste,"
      and is esteemed for "minor intellectual qualities of com-
      position, phraseology, and style." Another American work,
      <u>A Life in Pennsylvania</u>, is superior.

16   ANON. Notice of <u>A History of New York</u>. <u>New Monthly Magazine</u>,
      XIV (December 1820), 686.
         ". . . a singular work replete with sprightly and enter-
      taining remarks, philosophical views of human nature, and
      masterly sketches of character."

17   ANON. Review of <u>A History of New York</u>. <u>Edinburgh Magazine</u>
      <u>and Literary Miscellany</u>, VII (December 1820), 543-48.
         "This is a shrewd, clever, eccentric performance--a sort
      of historical heroicomic poem in prose. . . ." It is less
      varied and therefore less amusing than <u>The Sketch Book</u>, but
      is a more powerful and sustained effort. Irving's satire
      of philosophical systems is noteworthy.

18   ANON. Review of <u>A History of New York</u>. <u>Gold's London Maga-</u>
      <u>zine, and Theatrical Inquisitor</u>, II (December 1820),
      577-88.
         Irving is "a profound thinker; an acute observer; a hu-
      morous narrator." Long quotations, and digressions on
      American culture and English politics.

19   *ANON. Review of <u>A History of New York</u>. <u>London Magazine</u>
      (December 1820) [data incomplete].
         Unlocatable. Cited in Williams (1935.A1), Vol. 2,
      p. 277.

20   E. Review of <u>The Sketch Book</u>. <u>Western Review and Miscella-</u>
      <u>neous Magazine</u>, II (May 1820), 244-54.
         Discussion of <u>The Sketch Book</u> in terms of Western [Ken-
      tucky] attitudes and tastes. This book has great merit,
      though it is not quite up to the expectations raised by
      Irving's earlier works. <u>The Sketch Book</u> has fewer faults,
      but also less of his satiric genius. Summarizes some of
      the sketches with brief comments. "Rip Van Winkle" is a

1820

(E.)
very admirable tale, but the reviewer is "unable to conjecture how the story can be reconciled with reason or common sense."

21 H-s. Review of The Sketch Book. Revue Encyclopédique, VII (August 1820), 331-32.

22 [JEFFREY, FRANCIS.] Review of The Sketch Book. Edinburgh Review, XXXIV (August 1820), 160-76.
Praises the book's taste, style, humor, and imagination, primarily. Sees a lack of strength and originality in parts. Irving most directly imitates Addison, Goldsmith, and Mackenzie, to good effect. Quotes at length from "Rip Van Winkle" and "English Writers on America," with strong approbation.

23 [LOCKHART, JOHN G.] "Diedrich Knickerbocker's History of New York." Blackwood's Edinburgh Magazine, VII (July 1820), 360-69.
Enthusiastic review, lauding Irving as "by far the greatest genius that has arisen on the literary horizon of the new world." Mostly quotation.

24 _____. "On the Writings of Charles Brockden Brown and Washington Irving." Blackwood's Edinburgh Magazine, VI (February 1820), 554-61.
Comments on the early numbers of The Sketch Book. Some of the sketches are "very exquisite and classical pieces of writing, alike honourable to the intellect and the heart of their author."

1821 A BOOKS - NONE

1821 B SHORTER WRITINGS

1 ANON. Review of A History of New York. Monthly Review, XCIV (January 1821), 67-74.
Mostly summary and quotation. Irving is at his best with satire. "If he has not the terseness and concentration of Swift . . . but on the contrary plies us with a diffuseness and repetition of jokes . . . which become rather tiresome, still he has none of the nastiness of the witty Dean, or of his misanthropy."

2 ANON. Review of A History of New York. Edinburgh Monthly Review, V (February 1821), 232-48.

(ANON.)
Long quotations accompanied by humorous appreciative commentary, particularly on style and method.

3   ANON. Review of A History of New York. British Critic, N.S.
XV (March 1821), 261-72.
Generally complimentary to Irving, but expresses disappointment that most of the satire is incomprehensible to the British reader. Mostly quotation.

4   ANON. "Washington Irving, Esq." Port Folio, XI (March 1821),
131-36.
An article which quotes approvingly from remarks in "one of the most popular foreign journals" on Irving's debt to his English ancestry. Proposes that Irving write a series of novels on American life.

5   ANON. Review of The Sketch Book. Quarterly Review, XXV
(April 1821), 50-67.
Condescending praise for a fine American example of English literature. Says as much about British political attitudes toward America as about The Sketch Book. Particularly praises "Rip Van Winkle," "The Legend of Sleepy Hollow," and "The Spectre Bridegroom."

6   BAINBRIGGE, WILLIAM. "Ripvanwinkle." Blackwood's Edinburgh
Magazine, IX (May 1821), 225.
Letter to the editor suggesting that Irving modelled his story on the tale of Epimenides, as told by Diogenes Laertius.

1822 A   BOOKS - NONE

1822 B   SHORTER WRITINGS

1   [ALEXIS, WILLIBALD.] Review of Bracebridge Hall. Literarisches Conversationsblatt (8 November 1822), p. 1028;
(9 November), pp. 1031-32.

2   ANON. Review of Bracebridge Hall. New Monthly Magazine, 2nd
Ser., V (1822), 65-68.
It is well written, but quite inferior to The Sketch Book. Its characterization lacks reality and its style is not so "pure and select." Extensive quotation.

3   ANON. "Peter Klaus: The Legend of the Goatherd--Rip Van
Winkle." London Magazine, V (March 1822), 229-30.
Tells the story of Peter Klaus and comments that it is

1822

(ANON.)
"the undoubted source from which Geoffrey Crayon drew his Rip Van Winkle."

4   ANON. Review of Bracebridge Hall. Literary and Scientific Repository, IV (May 1822), 422-32.
      Irving seems to be merely going over old ground. Some passages, though, are fine examples of wit, description, and style. "[The sketches] embrace, indeed, a variety of subjects, and contain many sensible observations and just reflections, but the subjects want importance, the observations novelty, and the reflections force. The stories . . . are composed of the ordinary romance materials, and not very skilfully combined."

5   ANON. Review of Bracebridge Hall. Literary Chronicle and Weekly Review, IV (25 May 1822), 321-24.
      Irving is "the Goldsmith of the age." Bracebridge Hall is fully as interesting as The Sketch Book. Mostly quotation.

6   ANON. Review of Bracebridge Hall. Blackwood's Edinburgh Magazine, XI (June 1822), 688-92.
      Considers it good work, but inferior to The Sketch Book. Praises the portrayals of English manners, but finds the characterizations not true to life. Chides Irving for his attempt to promote good will between the United States and England.

7   ANON. Review of Bracebridge Hall. Literary Gazette, VI (1 June 1822), 339-41.
      Praises Irving as a talented and "pleasing" writer whose works would be of sufficient value to merit publication even if they had been written by an Englishman. Reprints "The Rookery."

8   ANON. Review of Bracebridge Hall. London Museum; or Record of Literature, Fine Arts, Science, Antiquities, the Drama, &c., I (1 June 1822), 83-85.
      Conciliatory--though lofty--remarks about the literary relations between England and America. Calls Irving a "very pleasant writer," and says, "if we find him occasionally gossiping and prosing, it must be confessed he does both very pleasantly."

9   ANON. Review of Bracebridge Hall. Edinburgh Magazine and Literary Miscellany, XI (July 1822), 91-96.
      Apologetic review, attempting to explain why the work seems inferior to The Sketch Book even though it is not.

(ANON.)
Briefly describes, and extracts from, the book. Recommends it for young people because of its innocuousness and moral attitudes.

10   ANON. Review of Bracebridge Hall. European Magazine, LXXXII (July 1822), 55-57.
Praises Irving's characterization, description, and style. The ease and spontaneity of the style surpasses that of The Sketch Book. Irving is in no sense a copyist-- he takes his descriptions directly from nature.

11   ANON. Review of Bracebridge Hall. Gentleman's Magazine, XCII (July 1822), 54-56.
This one is not as successful as A History of New York and The Sketch Book, primarily because no such beings as those in the book actually live in England nowadays. But Irving's work is still very amusing, and at times quite just; witty but not vulgar. Mostly quotation.

12   ANON. Review of Bracebridge Hall. Ladies' Monthly Museum, XVI (July 1822), 40.
Eulogistic comments on Irving's genius. Expresses surprise that an American could be so intimately acquainted with the fine points of British culture. Praises the style, subject matter, and imagination of the work.

13   ANON. Review of Bracebridge Hall. Leeds Correspondent, IV (July 1822), 185-95.
All but one paragraph is quotation. In that paragraph Irving is commended for being an attentive observer and for having a cultivated mind.

14   ANON. Review of Bracebridge Hall. New Edinburgh Review, II (July 1822), 151-77.
Brief, mainly laudatory comments. Mostly summary and quotation.

15   *ANON. Review of The Sketch Book. Literary Museum and Register of Arts, Sciences, Belles Lettres, Etc. (June 1822) [Incomplete data].
Unlocatable. Cited in Williams (1935.A1), II, 279.

16   ANON. Review of Bracebridge Hall. Monthly Magazine or British Register, LIII (1 July 1822), 548.
Irving's high reputation stands to gain still more from Bracebridge Hall. He succeeds in portraying an England of the past in which the characters are well drawn and humorous. His sketches of American characters are particularly valuable.

1822

17   ANON. Review of Bracebridge Hall. Monthly Censor, or Gen-
      eral Review of Domestic and Foreign Literature, I (August
      1822), 353-56.
           Bracebridge Hall confirms the praise given The Sketch
      Book; it has "wit, and humour, and learning, and good
      sense, and philosophy." America does not support belles
      lettres as does England.

18   ANON. Review of Bracebridge Hall. Monthly Review, 2nd Ser.,
      XCVIII (August 1822), 400-14.
           Irving's characterization and descriptive power are out-
      standing, and he charms the reader with his love for Brit-
      ish culture and his warm, romantic temperament. But he is
      "evidently fluttering his wings without rising," and might
      do well to rest awhile before attempting another book.

19   ANON. Review of Bracebridge Hall. British Critic, N.S.,
      XVIII (September 1822), 299-311.
           Highly commendatory review of Bracebridge Hall and of
      Irving's works in general. Praises his characterization
      and Addisonian style. Mostly quotation.

20   ANON. Review of Bracebridge Hall. Scottish Episcopal Review
      and Magazine, II (September 1822), 429-36.
           "Irvine" [sic] writes in a style that is "simple, pathet-
      ic, and terse." He handles difficult modes of composition
      with great ease, although his descriptions seem more from
      books than from life. On the whole, Bracebridge Hall con-
      tains "a good deal that is original, and very much that is
      beautiful and affecting." Reprints "The Stout Gentleman."

21   ANON. Review of Bracebridge Hall. London Magazine, VI (No-
      vember 1822), 436-39.
           Characterizes the book as "pleasant" and "agreeable,"
      but not equal in quality to The Sketch Book. Enumerates
      the various sketches.

22   ANON. Review of Erzählungen von Washington Irwing [sic].
      Literarisches Conversationsblatt (27 December 1822),
      p. 1188.
           Review of tales from The Sketch Book, translated by
      W. A. Lindau.

23   A[VENEL], M. Review of Voyage d'un Américain à Londres, ou
      Esquisses sur les moeurs anglaises et américaines. Revue
      Encyclopédique, XIII (February 1822), 442-43.
           Reviews a French translation of The Sketch Book.

24   [EVERETT, EDWARD.] Review of Bracebridge Hall. North Amer-
        ican Review, XV (July 1822), 204-24.
            Irving treated "as an auxiliary in the battle . . .
        waged in behalf of our country's reputation." Quotes from
        the London Morning Chronicle to the effect that Bracebridge
        Hall could not have been written by an American. Exten-
        sive quotation. Comments briefly and favorably on A His-
        tory of New York, mainly in relation to the same topic.

25   [JEFFREY, FRANCIS.] "Bracebridge Hall." Edinburgh Review,
        XXXVII (November 1822), 337-50.
            Irving is able to discuss national character while re-
        maining politically neutral; he has a spirit of kindness
        and good will toward all. Bracebridge Hall is a continua-
        tion of The Sketch Book, and quite as good.

26   [PRESCOTT, W. H.] "Essay Writing." North American Review,
        XIV (April 1822), 319-50.
            A review of two anonymous collections of essays, The
        Club Room and The Idle Man. A general survey of the essay
        in English literature, culminating in a discussion of The
        Sketch Book, which "certainly forms an epoch in the his-
        tory of this kind of literature." The works reviewed are
        compared unfavorably to The Sketch Book.

27   Q. Review of Bracebridge Hall. Examiner (London) (15 Decem-
        ber 1822), pp. 792-93.
            Says that both The Sketch Book and Bracebridge Hall are
        pleasant, "ingenious imitations of popular and well-known
        originals." Attacks Irving's aristocratic prejudices, and
        finds them very strange in an American.

1823 A   BOOKS - NONE

1823 B   SHORTER WRITINGS

 1   ANON. "Mr. Irving." New Monthly Magazine, 2nd Ser., VIII
        (1823), 193-202.
            Reports that a preacher with the name "Irving" is being
        mistaken by some for the author of The Sketch Book. A re-
        view of this Mr. Irving's oratory.

 2   ANON. Review of Bracebridge Hall. Port Folio, XV (February
        1823), 156-60.
            Reprinted from the London Magazine (November 1822). See
        item 1822.B21.

1823

3   ANON. Review of Bracebridge Hall. Eclectic Review, XXXVII
(March 1823), 233-43.
The Review congratulates itself for having been the first
to welcome "Mr. Irvine" to England, and contends, some
critics' views notwithstanding, that Bracebridge Hall is
not inferior to The Sketch Book.

4   ANON. "Literary and Scientific Intelligence." Port Folio,
XVI (July 1823), 85.
An extract from a letter written by Maria Edgeworth, commenting on Bracebridge Hall. She finds things to admire,
but says, "the fault of the book is that the workmanship
surpasses the work."

5   ANON. "Abendunterhaltungen." Literarisches Conversationsblatt (3 July 1823), pp. 609-12.
Review of a German translation of Bracebridge Hall.

6   ANON. Review of Salmagundi. Literary Chronicle and Weekly
Review, No. 239 (13 December 1823), pp. 791-93.
Mostly quotation. High praise of Irving as an essayist,
in which he is compared to Goldsmith. Favorable mention
of A History of New York.

7   ANON. Review of Salmagundi. Literary Sketch Book, I (13 December 1823), 275-96.
Irving is at his best when he joins "refined humour with
melancholy feeling." He mingles "the retrospection of
days gone by" with "a passive enjoyment of the present."
Salmagundi is juvenilia, but it contains the same qualities that blossomed more perfectly in The Sketch Book.
Extensive quotation.

8   *ANON. Review of Salmagundi. Literary Museum and Register of
Arts, Sciences, Belles Lettres, Etc., II (20 December
1823)[incomplete data].
Cairns (1922.B1) says the review praises Irving's other
work but criticizes Salmagundi: "'There is a juvenile
spirit--a freshness, an audacity about these nefarious
acts of humor and pathos perfectly intolerable.'"

9   [JEFFREY, FRANCIS,] Review of Bracebridge Hall. Museum of
Foreign Literature and Science, II (1823), 276-86.
Reprinted from Edinburgh Review, XXXVII (November 1822).
See item 1822.B25.

10   NEAL, JOHN. Randolph, a Novel. n.p., 1823, I, pp. 137-38.
Among comments on American writers inserted into this
epistolary novel, Irving is impressionistically described,

(NEAL, JOHN)
and his writing is compared to the work of the British
painter, Westall.

1824 A   BOOKS - NONE

1824 B   SHORTER WRITINGS

1   [ALEXIS, WILLIBALD.]   Review of Jonathan Oldstyle's Briefe.
    Literarisches Conversationsblatt (12 October 1824), p. 940.
        Reviews Spiker's German translation of Letters of Jona-
    than Oldstyle.

2   ANON. Review of Arthur Mervyn. Retrospective Review, IX
    (1824), 304-26.
        Among comments on American authors, Irving gets a para-
    graph (316-17). He is a fine imitator of Addison. "His
    humour (which is the best part of his genius) is neat and
    graceful; but his sketches of character are meagre, and
    his pathos is artificial and frail."

3   ANON. Review of Tales of a Traveller. European Review, V
    (1824), 124-35.
        Irving has forged his own style, combining English wit
    with American "wildness." With these Tales, he is becom-
    ing "less and less sentimental, while the graphic powers
    of description and the touches of satire rather improve."
    The book as a whole is uneven. Reprints "The Bold Dragoon"
    and "The Story of the Young Robber."

4   *ANON. Review of The Sketch Book. European Review (London)
    (1824)[data incomplete].
        Unlocatable. Cited in Williams (1935.A1), II, 279.

5   ANON. "Illustrations of the Works of Washington Irving, Esq."
    Port Folio, XVII (January 1824), 85-86.
        Enthusiastic note, quoted from the London Literary Ga-
    zette, on John Murray's publication of illustrations for
    The Sketch Book and A History of New York.

6   ANON. "Literary Intelligence." Port Folio, XVII (March
    1824), 252.
        Brief quotations from two British journals, praising
    Salmagundi.

7   ANON. Review of Letters of Jonathan Oldstyle, Gent. Monthly
    Critical Gazette, I (June 1824), 93-94.

1824

(ANON.)
> These observations on the New York theater twenty-two years ago can hardly be of interest to an English reader. The style is fine, but the content and the pompous manner typical of the very young writer makes these letters of little intrinsic merit. Publishers capitalizing on Irving's name by publishing his juvenilia do a real disservice to a distinguished author.

8   *ANON. Review of Tales of a Traveller. United States Literary Gazette, I (15 June 1824)[data incomplete].
> Unlocatable. Cited in Williams (1935.A1), II, 294.

9   ANON. Review of Tales of a Traveller. Literary Chronicle and Weekly Review, VI (28 August 1824), 545-49; (4 September), 563-67.
> The first part compares Irving favorably to Byron and Scott in terms of the time and care he takes with his works. Reprints "A Literary Dinner" and the "Story of the Young Robber." The second pronounces the longer tales, especially "Buckthorne," uninteresting, and reprints "The Young Italian" and "Kidd the Pirate."

10 ANON. Review of Tales of a Traveller. Literary Gazette, VIII (28 August 1824), 545-46; (4 September), 565-68.
> Though the work shows some talent, it is generally devoid of interest. Mostly quotation.

11 ANON. Review of Tales of a Traveller. London Literary Gazette, No. 397 (28 August 1824), pp. 545-46.
> Mostly summary and quotation. This book is not up to the standard set by Irving's earlier works, particularly The Sketch Book; the style is not enough to redeem the lack of interest in some of the tales.

12 ANON. "Letters of Timothy Tickler, Esq. to Eminent Literary Characters. No. XVIII. To Christopher North, Esq. On the last Edinburgh and Quarterly Reviews, and on Washington Irving's Tales of a Traveller." Blackwood's Edinburgh Magazine, XVI (September 1824), 291-304.
> Tales of a Traveller consists of old, hackneyed material that is far better in the original versions. Irving, seemingly, "cannot even make a robbery terrific, or a love-story tolerable." But when he writes about American scenes, he is "worthy of himself and his fame." He "has no inventive faculties at all" and "cannot write anything serious to much effect." He should concentrate on what he can do.

13   ANON. Review of <u>Tales of a Traveller</u>, Part I. <u>Atlantic</u>, I (September 1824), 390-91.

        Brief, enthusiastic review. Irving is almost unrivalled "in painting the lighter and livelier emotions of the mind, in every day life," and though he falls somewhat short in delineating the "stronger passions," he is "always natural."

14   ANON. Review of <u>Tales of a Traveller</u>. <u>Edinburgh Magazine and Literary Miscellany</u>, XV (September 1824), 325-36.

        The book is extremely disappointing. It lacks the refined humor and pathos of <u>Bracebridge Hall</u> and <u>The Sketch Book</u>, and at times is almost commonplace. The tone is cold and artificial, and many of the longer tales are not interesting. Irving lacks inventiveness.

15   ANON. Review of <u>Tales of a Traveller</u>. <u>European Magazine</u>, LXXXVI (September 1824), 251-54.

        Irving wastes his genius on inferior subjects. Reviewer expresses shock at the veiled "ribaldry" that runs throughout these stories, but has good words for "The Young Italian" and "Buckthorne," quoting long passages. Notes some errors in diction which the reviewer "hopes" are attributable to the printer.

16   ANON. Review of <u>Tales of a Traveller</u>. <u>Lady's Magazine and Museum of the Belles-Lettres</u>, N.S. V (September 1824), 484-91.

        These volumes do not really come up to expectations, but they are occasionally striking and "never contemptible." Extracts from "The German Student" and "The Young Robber"; brief comments on other sketches.

17   ANON. Review of <u>Tales of a Traveller</u>. <u>Kaleidoscope</u>, V (14 September 1824), 85-86.

        This new work is "decidedly inferior" to <u>The Sketch Book</u> and <u>Bracebridge Hall</u>. Some of the tales contain very little of interest, and the conclusions are generally tame and trite. Reprints "Adventure of the German Student."

18   ANON. Review of <u>Tales of a Traveller</u>, Part I. <u>United States Literary Gazette</u>, I (15 September 1824), 61-63.

        In writing <u>Bracebridge Hall</u> Irving followed the foolish advice of critics: he tried to give the work an artificial unity, and to temper his imagination's tendency to "run wild." In <u>Tales of a Traveller</u>, though, he has allowed his natural genius to rule. Brief comments on each of the tales.

1824

19   ANON. Review of <u>Tales of a Traveller</u>. <u>Kaleidoscope,</u> V (21
     September 1824), 93-94.
     Reprinted from the <u>Examiner</u>. <u>See</u> item 1824.B37.

20   ANON. "Washington Irving." <u>New York Mirror</u>, II (25 Septem-
     ber 1824), 70-71.
     The <u>Mirror</u> prints and attacks a review of <u>Tales of a</u>
     <u>Traveller</u> by a "contemptible miscreant," a Mr. Simpson, in
     the <u>Philadelphia Columbian Observer</u>. To Simpson, Irving
     is overrated, puerile, dull, and stupid. He especially
     attacks the writing of ghost stories in an enlightened age.

21   ANON. Critical Notice of <u>Tales of a Traveller</u>. <u>Ladies'</u>
     <u>Monthly Museum</u>, XX (October 1824), 222.
     The tales are dull, and some of them quite improbable.
     They will be read widely, but only because Irving is a
     popular author.

22   ANON. Review of <u>Tales of a Traveller</u>. <u>Metropolitan Literary</u>
     <u>Journal and General Magazine of Literature, Science and</u>
     <u>the Arts</u> (October 1824), pp. 538-45.
     Summarizes the <u>Tales</u>, concluding that they are "obvious"
     and unoriginal. Speculates as to their sources. Irving
     should write "reflections," but he should "shun tale-
     writing; it is not his forte."

23   ANON. Review of <u>Tales of a Traveller</u>. <u>Monthly Critical Ga-</u>
     <u>zette</u>, I (October 1824), 465-68.
     Caustic attack on <u>Tales of a Traveller</u>, condemning it as
     a cheap commercial venture cashing in on the name of a
     celebrated author. The <u>Tales</u> themselves are ill-made and
     filled with "puerility and absurdity." Quotes "A Literary
     Dinner" as the supreme example of "supercilious conceit"
     and "impudent ignorance."

24   ANON. Review of <u>Tales of a Traveller</u>. <u>Monthly Magazine</u>,
     LVIII (October 1824), 260.
     "Irwin" [sic] is all style and little substance. Praises
     the elegance and a certain "quaintness of exaggeration" in
     these <u>Tales</u>, but notes that the stories themselves are in-
     substantial.

25   ANON. Review of <u>Tales of a Traveller</u>. <u>Westminster Review</u>,
     II (October 1824), 334-46.
     A diatribe against aristocracy, "the empty jargon of
     Belles Lettres," and virtually every aspect of Geoffrey
     Crayon's work.

26   ANON. "Washington Irving's New Work." London Magazine, X
     (October 1824), 401-406.
          Review of Tales of a Traveller. It is inferior, and un-
     worthy of Irving, who had previously proven his exceptional
     talent for instructing by entertaining. It was probably
     "written against time" for a large profit.

27   ANON. Review of Tales of a Traveller, Part II. United States
     Literary Gazette, I (1 October 1824), 177-78.
          Though the tales are "exquisite delicacies," Part II is
     inferior to Part I. Of the second part, "we do not recol-
     lect anything in it which is not pretty good; neither can
     we recollect much that is more than pretty good." Exten-
     sive quotation.

28   ANON. Review of Tales of a Traveller. Literarisches
     Conversationsblatt, No. 231 (7 October 1824), pp. 922-23.
          Review dated 31 August 1824.

29   ANON. Review of Tales of a Traveller. Atlantic, II (Novem-
     ber 1824), 59-74.
          Suggests that Irving's charm lies in his "delicate
     appreciation of the beautiful united to a lively percep-
     tion of the ridiculous." Divides these tales into the
     "serious" and the "sprightly," promising to evaluate each
     story on its own terms. Treats the "serious" stories in
     this article. Long discussions of "The Young Italian" and
     "The Young Robber."

30   ANON. Review of Tales of a Traveller. Universal Review, II
     (November 1824), 259-72.
          Discusses Irving's popularity--his "rise" through The
     Sketch Book, and his "fall" through Tales of a Traveller--
     in terms of the general inferiority of American culture.
     The Tales in general are "not inferior" to Irving's other
     works; he has simply not improved, letting all the praise
     go to his head. Irving is at his best when writing about
     his own country.

31   ANON. Review of Bracebridge Hall. Leipziger Literatur
     Zeitung (5 November 1824), p. 2166.
          Reviews Spiker's German translation.

32   ANON. Review of Tales of a Traveller, Part III. United
     States Literary Gazette, I (15 November 1824), 228-29.
          Apparently Irving has become satiated with so many
     travels; freshness and enthusiasm have gone. Moreover,
     "we are bound to charge him with the vulgarism of indeli-
     cacy." Ascribes "The Painter's Adventure" and its two

1824

(ANON.)
sequels to a true account in the journal of an artist employed by Lucien Buonaparte.

33 ANON. Review of Tales of a Traveller. Atlantic, II (December 1824), 85-97.
A continuation of the review in the November 1824 Atlantic. See item 1824.B29. This article treats the "humorous" stories. Brief comments on each story expressing varying degrees of praise or disappointment, but concluding that nothing Irving has previously written surpasses these stories in humor or in the "picturing" of detail.

34 A., W. "Über Washington Irving." Hermes, Oder Kritisches Jahrbuch der Literatur, III (1824), 305-30.
Comments on Tales of a Traveller and The Sketch Book.

35 H. "A Remark on Knickerbocker." Port Folio, XVII (May 1824), 422.
A passage from the book is arranged as verse to show that Diedrich Knickerbocker "has a touch of the true poetic vein."

36 LEGIS, STUDENS. Review of Tales of a Traveller. New York American (31 August 1824) [incomplete data].
Praise of Irving and the first number of Tales of a Traveller. Irving appeals to the most universal emotions and draws out feelings in his characters we feel to be our own. "The Young Italian," in its "pathos and feeling," is the best story he ever wrote.

37 Q. Review of Tales of a Traveller. Examiner (London) (5 September 1824), pp. 563-65.
How could Irving, an American Republican, capitulate so entirely to the tastes and values of the English upper class? He models himself after Addison but does not even allow himself "a sentiment half so bold as even Addison's whiggism." Irving has a "light and pleasant power of combining reminiscences" but "of positive invention there is scarcely an iota." Surveys Tales of a Traveller, with comments on Irving's reticence and lack of originality. A footnote accuses him of plagiarism in A History of New York.

1825 A   BOOKS - NONE

1825 B   SHORTER WRITINGS

1   ANON. Review of Tales of a Traveller. Museum of Foreign Lit-
     erature and Science, VI (1825), 83-93.
     Reprinted from Westminster Review, II (October 1824). See
     item 1824.B25.

2   ANON. Review of Tales of a Traveller. Imperial Magazine, VII
     (January 1825), 82-85.
        The book is well praised for its "deep, thrilling inter-
     est," though acknowledged as inferior to The Sketch Book
     and Bracebridge Hall.

3   ANON. "Zeitung der Ereignisse und Unsichten." Gesellschafter
     oder Blätter für Geist und Herz, Blatt 7 (January 1825),
     pp. 35-36.
        Favorable review of Tales of a Traveller.

4   *ANON. Review of Tales of a Traveller. Abendzeitung (Dres-
     den), No. 31 (5 February 1825) [data incomplete].
        Unlocatable. Cited in Williams (1935.A1), II, 295.

5   ANON. "Memoir of Washington Irving, Esq." European Magazine
     and London Review, LXXXVII (March 1825), 197-201.
        A favorable overview of Irving's life and works to date.
     He is called "the Campbell of prose,"

6   ANON. Review of Salmagundi, A History of New York, Brace-
     bridge Hall, Tales of a Traveller. Quarterly Review, XXXI
     (March 1825), 473-87.
        A favorable evaluation of Irving's works in light of a
     recent decline in his prestige. Salmagundi is "unsparing"
     satire. Of A History of New York, "all that we understand"
     is good, though everything tends to be "over-done." Brace-
     bridge Hall exhibits "good taste and minute observation"
     though it is over long. Tales of a Traveller shows some
     "indolence," but it suggests that as a novelist, Irving
     might "prove no contemptible rival to Goldsmith."

7   ANON. "Memoir of Washington Irving." Port Folio, XIX (May
     1825), 436-40.
        A favorable overview (apparently reprinted from a British
     publication) of the chief details of Irving's life and
     career to date.

8   ANON. Review of Tales of a Traveller. Eclectic Review, XLII
     (July 1825), 65-74.
        Generally commendatory review, with some complaint about
     Irving having left many tales unfinished, and having some-
     times descended to vulgarity and profaneness.

1825

9   ANON. Review of Erzählungen eines Reisenden. Literarisches
      Conversationsblatt (18 July 1825), pp. 653-54.
        Reviews Spiker's German translation of Tales of a Trav-
      eller.

10   HAZLITT, WILLIAM. The Spirit of the Age; or, Contemporary
      Portraits. London: Henry Colburn, 1825.
        Brief remarks on Irving. The Sketch Book and Bracebridge
      Hall are "very good American copies" of British models such
      as Addison, Goldsmith, and Fielding. They are anachronisms
      and lack freshness.

11   [HUGHES, T. S.] Review of Salmagundi, A History of New York,
      Bracebridge Hall, Tales of a Traveller. Quarterly Review,
      XXXI (March 1825), 473-87.
        A discussion of all four books, which both praises and
      finds fault but is generally quite favorable. Lauds Irving
      as the equal of his British contemporaries.

12   N., C. Review of Contes d'un Voyageur. Revue Encyclopédique,
      XXV (January 1825), 213-14.
        Reviews a French translation of Tales of a Traveller.

13   NEAL, JOHN. "American Writers." Blackwood's Edinburgh Maga-
      zine, XVII (January 1825), 48-69.
        A long, detailed discussion of Irving in a long article
      on American writers. Treats each of Irving's works through
      Tales of a Traveller. Enthusiastic, though qualified
      praise for A History of New York, which is "altogether
      original," and The Sketch Book, "a timid, beautiful work."
      Irving's other works are seen as failures. Though there
      are passages of genuine poetry in Irving, he "has no idea
      of genuine romance; or love--or anything else, we believe,
      that ever seriously troubles the blood of men."

14   X. Review of Salmagundi. Literatur-Blatt (Supplement to
      Morgenblatt für gebildete Stände), No. 58 (22 July 1825),
      pp. 229-31.

1826 A   BOOKS - NONE

1826 B   SHORTER WRITINGS

1   ANON. "A Biographical Sketch of Thomas Campbell, Esq. by
      Geoffrey Crayon, Gent." Bolster's Quarterly Magazine, I
      (February 1826), 28-39.
        Reprint of the biographical essay, with appended note.
      Praises Irving's elegant and aristocratic style, his humor,

(ANON.)
and his philanthropic attitudes. Extremely favorable commentary.

1827 A   BOOKS - NONE

1827 B   SHORTER WRITINGS

1   ANON. Review of A History of New York. Le Globe (Paris), V
      (2 October 1827), p. 415.

2   D., E. "Amérique du Nord. Littérature des États-Unis. (IVe
      Article.) Prosateurs.--Washington Irving (I)." Le Globe
      (Paris) (31 March 1827), pp. 521-23.

1828 A   BOOKS - NONE

1828 B   SHORTER WRITINGS

1   ANON. Review of The Life and Voyages of Christopher Columbus.
      Literary Gazette (London), XII (2 February 1828), 65-67.
          This pre-publication notice, mostly quotation, finds the
      style and thought equal to that in Irving's previous works.
      In addition, this book, a history, is of justifiably higher
      pretensions than his others.

2   ANON. Review of The Life and Voyages of Christopher Columbus.
      Kaleidoscope, VIII (12 February 1828), 265-67.
          Hails Irving in his new role of historian and biographer.
      Stresses the importance of his research. Prints long ex-
      tract from the as yet unpublished work.

3   ANON. "Washington Irving's Life of Columbus." Athenaeum,
      No. 7 (12 February 1828), pp. 102-103; No. 9 (22 February),
      pp. 131-33; No. 10 (26 February), pp. 150-51.
          Irving's recent works have been insipid, and his reputa-
      tion, inflated even at first, has declined. The great
      merit of Columbus is its unaffected, clear style. But it
      adds little to our knowledge, and Irving is morally cul-
      pable for weakly excusing Spanish atrocities against the
      Indians.

4   ANON. "Life and Voyages of Columbus." London Weekly Review,
      II (16 February 1828), 97-99; (23 February 1828), 115-17.
          A two-part review (mostly quotation) which was preceded
      by a long excerpt on 9 February. Praises Irving's style
      and treatment. Calls the book ". . . a work which unques-

1828

(ANON.)
tionably entitles its author to rank among the ablest historians of the age."

5   ANON. Review of The Life and Voyages of Christopher Columbus. Literary Chronicle and Weekly Review, X (23 February 1828), 118-20; (22 March), 184-85.
     Attacks the "shallow criticism" of the work in most journals, and expresses high regard for Irving as an historian. Almost entirely quotation.

6   ANON. "Life and Voyages of Christopher Columbus." New Monthly Magazine, XXII (March 1828), 288-96.
     Extensive quotation of "spirited, elegant, and interesting" passages with brief mention of a few stylistic faults.

7   ANON. Review of The Life and Voyages of Christopher Columbus. American Quarterly Review, III (March 1828), 173-90.
     In writing history, Irving gives up many of his natural advantages, but his subject matter and style combine to produce excellence. Mostly quotation and paraphrase.

8   ANON. Review of The Life and Voyages of Christopher Columbus. Eclectic Review, N.S. XXIX (March 1828), 224-32.
     Essentially summary and quotation. "On the whole, [Irving] has given the details of his story fully, put them together skilfully, and narrated them in a most attractive manner."

9   ANON. Review of The Life and Voyages of Christopher Columbus. Ladies' Monthly Museum, XXVII (March 1828), 170-71.
     Highly favorable comment on Irving's literary talent and scholarly objectivity. Mainly a speculation on the long-range effects of Columbus' discovery of the New World.

10   ANON. Review of The Life and Voyages of Christopher Columbus. Lady's Magazine, N.S. IX (March 1828), 145-49.
     Irving is to be lauded for his diligence, accuracy, and his "agreeable style," but he has not come up with anything new. Prints extracts describing Isabella and Columbus, observing that "both portraits are drawn by the florid and emblazoning pencil of a rhetorician rather than with the strict fidelity of a dispassionate historian."

11   ANON. Review of The Life and Voyages of Christopher Columbus. London Magazine, 2nd Ser., X (March 1828), 281-325.
     ". . . an agreeable book; somewhat too prolix, and in many places feeble; but on the whole, four pleasant volumes, which would be much pleasanter if they were only

(ANON.)
three. The chief and pervading fault of the book is that
absence of all manly opinion--that skinless sensitiveness,
that shuddering dread of giving offence, by which all the
former productions of this writer are marked." Extensive
summary and quotation.

12   ANON. Review of The Life and Voyages of Christopher Columbus.
      New York Mirror, V (22 March 1828), 295.
          No one could have expected Irving to turn to serious his-
      tory, but he has done so to great advantage. The 3-volume
      work holds the reader's interest throughout, and by itself
      would be enough to guarantee Irving's literary immortality.

13   ANON. Review of The Life and Voyages of Christopher Columbus.
      Monthly Magazine or British Register, N.S. V (April 1828),
      407-10.
          Outlines the major events in the book and expresses a
      favorable opinion of it, but feels that Irving has been
      too partial and apologetic for Columbus, and has restricted
      himself too greatly by undertaking to write history.

14   ANON. Review of The Life and Voyages of Christopher Columbus.
      Monthly Review, N.S. VII (April 1828), 419-34.
          Objects to Irving's romanticizing of Columbus, who seems
      more like a hero of an historical novel than the object of
      a serious historical inquiry. Furthermore, the four-vol-
      ume work is needlessly long and prolix.

15   ANON. Review of The Life and Voyages of Christopher Columbus.
      Southern Review, III (August 1828), 1-31.
          Irving's earliest works, when he lived in America, were
      not only written in a correct style, but they were also
      full of "vivacity" and "racy humour." His European pro-
      ductions show too much restraint and deference. Irving
      is at his best when he writes on American themes, and "we
      rejoice" at this study of Columbus. Mostly summary and
      quotation.

16   ANON. Review of The Life and Voyages of Christopher Columbus.
      Western Monthly Review, II (September 1828), 227-36.
          The scope of Irving's book is truly epic. He grounds
      the romantic possibilities in well-researched fact. His
      delineation of character and his descriptions of tropical
      scenery are superb. Mostly quotation and summary.

17   ANON. "Cooper and Irving." Philadelphia Album, III (14 Sep-
      tember 1828), 134-35.
          A discussion of Irving's Life of Columbus and Cooper's

1828

(ANON.)
   Notions of the Americans. "Both these writers have attempted performances of an entirely different kind from
   those which have raised their fame. This experiment is
   always dangerous, almost uniformly fatal."

18   DEPPING. Revue of Histoire de la Vie et des Voyages de
   Christophe Colomb. Revue Encyclopédique, XXXIX (July
   1828), 95-109.
   Reviews a French translation of Columbus.

19   [JEFFREY, FRANCIS.] Review of The Life and Voyages of Christopher Columbus. Edinburgh Review, XLVIII (September
   1828), 1-32.
   An admirable work--one which will probably be the definitive treatment for years to come. Irving's style, treatment, temper, are all to be praised. Mostly summary and
   quotation.

1829 A   BOOKS - NONE

1829 B   SHORTER WRITINGS

1   ANON. Review of A Chronicle of the Conquest of Granada.
   American Quarterly Review, V (March 1829), 190, 221.
   Expresses disappointment that Irving chose to deal only
   with the destruction of the Moorish kingdom. Summarizes
   the history of the Moors. Irving's assuming the character
   of Fray Antonio Agapida gives his story poetic interest
   and legitimizes his approach to the subject. Though the
   narrative is sometimes overelaborated, it perpetually
   claims our attention.

2   ANON. Review of A Chronicle of the Conquest of Granada.
   Critic, I (25 April 1829), 400-404.
   Eulogistic commentary. The work is appropriately
   adapted to the character of Fray Antonio Agapida. Mostly
   quotation.

3   ANON. Review of A Chronicle of the Conquest of Granada.
   Philadelphia Album, III (6 May 1829), 386.
   Irving has been overrated. This work is a loose collection of sketches "calculated to please, but not thrill the
   mind of the reader."

4   ANON. Review of A Chronicle of the Conquest of Granada.
   London Literary Gazette (23 May 1829), pp. 329-31.
   This book fills an important gap in our knowledge of the

(ANON.)

history of Spain. The language is "chaste and animated," presenting a series of "splendid pictures" of chivalry, which are all the more surprising coming from "an American and a republican." Mostly quotation.

5   ANON. Review of A Chronicle of the Conquest of Granada. Ariel, II (30 May 1829), 23.
    Questions why the book has received relatively little attention in America. It delightfully combines history and humor, and "possesses all the striking peculiarities" of Irving's genius.

6   ANON. Review of A Chronicle of the Conquest of Granada. Edinburgh Literary Gazette, I (June 1829), 71-72.
    This book is "elegantly written and highly entertaining," but Irving's talents are better suited to fiction than history. Despite the soundness of his authorities, the romantic coloring of his account makes his book hard to accept as "sound and sober" history. The reviewer is confused about Fray Antonio Agapida. Mostly summary and quotation.

7   ANON. "Washington Irving's Conquest of Granada." London Magazine, 3rd Ser., III (June 1829), 529-56.
    Bitter attack on Irving for romanticizing war and distorting the facts of the conquest.

8   ANON. Review of A Chronicle of the Conquest of Granada. Edinburgh Literary Journal, II (6 June 1829), 1-4.
    Generally praises the book and recommends it to lovers of the chivalrous and splendid. Accepts Antonio Agapida as real, and criticizes Irving for following him too closely in his attitude toward the Moors.

9   ANON. Review of A Chronicle of the Conquest of Granada. Monthly Repository and Review, N.S. III (July 1829), 502-503.
    "There is more spirit and power in this book than in any which Mr. Washington Irving has yet put forth." Praises Irving's balanced view of chivalry and his use of Fray Antonio Agapida as a "naive" narrative voice.

10   ANON. Review of A Chronicle of the Conquest of Granada. Monthly Review, 3rd Ser., XI (July 1829), 430-45.
    Despite his complaints about the "pertinacious interposition" of Fray Antonio Agapida, and the occasional use of Froissart's style, the reviewer gives the book a good report as "a history written in the language and manner of romance."

1829

11   ANON. Review of <u>Histoire de la conquête de Grenade, tirée de</u>
      <u>la chronique manuscrite de Fray Antonio Agapida</u>. <u>Revue</u>
      <u>Encyclopédique</u>, XLIII (September 1829), 719-20.
          Reviews the French translation of <u>Granada</u> by J. Cohen.

12   ANON. "America and American Writers." <u>Athenaeum</u>, II (14 Oc-
      tober 1829), 637-39.
          Irving is given a paragraph, in which <u>A History of New</u>
      <u>York</u> is highly praised as an independent work of "genuine
      original humour." Irving gave up the character of Diedrich
      Knickerbocker, however, to become a "second-rate essayist,
      [and] a twelfth-rate historian."

13   ANON. Review of <u>Die Geschichte des Lebens und der Reisen</u>
      <u>Christoph's Columbus</u>, I-III. <u>Blätter für literarische</u>
      <u>Unterhaltung</u> (16 October 1829), pp. 953-54; (17 October),
      pp. 957-59; (19 October), pp. 961-62; (20 October), pp.
      965-67.
          Reviews von Meyer's German translation of <u>Columbus</u>, Vols.
      I-III.

14   [EVERETT, A. H.] Review of <u>The Life and Voyages of Chris-</u>
      <u>topher Columbus</u>. <u>North American Review</u>, XXVIII (January
      1829), 103-34.
          The book is "on the whole, more honorable to the litera-
      ture of the country than any [other] that has hitherto ap-
      peared among us." It may be compared to the finest narra-
      tive or epic poems. Also discusses <u>Salmagundi</u> and <u>A His-</u>
      <u>tory of New York</u>, and calls Irving the foremost American
      author.

15   KNAPP, SAMUEL LORENZO. <u>American Cultural History 1607-1829:</u>
      <u>A Facsimile Reproduction of</u> Lectures on American Literature
      <u>(1829)</u>. Eds. Richard Beale Davis and Ben Harris McClary.
      Gainesville, Florida: Scholars' Facsimiles & Reprints,
      1961.
          One page on Irving. Ranks him among the best American
      authors. Particularly praises his <u>Columbus</u>.

16   *<u>LADIES' MAGAZINE</u>, N.S. X (August 1829), 423 [data incomplete].
          Unobtainable. Cited in Williams (1935.A1), II, 312.

17   NAVARRETE, MARTIN FERNANDEZ de. <u>Coleccion de los Viages y</u>
      <u>Descubrimientos. . . .</u> Madrid: Imprenta Real, 1829. III,
      xiii-xiv.
          Favorable comments on Irving's <u>Columbus</u>.

18   [PRESCOTT, WILLIAM H.] Review of <u>A Chronicle of the Conquest</u>
      <u>of Granada</u>. <u>North American Review</u>, XXIX (October 1829),
      293-314.

([PRESCOTT, WILLIAM H.])
    Discussion of the different schools of historical writing
and Irving's brand of "narrative history." Survey of the
historical background and Irving's sources. Despite its
"dramatic coloring" and "romantic forms" of style, this is
an authentic and accurate historical treatment.

1830 A BOOKS - NONE

1830 B SHORTER WRITINGS

1   [ALEXIS, WILLIBALD.] Review of Die Eroberung von Granada.
        Blätter für literarische Unterhaltung (12 July 1830),
        769-71.
            Reviews Gustav Sellen's German translation of Granada.

2   ANON. Review of Die Geschichte des Lebens und der Reisen
        Christoph's Columbus, IV. Blätter für literarische Unter-
        haltung (31 January 1830), n.p.
            Reviews von Meyer's German translation of Columbus, Vol.
        IV.

3   ANON. Review of The Life and Voyages of Christopher Columbus
        (Abridged). Athenaeum, No. 115 (13 March 1830), pp. 148-
        49.
            The abridgement is superior to the "diffuse" original,
        and is "among the most beautiful specimens of biography in
        any language." It combines an appropriate enthusiasm with
        fine scholarship, and is notable for its full treatment of
        Columbus' personality. Mostly quotation.

4   ANON. Review of The Life and Voyages of Christopher Columbus
        (Abridged). Dublin Literary Gazette, I (13 March 1830),
        162-63.
            A delightful book, combining "the elegancies of the imag-
        ination with the sterling solidity of truth." Mostly sum-
        mary and quotation.

5   ANON. Review of The Life and Voyages of Christopher Columbus
        (Abridged). Edinburgh Literary Journal, III (13 March
        1830), 161.
            "Mr. Murray could not have made a more acceptable addi-
        tion to his Family Library than his present work, which is
        purely and classically written, and is replete with inter-
        est."

6   ANON. Review of The Life and Voyages of Christopher Columbus.
        Gentleman's Magazine, C (April 1830), 338-39.

1830

(ANON.)
   Primarily a disquisition on historical matters associated
   with Columbus. Calls the book "most interesting," and sees
   great human significance in the story it tells.

7   *ANON. Review of The Life and Voyages of Christopher Columbus.
      Missionary Chronicle, VIII (April 1830), 151.
         Unobtainable. Cited in Cairns (1922.B1).

8   ANON. "Geschichte." Allgemeine Literatur-Zeitung (Halle), IV
      (July 1830), Ergänzungsblätter, 671.
         Review of two German renditions of The Conquest of
      Granada.

9   ANON. Review of The Life and Voyages of Christopher Columbus
      (Abridged). Eclectic Review, 3rd Ser., IV (August 1830),
      97-98.
         Paragraph in an essay deprecating abridged, "family li-
      brary" editions, which praises Irving's abridgement of his
      Columbus over the full-length version.

10 INCE., H. "Comments of a Reader--No. 2." Olio, VI (23 Octo-
      ber 1830), 282-83.
         Retrospective thoughts on The Sketch Book and its accep-
      tance in England. Quotes William Godwin's praise, and con-
      cludes that Irving, a foreigner, has done more to enrich
      the literature of England than any native writer in the
      last fifty years.

11 [IRVING, WASHINGTON.] Review of A Chronicle of the Conquest
      of Granada. Museum of Foreign Literature and Science,
      XVII (September 1830), 253-65.
         Reprinted from the Quarterly Review, XLIII (May 1830).
      See item 1830.B12.

12 _____ Review of A Chronicle of the Conquest of Granada.
      Quarterly Review, XLIII (May 1830), 55-80.
         An enthusiastic, lengthy synopsis. Questions the wisdom
      of using Agapida. Quotes substantial passages, supplies
      missing historical background, and extends the history be-
      yond the point where the Chronicle leaves off.

1831 A BOOKS - NONE

1831 B SHORTER WRITINGS

1   ANON. Review of Voyages and Discoveries of the Companions of
      Columbus. Athenaeum, IV (1 January 1831), 9; (22 January),
      51-52.

(ANON.)
The book is written with "elegance, spirit, and simplicity." But its weakness is that it consists of unconnected
narratives, and is neither fully biographical nor historical. Irving should have written the history of the
period.

2   ANON. Review of Voyages and Discoveries of the Companions of
Columbus (Abridged). Edinburgh Literary Journal, V (22
January 1831), 63.
Brief, favorable appreciation of the value of Irving's
new work. Singles out Vasco Nuñez de Balboa as of special
interest, and reprints the chapter on his discovery of the
Pacific.

3   ANON. Review of Voyages and Discoveries of the Companions of
Columbus. Gentleman's Magazine, CI (February 1831), 143-
44.
Commentary on the immorality of the Spanish conquests,
and the lessons to be drawn therefrom. No critical remarks.

4   ANON. Review of Voyages and Discoveries of the Companions of
Columbus. Monthly Review, N.S. I (February 1831), 244-53.
Praises the subject matter and the style of execution.
Summarizes the story of Vasco Nuñez de Balboa. Mostly
quotation.

5   ANON. Review of Voyages and Discoveries of the Companions of
Columbus. American Quarterly Review, IX (March 1831),
163-86.
Copious quotations, summary, and praise followed by more
specific comments on Irving's style. Replies to the ob-
jection that Irving's style is too elaborate, sacrificing
strength of expression. Argues that Irving's refinement
is suited to his purposes for "he never endeavoured to
call up violent emotions." Columbus and Companions of
Columbus exhibit "a different manner" for Irving, but one
that in its unobtrusiveness is equally appropriate to his
subject.

6   ANON. Review of Voyages and Discoveries of the Companions of
Columbus. Monthly Magazine or British Register, N.S. XI
(May 1831), 571-72.
Summary of the events of the work; pronounces it "inter-
esting" but makes no critical comment.

7   ANON. Review of Voyages and Discoveries of the Companions of
Columbus. Southern Review, VII (May 1831), 214-46.

1831

(ANON.)
>Mostly summary and quotation. The review argues, though, that the Spanish explorers, contrary to Irving's view, were motivated more by cupidity than by chivalry.

8 ANON. "Washington Irving's Reisen der Gefährten des Colombo." Blätter für literarische Unterhaltung (27 May 1831), pp. 643-44.
>Reviews the Companions of Columbus.

9 ANON. "Gallery of Literary Characters: Washington Irving." Fraser's Magazine, IV (November 1831), 435.
>Portrait, with comments as to how Irving is a contrast to most Englishmen's image of Americans. Today, Irving is not only totally accepted, but he is "a standard writer among British men of genius."

10 C. "Americans in London." New York Mirror, VIII (12 March 1831), 284.
>Contains a brief report of a conversation with Irving in London. Discussed were New York places and people, including William Cullen Bryant.

11 U. Review of A Chronicle of the Conquest of Granada. Jahrbücher der Literatur (Vienna), LIII (January-March 1831), 123-53.

1832 A BOOKS - NONE

1832 B SHORTER WRITINGS

1 [ALEXIS, WILLIBALD.] "Die--Das--Alhambra." Blätter für literarische Unterhaltung (18 October 1832), 1229-31.
>A review.

2 ANON. "Washington Irving." New York Mirror, IX (4 March 1832), 273-74.
>A laudatory overview of Irving's life and works. Portrait.

3 ANON. "Salmagundi." New York Mirror, IX (17 March 1832), 295.
>Attributes authorship of the Salmagundi papers as follows: "All the poetry, and two of the prose articles were from the hand of William Irving; the rest were furnished, in about equal parts, by Washington Irving and J. K. Paulding."

30

4   ANON. Review of The Alhambra. Literary Gazette, XVI (28
       April 1832), 257–60; (5 May), 278–80.
          Gives credit to Irving for having established American
       literature and having cultivated friendly relations between
       Great Britain and the United States. Praises his kindly
       sentiments, humor, pathos, and poetic style. Comments
       briefly on the romance of the Alhambra, and quotes long
       passages from the book.

5   ANON. Review of The Alhambra. Athenaeum, No. 236 (5 May
       1832), pp. 283–84.
          Comments on Irving's general strengths and weaknesses.
       His writing has elegance rather than power, and he is most
       successful at delineating American characters. The book
       may not increase Irving's fame, but it is high praise to
       say that it will not diminish it.

6   ANON. "Washington Irving's New 'Sketch Book.'" Literary
       Guardian, II (5 May 1832), 65–68.
          Review of The Alhambra. Even though he is not an
       Englishman, "Washington Irving is decidedly the first
       English prose-writer of the day." Scott is a great ro-
       mancer, but Irving "is as great in biography as in fic-
       tion." Prints long extract from the as yet unpublished
       Alhambra.

7   ANON. Notice of The Alhambra. New Monthly Magazine, XXXVI
       (June 1832), 242.
          Praises Irving's romanticism.

8   ANON. Review of The Alhambra. Monthly Review, N.S. II (June
       1832), 221–47.
          All of Irving's works since Bracebridge Hall are inferior
       productions. Tales of a Traveller was a total failure;
       The Alhambra is somewhat better but still mediocre. Sum-
       marizes, and reprints substantial extracts.

9   ANON. Review of The Alhambra and A Chronicle of the Conquest
       of Granada. Eclectic Review, VIII (July 1832), 1–8.
          Criticizes the use of a persona in Granada, but speaks
       highly of the work otherwise. Praises the quiet humor,
       easy style, and rich description in The Alhambra and in
       Irving's works as a whole.

10   ANON. "The Irving Dinner." New York Mirror, IX (9 June
       1832), 386–87, 390–91.
          A full report of a testimonial dinner for Irving, held
       on May 30, 1832 in New York, including the speeches of the
       notables attending.

1832

11   ANON. Review of The Alhambra. New York Mirror, IX (23 June
      1832), 401-403.
          These tales are brilliant and striking, but compared to
      The Sketch Book and Bracebridge Hall they are disappoint-
      ing. Extensive quotation.

12   ANON. Review of The Alhambra. New England Magazine, III
      (July 1832), 81-82.
          Irving rather exhausted his materials in his other Span-
      ish books. The Alhambra is good, but below the standard
      set by The Sketch Book and A History of New York.

13   ANON. "Washington Irving's Alhambra." Westminster Review,
      XVII (July 1832), 132-45.
          Irving's art is compared to painting. High praise of
      both his style and subject. Extensive quotation.

14   ANON. Review of The Alhambra. American Monthly Review, II
      (September 1832), 177-89.
          Praises Irving's imagination, humor, pathos, and power
      of description. Criticizes his style as vague, artificial,
      and circumlocutory. Extensive quotation.

15   [EVERETT, A. H.] "Irving's Alhambra." North American Review,
      XXXV (October 1832), 265-82.
          Reflections on the history and culture of Spain, and what
      a fertile ground it has proved for Irving's "poetical tem-
      perament." Welcomes Irving back to America, and hopes that
      the New World will inspire him as did the old. Extensive
      summary and quotation.

16   FAY, T. S. Dreams and Reveries of a Quiet Man. 2 vols. New
      York: J. & J. Harper, 1832.
          In Vol. II is a short essay entitled "The Alhambra,"
      which praises the book very highly, while calling Irving's
      works in general "the perfection of refined and elegant
      writing."

17   FONTANEY, A. "La Littérature américaine. Washington
      Irving.--The Alhambra." Revue des Deux Mondes, VI (1 June
      1832), 516-49.
          Seven pages of commentary accompanying extensive quota-
      tions from the text.

18   MONTGOLFIER, ADÉLAÏDE. Review of The Alhambra. Revue
      Encyclopédique, LV (July 1832), 153-56.

32

1833 A   BOOKS - NONE

1833 B   SHORTER WRITINGS

1   ANON. "The Alhambra." Royal Lady's Magazine, V (January
      1833), 30-32.
          In arousing high expectations, Irving's earlier works
      "are the greatest enemies his future productions will prob-
      ably meet." Though there is nothing "striking" in this
      volume, there is no reason for disappointment. The Alham-
      bra is graceful and imaginative, and Irving involves the
      reader in his subject. His portraits of women are a source
      of delight.

2   ANON. "Scraps from the Book Kept at Stratford-upon-Avon."
      New York Mirror, XI (26 October 1833), 136.
          Prints a quatrain written there by Irving.

3   VERPLANCK, GULIAN C. "Historical Discourse." Discourses and
      Addresses on Subjects of American History, Arts, and Liter-
      ature. New York: J. & J. Harper, 1833, pp. 63-64.
          Originally delivered before the New York Historical So-
      ciety, Dec. 7, 1818. Expresses concern that a writer such
      as Irving has done so much to denigrate the Dutch in A His-
      tory of New York. Irving's great promise as a serious
      writer has recently been fulfilled, according to a new
      footnote, by Life of Columbus.

1834 A   BOOKS - NONE

1834 B   SHORTER WRITINGS

1   ANON. Review of The Alhambra. Morgenblatt für Gebildete
      Stände, Literatur-Blatt (Stuttgart and Tübingen), No. 9
      (1 January 1834), pp. 35-36.
          Short review of a German translation of The Alhambra.

2   ANON. "Outre-Mer." North American Review, XXIV (October
      1834), 459-67.
          A review of Longfellow's Outre-Mer. In his opening para-
      graph the reviewer notes that Longfellow has adopted the
      form of a series of tales and sketches used with so much
      success by Irving.

1835 A   BOOKS - NONE

1835

1835 B   SHORTER WRITINGS

1   ANON. Review of A Tour on the Prairies. Magazin für die
       Literatur des Auslands, VII (25 March 1835), 141-42.

2   ANON. Review of A Tour on the Prairies. Knickerbocker, V
       (April 1835), 352-55.
         Brief review with an extract from the as yet unpublished
       work. Praises Irving's "painter-like style."

3   ANON. Review of A Tour on the Prairies. Monthly Review, 4th
       Ser., I (April 1835), 467-79.
         Expresses delight with the style, sentiments, subjects,
       and scenes of the book.

4   ANON. Review of A Tour on the Prairies. Southern Literary
       Messenger, I (April 1835), 456-57.
         Despite Irving's agreeable, fresh, and highly descriptive
       style, his subject--the vast solitudes of the western
       prairies--wearies the mind with its monotony. Considering
       his famed purity of style, it is surprising to find the ex-
       pression "he set off like mad" repeated again and again.

5   ANON. "Washington Irving's neuestes Gemälde: 'A Tour on the
       Prairies.'" Blätter für literarische Unterhaltung (21
       April 1835), 459-60; (22 April), 462-63.
         Review of A Tour on the Prairies.

6   ANON. "Irving's Tour on the Prairies." Dublin University
       Magazine, V (May 1835), 554-72.
         Largely quotation, mixed with commentary on the Indian
       situation in the United States. High praise for Tour, and
       mixed comments on the earlier works.

7   ANON. Review of A Tour on the Prairies. Portland Magazine,
       I (1 May 1835), 255-56.
         Irving is essentially a "Yankee." When writing about
       foreign subjects, his genius suffers. A Tour on the
       Prairies is evidence that when he writes about America he
       is at his best.

8   ANON. Review of Abbotsford and Newstead Abbey. Athenaeum,
       No. 393 (9 May 1835), pp. 345-46.
         The book is overly long and contains little not already
       well-known or better handled by others.

9   ANON. Review of Abbotsford and Newstead Abbey. Magazin für
       die Literatur des Auslands, VII (27 May 1835), 249-51.

10   ANON. Review of <u>Abbotsford and Newstead Abbey</u>. <u>Knicker-</u>
      <u>bocker</u>, V (June 1835), 559.
            This second volume of Irving's <u>Crayon Miscellany</u> is even
      better than <u>A Tour on the Prairies</u> since the sketches of
      the estates of Scott and Byron "have more of an interest
      in them for the true lover of literary merit." Irving is
      "the purest writer of his age."

11   ANON. Review of <u>A Tour on the Prairies</u>. <u>American Quarterly</u>
      <u>Review</u>, XVII (June 1835), 532-33.
            Wit, morality, honesty enrich the account of western
      travels. Irving's descriptive skills give special interest
      to the scenes.

12   ANON. Review of <u>A Tour on the Prairies</u>. <u>Western Monthly</u>
      <u>Magazine</u>, III (June 1835), 329-37.
            Generalizations about Irving's greatness. Bulwer is a
      brilliant meteor who will soon fade away, but Irving will
      shine mildly, but steadily, for all time. Irving, the best
      essayist of his time, in turning his attention to the West,
      has left behind purely thoughtful musings for lively nar-
      ration.

13   ANON. "Washington Irving's neuestes Werk." <u>Blätter für</u>
      <u>literarische Unterhaltung</u> (29 June 1835), pp. 743-44.
      A review of <u>Abbotsford and Newstead Abbey</u>.

14   ANON. Review of <u>Abbotsford and Newstead Abbey</u>. <u>Southern</u>
      <u>Literary Messenger</u>, I (July 1835), 646-48.
            The volume "is the tribute of genius to its kindred spir-
      its, and it breathes a sanctifying influence over the
      graves of the departed." Extensive quotation.

15   ANON. Review of <u>Salmagundi</u>. <u>Knickerbocker</u>, VI (July 1835),
      73-75.
            Review of <u>Salmagundi</u> as published in Paulding's <u>Works</u>.
      Praises its humor and "thoughtful beauty," adding that the
      book seems to have increased rather than diminished in
      richness over time.

16   ANON. Review of <u>A Tour on the Prairies</u>. <u>Southern Literary</u>
      <u>Journal</u>, I (September 1835), 8-12.
            Praises Irving's "simple grace of style," graphic descrip-
      tion, good humor, and indulgent attitude toward human
      frailties. Mostly quotation.

17   ANON. "Washington Irving's Miscellanies." <u>Fraser's Magazine</u>,
      XII (October 1835), 409-15.

1835

(ANON.)
Unfavorable English review of A Tour on the Prairies. Criticizes it for lack of realism, tasteless humor, and its treatment of a barbaric topic. Concludes with more neutral comments on Abbotsford and Newstead Abbey.

18 [BUCKINGHAM, J. T.] Review of A Tour on the Prairies. New England Magazine, VIII (May 1835), 409–10.
Irving captures natural scenery through incisive and suggestive images. Quotes appropriate passages and comments on them.

19 CHASLES, PHILARÈTE. "De la littérature dans l'Amérique du nord." Revue des Deux Mondes, III (15 July 1835), 169–202.
Brief remarks on Irving. See in particular p. 193.

20 [EVERETT, EDWARD.] Review of A Tour on the Prairies. North American Review, XLI (July 1835), 1–28.
Irving is, as has been said before, the "best living writer of English prose." The present book defies classification. It blends elements of the travel book, novel, and romance. Extensive quotation.

21 [POE, EDGAR ALLAN.] Review of Legends of the Conquest of Spain. Southern Literary Messenger, II (December 1835), 64–65.
"To snatch from [history] a few striking and picturesque legends, possessing, at the same time, some absolute portion of verity, and to adorn them in his own magical language is all that Mr. Irving has done in the present instance. But that he has done this very well it is needless to say."

22 SOMNER, WILLIAM S. "Washington Irving." New York Mirror, XIII (19 December 1835), 197.
A "literary portrait." dealing with the qualities of Irving's writings in general. His forte is delicate humor.

1836 A BOOKS - NONE

1836 B SHORTER WRITINGS

1 A. "Vermischte Schriften." Allgemeine Literatur-Zeitung (Halle), III (July 1836), Ergänzungsblätter, 502–504.
Review of Abbotsford and Newstead Abbey and Legends of the Conquest of Spain.

2   ANON. Review of Legenden aus der Zeit der Eroberung von
    Spanien. Magazin für die Literatur des Auslands, IX (11
    January 1836), 19-20.
        Legends of the Conquest of Spain (Crayon Miscellany).

3   ANON. Review of Legends of the Conquest of Spain. Fraser's
    Literary Chronicle, I (23 January 1836), 117-18.
        ". . . a more delightful narrative of historical romance
    it has seldom been our lot to peruse."

4   ANON. "Washington Irving." New York Mirror, XIII (23 January
    1836), 235.
        Quotes and agrees with an unidentified London critical
    journal which suggests that Irving write books treating the
    United States as he did Spain. Adds that Legends of the
    Conquest of Spain has not received the public attention it
    deserves.

5   ANON. Review of Legends of the Conquest of Spain. Metropol-
    itan Magazine, XV (February 1836), 34.
        Brief review, summarizing some of the legends. Irving
    could not fail with such material, and he turns it to its
    best advantage.

6   ANON. "Irving's Miscellanies: Legends of the Conquest of
    Spain." New York Mirror, XIII (6 February 1836), 251.
        Quotes a lengthy passage describing Florinda. This de-
    scription, in its delicacy of style and sweetness of lan-
    guage, is unsurpassed, even by Irving.

7   ANON. "Knickerbocker's History of New York." Tait's Edin-
    burgh Magazine, III (March 1836), 201.
        Brief note. ". . . the very flower of Washington
    Irving's works!"

8   ANON. Review of Legends of the Conquest of Spain. Blätter
    für literarische Unterhaltung (26 April 1836), pp. 502-504.

9   ANON. Review of Astoria. Western Monthly Magazine, V (Novem-
    ber 1836), 685-87.
        Irving is to be admired because, despite his active imag-
    ination, he works within a framework of historical accu-
    racy. The review quotes passages from Astoria, but says
    little specifically about it.

10 ANON. Review of Astoria. Monthly Review, 4th Ser., II (De-
    cember 1836), 487-98.
        The best thing by Irving since, perhaps, The Sketch Book.
    The "history of a magnificent mercantile speculation."

1836

11   [CLARK, WILLIS GAYLORD.] "Ollapodiana." Knickerbocker, VIII
     (October 1836), 459-72.
         The author expresses his reverence for Irving: "I read
     [A History of New York] regularly once a year." Describes
     the last time he saw Irving, and the brilliance of his con-
     versation.

12   M. "Legends of the Conquest of Spain." Monthly Repository,
     N.S. X (February 1836), 81-89.
         Mostly summary and quotation from this volume of The
     Crayon Miscellany. The only fault of the volume is that
     it deals too much in details of battles.

13   *SOMNER, WILLIAM S. "The Writings of Washington Irving."
     Parterre, IV (26 March 1836), 196-98.
         Cited in Gohdes (1944.B3).

1837 A BOOKS - NONE

1837 B SHORTER WRITINGS

1   ANON. Review of Astoria. Knickerbocker, IX (January 1837),
     88-90.
         Essentially a long quotation with an adulatory introduc-
     tion.

2   ANON. "Astoria, or, Enterprise beyond the Rocky Mountains."
     Dublin University Magazine, IX (February 1837), 167-76.
         Mostly summary and quotation. "The book has all the in-
     terest of a work of fiction, combined with the accuracy of
     a historical narrative."

3   *ANON. Review of Astoria. Blätter für literarische Unter-
     haltung (28 February 1837) [Incomplete data].
         Unlocatable. Cited in Hewett-Thayer (1958.B3), p. 22.

4   ANON. Review of Astoria. American Quarterly Review, XXI
     (March 1837), 60-74.
         Praises both author and book. Suggests that Irving
     should have spent more time on the fine character of Astor
     and less on the secondary figures in the enterprise.

5   ANON. Review of Adventures of Captain Bonneville. Monthly
     Review, 4th Ser., II (June 1837), 279-90.
         A work of stylistic ease and grace, but three times as
     long as it should be.

6   ANON. Review of <u>Adventures of Captain Bonneville</u>. <u>Magazin</u>
      <u>für die Literatur des Auslands</u>, XI (28 June 1837), 305–
      306; (30 June), 311–12.

7   ANON. Review of <u>Adventures of Captain Bonneville</u>. <u>New York</u>
      <u>Review</u>, I (October 1837), 439–40.
         Irving "has shown us that here, in these worn-out times
      of the world, there is a last foothold left for a remnant
      of chivalry in the wild life of the Far West." May he
      write more such delightful books!

8   [EVERETT, EDWARD.] Review of <u>Astoria</u>. <u>North American Review</u>,
      XLIV (January 1837), 200–37.
         Thoughts on commercial exploitation of new lands through-
      out history, and on the implications of Astor's fur trade.
      Irving's book is extensively quoted and summarized.

9   LOCKHART, J. G. <u>Memoirs of the Life of Sir Walter Scott,</u>
      <u>Bart.</u> Edinburgh: Robert Cadell; London: John Murray and
      Whittaker and Company, 1837. IV, 87–95.
         Account of Irving's stay with Scott. Quotes extensively
      from <u>Abbotsford</u>. Suggests correctly that the visit was
      not in 1816, as Irving has it, but in 1817.

10   M., A. G. Review of <u>Astoria</u>. <u>Southern Literary Journal</u>, III
      (March 1837), 30–41.
         Mostly summary. Praises Irving, but points out certain
      "ungrammatical" passages. Especially quarrels with
      Irving's adoption of "American" spelling.

11   [POE, EDGAR ALLAN.] "Astoria." <u>Southern Literary Messenger</u>,
      III (January 1837), 59–68.
         This review of <u>Astoria</u> is essentially a history of the
      fur trade. Irving's work is thoroughly summarized and
      highly praised, but there is almost no attempt at literary
      criticism. Lists a few errors in the hope that they will
      be corrected in future editions.

12   R., J. A. Review of <u>Astoria</u>. <u>Westminster Review</u>, XXVI
      (January 1837), 318–48.
         Lengthy abstract of the work, with quotation. Praises
      Irving's skill in using primary documents to "weave a con-
      nected and exciting narrative."

1838 A   BOOKS - NONE

1838

1838 B SHORTER WRITINGS

   1   ANON. Review of A History of the Reign of Ferdinand and Isa-
        bella, the Catholic, by William H. Prescott. North Amer-
        ican Review, XLVI (January 1838), 234-46.
           Includes a comparison of Prescott's treatment of the
        Moorish wars with Irving's in The Conquest of Granada.
        Irving intends to amuse through a fanciful retelling of
        stories, Prescott to instruct through sober facts. Both
        approaches are valid.

   2   ANON. "American Lions." Bentley's Miscellany, IV (1 October
        1838), 405-12.
           Condescending treatment of American notables which turns
        respectful when mentioning Irving, but which makes fun of
        Americans' adulation of their one true literary figure.

   3   BROOKS, N[ATHAN] C. "American Authors. No. I. Washington
        Irving." American Museum of Literature and the Arts, I
        (September 1838), 1-7.
          A "short memoir" of Irving's life, generally praising
        his literary accomplishments, but also noting weaknesses,
        and contending that "much of the reputation he enjoys is
        adventitious, and belongs to the pioneer in letters, and
        the foreign courtier, as well as the author."

1839 A BOOKS - NONE

1839 B SHORTER WRITINGS

   1   ANON. "Want of a National Name." New York Mirror, XVII
        (7 September 1839), 7.
          Editorial concurring with Irving's views in his essay on
        "National Nomenclature." Quotes extensively, and heartily
        seconds Irving's proposal to change the name "America" to
        "Alleghania."

   2   [GALLAGHER, WILLIAM DAVIS.] Review of Hyperion by Henry
        Wadsworth Longfellow. Hesperian, III (October 1839), 420.
          Ranks Irving, Hawthorne, and Longfellow as the best
        American writers, though all three "lack force, comprehen-
        siveness, intensity."

1841 A BOOKS - NONE

1841 B   SHORTER WRITINGS

1   ANON. "Navarrete on Spain." Southern Literary Messenger,
       VII (March 1841), 231-39.
           Attacks Irving at length for misrepresenting in his
       Columbus his great debt to the work of Don Martin
       Navarrete. See also items 1842.B1-B4, 1843.B1.

2   ANON. Review of Biography and Poetical Remains of the Late
       Margaret Miller Davidson. Knickerbocker, XVIII (July
       1841), 71-72.
           Focuses mainly on the life and talents of Margaret and
       her sister Lucretia, commenting that "it is well that the
       writings of such an uncommon genius have fallen into the
       hands of an editor like Mr. Irving."

3   ANON. "Washington Irving." Democratic Review, IX (December
       1841), 593-97.
           Eulogistic praise of Irving for having raised the quality
       of American literature and increased its respectability in
       British eyes. Portrait.

4   *GIL, ENRIQUE. Pensamiento (Madrid) (1841), pp. 271 ff.
           Unobtainable. Cited in Williams (1935.A1), II, 300. On
       Irving's Columbus and Navarrete.

5   [HILLARD, A. S.] Review of Biography and Poetical Remains of
       the Late Margaret Miller Davidson. North American Review,
       LIII (July 1841), 139-46.
           Irving's memoir is "feeling and graceful." Extensive
       quotation.

6   POE, EDGAR A. "A Chapter on Autography." Graham's Magazine,
       XIX (December 1841), 273-86.
           On p. 279 Poe observes: "Irving's style is inimitable in
       its grace and delicacy; yet few of our practised writers
       are guilty of more frequent inadvertences of language. In
       what may be termed his mere English, he is surpassed by
       fifty whom we could name."

7   _____. Review of Biography and Poetical Remains of the Late
       Margaret Miller Davidson. Graham's Magazine, XIX (August
       1841), 93-94.
           "Few books have interested us more profoundly." (Poe's
       interest, however, is focused mainly on Margaret's sister,
       Lucretia, "a fairy-like child" and precocious poetic ge-
       nius who died at seventeen.) As for Irving, he has grace-
       fully let the material speak for itself; but in saying that

1841

([POE, EDGAR ALLAN.])
there has never been any poetry "more truly divine in its inspiration" than Lucretia's, he overstates the case.

1842 A BOOKS - NONE

1842 B SHORTER WRITINGS

1 ANON. "Spain." Southern Literary Messenger, VIII (May 1842), 305-17.
On p. 306 is a paragraph chiding Irving for his barely acknowledged use of Navarrete's work in his Columbus, and for taking all the credit for the laborious gathering of materials for the book. See items 1841.B1, 1842.B2-B4, and 1843.B1.

2 ANON. "Editor's Table." Knickerbocker, XX (July 1842), 97.
An attack on an unfavorable review of Columbus in the Southern Literary Messenger which accused Irving of plagiarism. See items 1841.B1, 1842.B1, B3-B4, 1843.B1.

3 ANON. "Editor's Table." Knickerbocker, XX (August 1842), 194-98.
Long attack on the plagiarism charge in the Southern Literary Messenger. Defends Irving's scholarship in his Columbus. See items 1841.B1, 1842.B1-B2, B4, 1843.B1.

4 ANON. "Mr. Washington Irving, Mr. Navarrete, and the Knickerbocker." Southern Literary Messenger, VIII (November 1842), 725-35.
Third and longest in a series of comments—by now a debate with the Knickerbocker Magazine—about the extent of Irving's reliance, in his Columbus, on the work of Navarrete. See items 1841.B1, 1842.B1-B3, and 1843.B1.

5 [POE, EDGAR ALLAN.] Review of Twice Told Tales by Nathaniel Hawthorne. Graham's Magazine, XX (April 1842), 254; (May), 298-300.
The only American tales of real merit are Hawthorne's and Tales of a Traveller. Compares Hawthorne to Irving; both writers have a certain quality of "repose," but Irving's "consists chiefly in the calm, quiet, unostentatious expression of commonplace thoughts, in an unambitious unadulterated Saxon."

1843 A BOOKS - NONE

1843 B SHORTER WRITINGS

1   ANON. "The Knickerbocker, Mr. Irving, and Sr. Navarrete."
     Southern Literary Messenger, IX (January 1843), 15-16.
          The last item on this side of the drawn-out controversy
     with the Knickerbocker Magazine on Irving's debt to
     Navarrete in his Columbus. This one attacks the Knicker-
     bocker, not Irving. See items 1841.B1 and 1842.B1-B4.

2   *OLLIFFE, CHARLES, ed. Extracts from the Complete Works of
     Washington Irving. Paris: Baudry, 1843.
          Contains a preface by the editor.

1844 A BOOKS - NONE

1844 B SHORTER WRITINGS

1   [ALEXIS, WILLIBALD.] Review of Life and Poetical Remains of
     Margaret M. Davidson. Blätter für literarische Unter-
     haltung (29 March 1844), pp. 355-56.
          Review of a German translation.

2   CLARK, LOUIS G., ed. The Literary Remains of the Late Willis
     Gaylord Clark. New York: Burgess, Stringer and Company,
     1844.
          On pp. 278-79 is a brief defense of Irving, included as
     part of an attack on an unnamed Philadelphia reviewer.

1845 A BOOKS - NONE

1845 B SHORTER WRITINGS

1   ANON. Review of Astoria. Magazin für die Literatur des
     Auslands, XXVIII (15 July 1845), 333; (17 July), 339-40.

2   D., E. Review of The Works of Washington Irving (2 vols.).
     Philadelphia: Lea and Blanchard, 1840. Southern Quarterly
     Review, VIII (July 1845), 69-93.
          Tribute to Irving for his role in establishing American
     literature, and his influence in educating the masses and
     raising national pride. Praises his "pure and faultless
     character," his humor, and his polished style.

3   PRESCOTT, WILLIAM H. "Irving's Conquest of Granada." Bio-
     graphical and Critical Miscellanies. London: R. Bentley,

1845

(PRESCOTT, WILLIAM H.)
1845, pp. 82-113.
Originally appeared in the North American Review. See item 1829.B18.

1846 A   BOOKS - NONE

1846 B   SHORTER WRITINGS

1   ANON. "Washington Irving." Bentley's Miscellany, XIX (1846), 622-23.
Brief tribute to Irving's literary talent and fine character. Portrait.

1847 A   BOOKS - NONE

1847 B   SHORTER WRITINGS

1   ANON. Notice of Life and Voyages of Christopher Columbus (Abridged). Brooklyn Daily Eagle, 12 March 1847.
"The life of Columbus should be read by every American young man and woman. And for most of them, this is probably the best form in which it can reach them."

2   GRISWOLD, RUFUS W. "Washington Irving." The Prose Writers of America. Philadelphia: Carey and Hart, 1847, pp. 201-22.
Contains a five-page essay on Irving and sixteen pages of selections from his works. A History of New York is called the "finest monument of his genius," and his other works treated with general approbation. Irving is not more English than American, and though his grammar is sometimes incorrect, his stylistic skills "place him in the very front rank of the masters of our language." Portrait.

3   MAYER, P. H. "Washington Irving." Democratic Review, XXI (December 1847), 488-94.
Glowing tribute to Irving as a great American writer and an inspiration to his successors.

1848 A   BOOKS - NONE

1848 B   SHORTER WRITINGS

1   ANON. "Washington Irving as a Writer." Ladies' Repository, VIII (July 1848), 217-20.

1848   (ANON.)
            An overview. High praise of his work, with the one qual-
            ification that, except for The Sketch Book and Columbus,
            he might have chosen more substantial subjects.

   2   *ANON. "Washington Irving." Hogg's Weekly Instructor, N.S. I
            (August 1848), 401-403.
                Cited in Gohdes (1944.B3). See item 1848.B7.

   3   ANON. Review of The Life of Oliver Goldsmith. Southern Lit-
            erary Messenger, XV (September 1848), 138.
                Comments on the previous biographies of Goldsmith. This
            latest one is "written by him, who, of all others, more
            nearly resembles Goldsmith in the purity and freedom of
            his style."

   4   ANON. Review of A History of New York. Literary World, III
            (2 September 1848), 604-607.
                Review occasioned by the publication of the Author's Re-
            vised Edition of the work. The book has "spontaneity of
            feeling" in addition to its other virtues. Its satire is
            still applicable forty years after being written.

   5   ANON. "Washington Irving." American Literary Magazine, III
            (October 1848), 195-201.
                Praises Irving as the greatest American master of belles
            lettres. An overview of his life and works.

   6   ANON. Review of The Sketch Book. Literary World, III (7 Oc-
            tober 1848), 703-704.
                Highly laudatory review of the Author's Revised Edition--
            critical of its pathos, but enchanted by everything else.

   7   ANON. "Washington Irving." Eclectic Magazine, XV (November
            1848), 412-15.
                Laments the unfortunate ideological antagonism between
            the U. S. and England, and praises Irving as a promoter of
            friendly relations. Briefly sketches his career and writ-
            ings. Reprinted from Hogg's Weekly Instructor. See item
            1848.B2.

   8   LOWELL, JAMES R. A Fable for Critics. New York: G. P. Put-
            nam, 1848, p. 65.
                Twenty lines of versified criticism on Irving. Mix "a
            true poet-heart" with "the fun of Dick Steele," "Throw in
            all of Addison, minus the chill"--
                And you'll find a choice nature, not wholly deserving
                A name either English or Yankee,--just Irving.

1849

1849 A BOOKS - NONE

1849 B SHORTER WRITINGS

1   ANON. "Washington Irving." Holden's Dollar Magazine, III
    (April 1849), 206-209.
        Irving's purity of taste and elegant manner are praised.
    As an example of his "elaborate simplicity," "The Voyage,"
    from The Sketch Book, is quoted whole.

2   ANON. Review of A Book of the Hudson. Literary World, IV
    (21 April 1849), 355.
        Enthusiastic reception of these reprinted tales and
    sketches.

3   ANON. Review of A Book of the Hudson. Holden's Dollar Maga-
    zine, III (June 1849), 373.
        "This is the Book of the Hudson." An enthusiastic note.

4   ANON. Review of Adventures of Captain Bonneville. Literary
    World, IV (16 June 1849), 515.
        Irving made a good book out of the raw materials provided
    by Bonneville. He is a master of literary felicity.

5   ANON. Review of The Life of Oliver Goldsmith. Literary
    World, V (1 September 1849), 173-74.
        Reviews the work of Goldsmith's previous biographers, and
    lauds Irving's work in bringing Goldsmith to life by inte-
    grating all the materials into a smooth narrative. "You
    feel that you are in the company of the hero of the story
    rather than of his biographer."

6   ANON. Review of The Life of Oliver Goldsmith. Holden's Dol-
    lar Magazine, IV (October 1849), 633.
        Irving's work leaves nothing more to be done. Of all
    his books, "this is the one for which literary men have the
    most reason to be grateful. It is a vindication of the
    literary character."

7   ANON. Review of The Life of Oliver Goldsmith. Knickerbocker,
    XXXIV (October 1849), 348-51.
        "We have no hesitation in pronouncing this one of the
    most delightful pieces of biography that we have ever pe-
    rused." Quotes passages with brief comments.

8   ANON. Review of Mahomet and His Successors. Literary World,
    V (22 December 1849), 537-39; (29 December), 560-61.
        Irving's eye is for the picturesque; he does not probe
    the most serious issues in the life of Mahomet. Mostly
    quotation.

9   [BOWEN, F.] Review of Astoria and The Crayon Miscellany.
     North American Review, LXIX (July 1849), 175-96.
          A review of books, by Irving and others, of interest be-
     cause of the emigration to California in search of gold.
     Irving is "the most delightful writer of English prose now
     living." It is good to know that the age "has not lost its
     relish for the unostentatious and inimitable graces, the
     fine taste and warm imagination of Irving."

1850 A BOOKS - NONE

1850 B SHORTER WRITINGS

1   ANON. Notice of Mahomet and His Successors. New Englander,
     VIII (February 1850), 153; (August), 481.
          The style, organization, unobtrusive philosophical con-
     text, and fairness of judgment distinguish Irving's work.
     He is a better historian than Goldsmith.

2   ANON. Review of Mahomet and His Successors. North British
     Review, XIII (February 1850), 189-224.
          Long essay on Mahomet and the Koran with only brief com-
     ments on Irving's biography: Irving's book "is an elegant
     but jejune compilation of legends relating to Mahomet, and
     by no means such a Life of the Prophet as ought by this
     time to have been laid before the English public."

3   ANON. Review of Mahomet and His Successors. Southern Quar-
     terly Review, XVII (April 1850), 248; (July), 529.
          A pleasing biography; but to one who has read Carlyle's
     "Mahomet" in Heroes and Hero Worship, Irving's work seems
     tame. Irving's delicacy ill accords with his subject's
     dramatic intensity.

4   ANON. "Washington Irving's Works." Christian Review, XV
     (April 1850), 203-14.
          A review of the Author's Revised Edition of Irving's
     works, and other Irving publications. Ardent admiration of
     Irving as a preserver of tradition. He modelled his style
     on the great literature of the past, particularly on Gold-
     smith; his works have become classics in their own time.

5   ANON. Review of Mahomet and His Successors, Vol. II. Liter-
     ary World, VI (27 April 1850), 415-16.
          A languid but marvellous history. Irving does best in
     the biographical, not the political parts, and the tales
     are told inimitably.

1850

6   ANON. "Washington Irving's Leben Muhammed's und seiner Nach-
     folger." Magazin für die Literatur des Auslands, XXXVII
     (4 May 1850), 213-15.
        On Mahomet and His Successors.

7   ANON. Review of A Chronicle of the Conquest of Granada.
     Holden's Dollar Magazine, VI (October 1850), 630.
        The work has the "finished elegance of style" character-
     istic of all Irving's writings. It is a beautiful, poet-
     ical romance and reliable history as well.

8   [COBB, J. B.] "The Genius and Writings of Washington Irving."
     American Whig Review, XII (December 1850), 602-16.
        High praise of Irving's genius and his contribution to
     the establishment of a truly American literature.

9   [KIRKLAND, MRS. C. M.] Review of The Life of Oliver Gold-
     smith. North American Review, LXX (April 1850), 265-89.
        Irving's book is reviewed along with Prior's Miscellane-
     ous Works of Goldsmith. The article essentially consists
     of reflections on Goldsmith, with few comments on Irving's
     contribution. Irving, however, is hailed as a successor
     to Goldsmith.

10   _____. Review of Mahomet and His Successors. North American
     Review, LXXI (October 1850), 273-307.
        Considers both Irving's book and another work on Mahomet.
     Mostly a retelling of the life. Of Irving's work, "the
     lack of potential passion in his own nature" enables him
     to treat his subject with detachment and a lack of preju-
     dice. "Mr. Irving possesses the rare power . . . of throw-
     ing his own mind into the mind he steadfastly contemplates,
     so as to see with its eyes, understand with its understand-
     ing, and feel with its passions."

1851 A BOOKS - NONE

1851 B SHORTER WRITINGS

1   ANON. Review of The Alhambra. Literary World, VIII (3 May
     1851), 356.
        Highest praise for this "flower-wreathed porch to Ara-
     bian History." A brief note.

2   *ANON. "Lives of Mahomet and His Successors." Christian Ob-
     server, CLXII (June 1851), 378.

3   *CHASLES, PHILARÈTE. Études sur la Littérature et les moeurs
      des Anglo-Américains au XIXe siècle. Paris: Amyot, 1851.
      Translated into English: See item 1852.B1.

4   CLARKE, EDWARD P. "Goldsmith and Irving." Holden's Dollar
      Magazine, VII (February 1851), 72-74.
           A comparison, biographical and literary, in which Irving
      is well-praised for his style, humor, and urbanity.

5   MARVEL, IK [D. G. MITCHELL.] "Dedicatory Letter." Dream
      Life: A Fable of the Seasons. New York: Charles Scrib-
      ner, 1851, pp. i-iii.
           Prefaced "Dedicatory Letter" is to Irving, "who has
      wrought our language into the most exquisite forms of
      beauty." See item 1863.B3.

6   [RIPLEY, G.] "Washington Irving." Harper's Monthly Magazine,
      II (April 1851), 577-80.
           A glowing essay on Irving's career, his style, and his
      personal virtues. He is down-to-earth without being pro-
      saic or dull; he "exalts and glorifies the actual without
      losing it in the clouds of a vaporous ideal." He balances
      many extremes, both in philosophy and style. Illustrated.

7   W., C. A. "Islamism." Southern Quarterly Review, N.S. IV
      (July 1851), 173-206.
           Long summary of Mahomet and His Successors, which is a
      "very grateful compilation," but which in intensity and
      imagination fails to do justice to the subject.

1852 A   BOOKS - NONE

1852 B   SHORTER WRITINGS

1   CHASLES, PHILARETE. Anglo-American Literature and Manners.
      New York: Charles Scribner, 1852.
           A translation from the French. See item 1851.B3. Irving
      is given five pages. His excellence lies primarily in his
      beautiful style, which is essentially English, not Amer-
      ican. His native New York was a strong influence, and his
      "most loveable works" are "those in which the delicate ob-
      servation of his youth is naïvely set forth." Index.

1853 A   BOOKS - NONE

1853

1853 B   SHORTER WRITINGS

1   ANON. "Washington Irving." Eclectic Magazine, XXIX (June
         1853), 155-62.
            Reprinted from New Monthly Magazine (April 1853). See
         item 1853.B3.

2   ANON. "American Authorship. No. I--Washington Irving."
         Littell's Living Age, XXXVII (11 June 1853), 646-52.
            Reprinted from New Monthly Magazine (April 1853). See
         item 1853.B3.

3   SIR NATHANIEL. "American Authorship. No. I--Washington
         Irving." New Monthly Magazine, XCVII (April 1853), 424-33.
            Characterizes Irving as a classic in his own time--the
         most popular author, though not necessarily the greatest
         in every respect. Surveys most of his works.

4   TUCKERMAN, H. T. "Washington Irving." Homes of American
         Authors. New York: George P. Putnam, 1853.
            A combination of biography, literary criticism, descrip-
         tion of the Hudson Valley, and brief comments on Sunnyside.

1854 A   BOOKS - NONE

1854 B   SHORTER WRITINGS

1   *ANON. An article on Washington Irving at home. Leisure Hour,
         III (1854?), 452-[Incomplete data].
            Cited in Poole's Index. Unlocatable.

2   HERRIG, L. Handbuch der nordamericanischen National-literatur.
         Braunschweig: George Westermann, 1854.
            Irving is treated on pp. 90-95.

1855 A   BOOKS - NONE

1855 B   SHORTER WRITINGS

1   ANON. "By the Fireside in the Frost." Dublin University
         Magazine, XLV (March 1855), 369-78.
            A rambling essay praising Irving's sketches of people
         and scenes in Wolfert's Roost, and his literary powers in
         general, as displayed in all his works.

2   ANON. "Washington Irving." Eclectic Magazine, XXXIV (April
         1855), 546-53.

(ANON.)
Reprinted from <u>Dublin University Magazine</u>. <u>See</u> item 1855.B1.

3   ANON. "Washington Irving; His Home and His Works." <u>New York Quarterly</u>, IV (April 1855), 66-83.
     A rambling essay, popular in tone, with many quotations from Irving's letters and works, and comments on a visit with him at Sunnyside.

4   ANON. Review of <u>The Life of George Washington</u>. <u>Knicker-bocker</u>, XLVI (July 1855), 74-76.
     Predicts eternal fame for the work and quotes from reviews by George Ripley and William Cullen Bryant. Ripley honors Irving for having overcome enormous difficulties inherent in such a project. Though the facts of Washington's career are well known, Irving has made them seem fresh; he presents Washington "as a living personality, not as a political or military automaton." Bryant appreciates the presentation of the great hero as a man with distinctly human weaknesses and uncertainties.

5   ANON. Review of <u>Wolfert's Roost</u>. <u>New Monthly Magazine</u>, 2nd Ser., CIV (July 1855), 297-99.
     Enumeration and glowing description of the sketches in the volume.

6   SACHOT, OCTAVE. Review of <u>Wolfert's Roost</u>. <u>Athenaeum français</u>, IV (12 May 1855), 384-86.

7   [STEVENS, A.] "Irving's Last Volume." <u>National Magazine</u>, VI (May 1855), 385-94.
     Favorable review of <u>Wolfert's Roost</u> and of Irving's works in general. Emphasizes the high moral quality of the writings, in contrast to most other works of the age.

1856 A BOOKS - NONE

1856 B SHORTER WRITINGS

1   [ALLYN, R.] "Irving's Works." <u>Methodist Quarterly Review</u>, XVI (October 1856), 537-49.
     Generally laudatory survey of Irving's accomplishments which sees his great flaw as lack of originality. Hence, <u>A History of New York</u>, "Rip Van Winkle," "The Legend of Sleepy Hollow," and some others will survive "because they are alive," while the rest will perish.

1856

2   ANON. Review of The Life of George Washington. Knicker-
     bocker, XLVII (March 1856), 304-306.
          "For clearness, richness, conciseness of arrangement,
     truthful grouping of incidents and scenes, it is unsur-
     passed by any modern work."

3   ANON. "Washington Irving." Littell's Living Age, LI (15 No-
     vember 1856), 435.
          Note on Irving's genealogy, expressing pride that such a
     distinguished American is of British descent. Reprinted
     from the London Literary Gazette.

4   [KIRKLAND, MRS. C. M.] Review of The Life of George Washing-
     ton North American Review, LXXXIII (July 1856), 1-30.
          Diffuse praise for Irving, and a long, philosophical sum-
     mary of Washington's life and career.

5   MOORE, THOMAS. Memoirs, Journal, and Correspondence of Thomas
     Moore. Ed. Lord John Russell. 8 vols. London: Longman,
     Brown, Green, and Longmans, 1856.
          Scattered references to Irving in Moore's Journal. Notes
     dinners, publishing arrangements, and allusions Irving
     makes to his works. Mentions telling Irving the story that
     was to develop into "Adventure of the German Student."
     Index.

6   [RICHARDS, T. A.] "Sunnyside, the Home of Washington Irving."
     Harper's Monthly Magazine, XIV (December 1856), 1-21.
          A long, discursive tour of the Hudson Valley and of Sun-
     nyside, interspersed with anecdotes about Irving and the
     region. Illustrated.

7   WALLACE, H. B. "Washington Irving: His Works, Genius, and
     Character." Literary Criticisms and Other Papers. Phila-
     delphia: Parry and McMillan, 1856, pp. 67-91.
          An essay on the aesthetics of Irving's writings.
     Irving's imagination and intellectual powers are actually
     quite commonplace. He pleases from the sheer force of his
     character and by inducing calm rather than excitement. In
     observation and visual descriptions, Irving reveals his
     genius.

1857 A BOOKS - NONE

1857 B SHORTER WRITINGS

1   ANON. "Washington Irving's Biographie Georg Washingtons."
     Blätter für literarische Unterhaltung (6 August 1857),
     p. 585-89.
          Review of the Life of George Washington.

2   ANON. Review of The Life of George Washington, Vol. 4. Lit-
    tell's Living Age, LV (17 October 1857), 177-81.
        Mostly quotation and summary. No critical commentary.
    Reprinted from the Athenaeum.

3   H. "Washington and Hamilton." Littell's Living Age, LIV (25
    July 1857), 250-53.
        Takes issue with Irving on his treatment of a Washington-
    Hamilton dispute in his Life of Washington. Reprinted from
    the National Intelligencer.

4   WHITMAN, WALT. "Reminiscences of Brooklyn." Brooklyn Daily
    Times (3 June 1857).
        The Dutch have made "grand" contributions to America,
    but as yet are only known "through some shallow burlesque,
    full of clown's wit like Irving's Knickerbocker 'history.'"
    The article is reprinted in Emory Holloway's Uncollected
    Poetry and Prose of Walt Whitman. Garden City, New York:
    Doubleday, Page, and Company, 1921, II, 5.

5   W[ILLIS], N. P. "Willis at Sunnyside." Littell's Living Age,
    LIV (12 September 1857), 699-702.
        Willis recounts, in a letter headed "Idlewild," his tour
    of Irving's estate and conversation with the author.
    Irving reminisces. Reprinted from The Home Journal (15
    August).

6   _____. "Willis at Sunnyside. No. II." Littell's Living Age,
    LV (24 October 1857), 241-43.
        A second letter, continuing that printed 12 September.
    Willis and Irving take an afternoon drive through Sleepy
    Hollow. Reprinted from The Home Journal.

1858 A   BOOKS - NONE

1858 B   SHORTER WRITINGS

1   ANON. "Four American Authors." Irish Quarterly Review, VIII
    (October 1858), 915-76.
        On Irving, basically a biographical sketch. Praises his
    "simple, direct and natural style," his "cosmopolitan tone
    of mind," and his contribution to American literature.
    Sees him as both a belles-lettrist and preserver of tradi-
    tion.

1858

2   [GREENE, G. W.] Review of The Life of George Washington.
     North American Review, LXXXVI (April 1858), 330–58.
        Eulogistic praise for all aspects of the work. Re-
     printed in Greene's Biographical Studies. See item 1859.B7.

1859 A BOOKS

1   *CREIGHTON, WILLIAM. Sermons on the Occasion of the Death of
     the Late Washington Irving. New York: Pudney & Russell,
     1859.
        Preached in Christ Church, Tarrytown, by Rev. William
     Creighton, and Rev. J. Seldon Spencer. Cited in Williams
     and Edge (1936.A1).

1859 B SHORTER WRITINGS

1   *ANON. Review of Lebensgeschichte Georg Washingtons. Magazin
     für die Literatur des Auslands, LVI (18 November 1859)
     [incomplete data].
        Life of George Washington. Unlocatable. Cited in
     Hewett-Thayer (1958.B3), p. 23.

2   ANON. "Death of Washington Irving." Littell's Living Age,
     LXIII (24 and 31 December 1859), 816–17.
        Obituary expressing appreciation for his genial character
     and literary achievement. Reprinted from the New York
     Evening Post.

3   ASPINWALL, THOMAS. "Remarks of Col. Aspinwall." Proceedings
     of the Massachusetts Historical Society, IV (December
     1859), 404–408.
        Personal reminiscence by Irving's friend and literary
     agent. "It was a marked peculiarity of Washington Irving
     to need sympathy, support, and cheering encouragement.
     When these were withheld, he was shorn of half his
     strength." Account of Irving's careful composition of The
     Sketch Book to disarm British criticism.

4   [CLARK, LOUIS GAYLORD.] "Editorial Narrative-History of the
     Knickerbocker Magazine: Number Seven." Knickerbocker,
     LIV (October 1859), 424–31.
        Account of how Irving became a contributor. Quotes ex-
     tensively from some of his early columns--"The Crayon
     Papers."

5   EVERETT, EDWARD. "Remarks of Mr. Everett." Proceedings of
     the Massachusetts Historical Society, IV (December 1859),
     395–403.

(EVERETT, EDWARD)
Survey of Irving's life. Detailed comparison of Irving and Addison. Addison is more learned, but in humor, characterization, and moral judgment they are equal. Irving is his superior in the "poetical faculty" and in "human sympathies." As for style, both are "remote from the tiresome stateliness of Johnson and Gibbon" but otherwise their resemblance has been overstated. Honors Irving as a great historian.

6 FELTON, C. C. "Remarks of Professor Felton." Proceedings of the Massachusetts Historical Society, IV (December 1859), 408-18.
Anecdotes and tribute on the occasion of Irving's death. Quotes letter from Irving to Felton dated 17 May 1859.

7 GREENE, GEORGE WASHINGTON. Biographical Studies. New York: G. P. Putnam, 1859.
Includes an adulatory essay on Irving's literary excellences, and another one of fulsome praise for his life of Washington which is reprinted from North American Review LXXXVI (April 1858). See item 1858.B2.

8 HOLMES, OLIVER WENDELL. "Dr. Holmes's Remarks." Proceedings of the Massachusetts Historical Society, IV (December 1859), 418-22.
Reminiscences. Account of his first visit with Irving and a discussion of Irving's medical problems.

9 LANMAN, CHARLES. "A Day With Washington Irving." Once A Week (31 December 1859), pp. 5-8.
Excerpt from a letter. Details of a long conversation with Irving while he was working on his Life of Washington. Irving reminisces on his life and literary work.

10 LONGFELLOW, HENRY WADSWORTH. "Remarks of Mr. Longfellow." Proceedings of the Massachusetts Historical Society, IV (December 1859), 393-95.
The first of a series of remarks in a special meeting of the Society on the occasion of Irving's death. "Every reader has his first book: I mean to say, one book, among all others, which, in early youth, first fascinates his imagination, and at once excites and satisfies the desires of his mind. To me, this first book was the 'Sketch Book' of Washington Irving." Warmly praises Irving as a writer and as a man. Introduces a resolution of honor and sympathy to be sent to his family.

WASHINGTON IRVING: A REFERENCE GUIDE

1859

11   SUMNER, GEORGE. Letter to the Massachusetts Historical So-
      ciety on the death of Irving. Proceedings of the Massa-
      chusetts Historical Society, IV (December 1859), 422-23.
      Points out Irving's diplomatic accomplishments.

12   TILTON, THEODORE. "Half an Hour at Sunnyside. A Visit to
      Washington Irving." Independent, XI (24 November 1859), 1.
      An interview with Irving at age 76, shortly before his
      death. He reminisces on his writing career.

13   _____. "A Visit to Washington Irving." Littell's Living Age,
      LXIII (24 and 31 December 1859), 822-24.
      Reprinted from the Independent (24 November). See item
      1859.B12.

1860 A BOOKS

1   IRVINGIANA: A MEMORIAL OF WASHINGTON IRVING. Comp. E. A.
      Duyckinck. New York: C. B. Richardson, 1860.
      A heterogeneous collection of anecdotes, poems, biograph-
      ical sketches, speeches, reminiscences, and assorted notes,
      concerning Irving's life, character, works, influence, and
      death (which the volume commemorates), much of it re-
      printed. The most significant contributors are Duyckinck,
      Longfellow, George Bancroft, and Edward Everett. Also in-
      cludes several Irving poems and letters.

1860 B SHORTER WRITINGS

1   ANON. "Death of Washington Irving." Eclectic Magazine, XLIX
      (January 1860), 139.
      Brief obituary, emphasizing Irving's literary success
      and his role as founder of American literature.

2   ANON. "Death of Washington Irving." Knickerbocker, LV (Jan-
      uary 1860), 96-99.
      Long obituary. Quotes eulogies in other publications.

3   ANON. "Gossip With Readers and Correspondents." Knicker-
      bocker, LV (May 1860), 552-53.
      Prints a long letter from a correspondent extolling the
      associations that Irving's works can provoke. Quotes and
      discusses an imitation of Irving's "Roscoe." Praises
      Bryant's tribute to Irving. Quotes from Edward Everett's
      eulogy. Mentions Paulding's death in connection with
      Irving's.

4   ANON. Obituary of Washington Irving. <u>Southern Literary Mes-</u>
      <u>senger</u>, XXX (January 1860), 73-74.
          Praises Irving's character, literary and diplomatic ca-
      reers, and graceful genius. Includes a eulogistic account
      of Irving's funeral by H. Tuckerman.

5   BANCROFT, GEORGE. "George Bancroft on Washington Irving."
      <u>Littell's Living Age</u>, LXV (9 June 1860), 620-21.
          Sentimental eulogy, delivered at a special meeting of the
      New York Historical Society, praising particularly Irving's
      historical works. Suggests that the merchants of New York
      raise a statue to his memory.

6   BRYANT, WILLIAM CULLEN. <u>A Discourse on the Life, Character</u>
      <u>and Genius of Washington Irving, Delivered Before the New</u>
      <u>York Historical Society, at the Academy of Music in New</u>
      <u>York, on the 3d of April, 1860.</u> New York: G. P. Putnam,
      1860.
          A laudatory, short literary biography in which Bryant
      comments that Irving paved the way, with <u>The Sketch Book</u>,
      for the rapid growth and acceptance of American literature.
      Includes warm remarks on the Irving-Bryant relationship.

7   _____. "The Life, Writings, and Genius of Washington Irving."
      <u>Littell's Living Age</u>, LXV (5 May 1860), 298-312.
          Transcription of Bryant's speech before the New York
      Historical Society, April 3, 1860. Detailed biographical
      sketch expressing deep reverence for Irving and his liter-
      ary accomplishments. Reprinted from the New York <u>Evening</u>
      <u>Post</u>.

8   BUCHANAN, W. W. "Dr. Buchanan's Reminiscences. Washington
      Irving." <u>Historical Magazine</u>, IV (May 1860), 138.
          Recollections about a children's literary club which in-
      cluded Irving. <u>See</u> the ed. note in the August 1860 issue
      (p. 244) explaining that the doctor had probably mistaken
      Irving for one of his older brothers.

9   _____. "Washington Irving and Adet Kissam." <u>Historical</u>
      <u>Magazine</u>, IV (August 1860), 245.
          A brief anecdote, by Dr. W. W. Buchanan, on Irving's
      having heard a false report of Kissam's death.

10   CLARK, LOUIS G., et al. "Memorial of Washington Irving."
      <u>Knickerbocker</u>, LV (January 1860), 113-28.
          This commemoration includes "Reminiscences of the Late
      Washington Irving" by Clark, with details of his associa-
      tion with Irving and recollections of his funeral; Dr.

1860

(CLARK, LOUIS G., et al.)
James O. Noyes' "Washington Irving as an Invalid"--a sec-
ondhand account; "Address of the Hon. George Bancroft, Before the N. Y. Historical Society"--a eulogy; "Extracts
from Dr. John W. Francis' Remarks Before the Historical
Society"--comments by a childhood friend; "From Mr. Willis'
'Idlewild' Letter"--reminiscences on the old Irving; and
"From Theodore Tilton's 'Half-Hour at Sunnyside'"--more
reminiscences on Irving's old age.

11   [CLARK, LOUIS GAYLORD.] "Narrative of the Knickerbocker Magazine: Number Twelve." Knickerbocker, LV (April 1860),
430-38.
Includes an account of how Irving helped Henry Cary pub-
lish a story in Knickerbocker. Cary, who wrote under the
name "John Waters," became an important contributor.

12   _____. "Reminiscences of the Late Washington Irving."
Knickerbocker, LV (April 1860), 439-44.
Primarily letters to the editor concerning Irving the man
and writer. Quotes an anecdote from the New York Spirit of
the Times. Prints two Irving letters.

13   _____. "Reminiscences of the Late Washington Irving: Number
Two." Knickerbocker, LV (February 1860), 222-23.
Anecdotes and personal recollections of Irving. Prints
an account of Irving's life by E. Lord and an article from
the Albany Evening Journal. Quotes Irving's pastor, Dr.
Creighton, on Irving's religious beliefs. Prints five letters from Irving to Clark and one letter to A. S. Thurston.

14   EVERETT, EDWARD. "Edward Everett on Washington Irving."
Eclectic Magazine, XLIX (February 1860), 290-93.
Commemorative speech, read to the Massachusetts Histor-
ical Society at a special meeting held in tribute to
Irving. See item 1859.B5.

15   LESLIE, C. R. Autobiographical Recollections. 2 vols. London: John Murray, 1860.
Memoirs of Irving's friend, an English artist who illustrated some of his writings. Gives an account of the composition of "The Stout Gentleman." The second volume consists largely of correspondence between the two. Portrait.

16   [PUTNAM, G. P.] "Recollections of Irving. By His Publisher."
Atlantic Monthly, VI (November 1860), 601-12.
Anecdotes and fond memories.

17   REDDING, CYRUS. "Washington Irving." New Monthly Magazine,
         CXVIII (February 1860), 213-21.
            Memoir and eulogy by a British acquaintance. Focuses on
         Irving's attitudes toward Great Britain, his promotion of
         international good will, his affable personality, and his
         contributions to literature in general.

18   THACKERAY, WILLIAM. "Nil Nisi Bonum." Cornhill Magazine, I
         (February 1860), 129-34.
            Eulogy, written shortly after Irving's death. Praises
         his gentle character and the good will towards England ex-
         pressed in his works.

19   _____. "Nil Nisi Bonum." Littell's Living Age, LXIV (10
         March 1860), 636-69.
            Reprinted from Cornhill Magazine, I (February 1860), 129-
         34. See item 1860.B18.

20   WINTHROP, R. C. Extract from a letter on the death of Irving.
         Proceedings of the Massachusetts Historical Society, IV
         (January 1860), 427-29.
            Mourns Irving's death and refers to the great impression
         he made in Europe.

1861 A   BOOKS - NONE

1861 B   SHORTER WRITINGS

1   ANON. Review of The Life of Oliver Goldsmith. Knickerbocker,
         LVII (May 1861), 548-49.
            Praises the Putnam edition of Irving's works. This work
         is "one of the best, the most entertaining, the most natu-
         ral biographies of the last three centuries." Compares
         Irving with Goldsmith and appreciates Irving's portrait of
         Boswell.

1862 A   BOOKS

1   IRVING, PIERRE M., ed. The Life and Letters of Washington
         Irving. 4 vols. New York: G. P. Putnam, 1862-1864.
            The authorized biography, by Irving's nephew. Irving's
         letters are placed in the context of his public and private
         life.

1862

1862 B   SHORTER WRITINGS

1   ANON. "Recollections of Washington Irving." Continental
      Monthly, I (June 1862), 689-700.
           Biographical essay by "one of his friends," which places
      great stress on Matilda Hoffman and her effect on Irving's
      life. If not for her death, the writer thinks, Irving
      would not have become a great author.

2   DUYCKINCK, E. A. "Washington Irving." National Portrait Gal-
      lery of Eminent Americans. New York: Johnson, Fry and
      Company, 1862. II, 99-109.
           A flattering biographical essay. Irving's character is
      praised, as are his achievements in literature and public
      life.

3   IRVING, PIERRE. "Why Irving Was Never Married." Knicker-
      bocker, LIX (May 1862), 485-87.
           From the Boston Post. Irving and the death of Matilda
      Hoffman. See item 1862.B4.

4   "NOR'WESTER." "Why Irving was Never Married." Eclectic Mag-
      azine, LVI (May 1862), 135-37.
           The story of Matilda Hoffman, quoted from an Irving let-
      ter to someone who inquired why he had never married. Re-
      printed from the Boston Post, 3 April 1862.

5   [WYNNE, J.] "Washington Irving." Harper's New Monthly Maga-
      zine, XXIV (February 1862), 349-56.
           A friend's recollections of Irving, his habits and per-
      sonality traits, his interaction with those around him.

1863 A   BOOKS - None

1863 B   SHORTER WRITINGS

1   ANON. "Washington Irving's Sketch-Book." Spectator, XXXVI
      (21 March 1863), 1786-87.
           Highly complimentary remarks occasioned by a new edition
      of The Sketch Book. Irving may be predominantly English
      in his art, but he is American in his feelings. His sense
      of nature and his depiction of American rural life are
      particularly noteworthy. Though some call his writings
      flimsy, their beauty of style renders them immortal; and
      their importance to the growth of American literature will
      keep them high in the opinion of scholars.

2   CURTIS, GEORGE W. "Longfellow." Atlantic Monthly, XII (December 1863), 769-75.
     In part, a comparison of Outre-Mer with The Sketch Book, discussing the particular qualities of each.

3   MITCHELL, D. G. "Preface." Dream Life: A Fable of the Seasons. New York: Charles Scribner's Sons, 1863, pp. v-xiii.
     A new preface on the author's friendship and conversations with Irving. Recounts conversations on Irving's habits of composition and on a novel he had intended to write about one of the "regicide Judges" who had fled to New England. Includes a letter from Irving to Mitchell dated November 1851, and miscellaneous biographical glimpses. See item 1851.B5.

4   THACKERAY, W. M. "Nil nisi bonum." Roundabout Papers. London: Smith, Elder and Company, 1863. pp. 339-52.
     Thackeray's eulogy on Irving, reprinted from Cornhill Magazine. See item 1860.B18.

1864 A   BOOKS - NONE

1864 B   SHORTER WRITINGS

1   ANON. "Irving at Sunnyside." New Monthly Magazine, CXXXI (July 1864), 297-309.
     Biographical sketch of Irving in his later years, based on Vol. IV of Pierre Irving's Life and Letters. Emphasizes his material success, happiness, and admirable character.

2   EYMA, XAVIER. "Les Historiens de L'École américaine. IV, Washington Irving." Revue contemporaine, XL (31 August 1864), 656-80.

3   [MITCHELL, D. G.] "Washington Irving." Atlantic Monthly, XIII (June 1864), 694-701.
     A biographical essay, with some personal reminiscences, occasioned by the publication of Pierre Irving's Life and Letters. Sees Irving, finally, as "the man whom all men loved."

1865 A   BOOKS - NONE

1865

1865 B   SHORTER WRITINGS

1   ANON. "A Visit to Sunniside, [sic] on the Banks of the Hudson: The Residence of the Late Washington Irving." Leisure Hour, XIV (1865), 103–106.
     Biographical sketch of Irving, description of his home, and an account of conversations with him.

2   ANON. "A Visit to Sunnyside." Eclectic Magazine, LXIV (N.S. I) (April 1865), 497–501.
     Reprinted from Leisure Hour; See item 1865.B1.

3   COOKE, JOHN ESTEN. "Irving at Sunnyside in 1858." Hours at Home, I (October 1865), 507–12.
     Sentimental memoir of an afternoon's visit with Irving the summer before his death. Character sketch of Irving.

1866 A   BOOKS – NONE

1866 B   SHORTER WRITINGS

1   [DENNETT, J. R.] "Irving's New Volumes." Nation, III (4 October 1866), 265–66.
     Review of Spanish Papers and Other Miscellanies. Characterizes Irving as a writer of the past, and calls his work entertaining but not great.

1867 A   BOOKS – NONE

1867 B   SHORTER WRITINGS

1   ANON. "Washington Irving's Spanish Papers and Miscellanies." Littell's Living Age, XCIV (14 September 1867), 692–95.
     Mostly summary. Praises Irving's "grace and ease of style," and his "generous and kindly sentiments," but objects to the confusion of fact and fiction. Reprinted from Saturday Review.

2   ANON. "Washington Irving's Miscellanies." Littell's Living Age, XCV (28 December 1867), 817–20.
     Deplores Pierre Irving's efforts in collecting inferior writings. Deprecates particularly W. Irving's critical articles, his lack of originality, and his hesitancy to state his opinions openly. Reprinted from the London Review.

3   WALDRON, WILLIAM WATSON. "Sketch One: Washington Irving." <u>Washington Irving and Cotemporaries, in Thirty Life Sketches</u>. New York: W. H. Kelley and Co., [1867], pp. 17-54.

A survey of Irving's life and career, including quotations from reviews. The book's preface comments on the author's friendship with Irving, and their correspondence.

1868 A BOOKS - NONE

1868 B SHORTER WRITINGS

1   [TAYLOR, BAYARD.] "By-ways of Europe: The Kyffhauser and Its Legends." <u>Atlantic Monthly</u>, XXI (May 1868), 614-26.

On p. 623 cites the legend of Peter Klaus as the source of "Rip Van Winkle." Although almost every feature is taken from the legend, Irving has worked the material into a new creation. "Peter Klaus is simply a puppet of the people's fancy, but Rip Van Winkle has an immortal vitality of his own."

1869 A BOOKS - NONE

1869 B SHORTER WRITINGS

1   CLARK, L[OUIS] GAYLORD. "Recollections of Washington Irving." <u>Lippincott's Monthly Magazine</u>, III (May 1869), 552-60.

Clark's account of his friendship with Irving. Includes parts of conversations, anecdotes, and extracts from letters and notes.

1870 A BOOKS

1   ADAMS, CHARLES. <u>Memoir of Washington Irving. With Selections from His Works, and Criticisms</u>. New York: Carlton and Lanahan, 1870.

". . . a brief and direct history of Irving, . . . including slight specimens of some of his more popular compositions. . . ." Not written for "the <u>literati</u>, professional men, and students. . . ."

1870 B SHORTER WRITINGS

1   LOWELL, JAMES R. <u>Among My Books</u>. London: MacMillan and Co., 1870.

<u>A History of New York</u> looks at history in the "daylight"

1870

(LOWELL, JAMES R.)
of a modern vantage point, making the historical figures
seem "ludicrously small, when contrasted with the semi-
mythic grandeur in which we have clothed them." See
Lowell's p. 221.

1871 A   BOOKS - NONE

1871 B   SHORTER WRITINGS

1   PUTNAM, G. P. "Memories of Distinguished Authors. Washington
      Irving." Harper's Weekly (Supplement), XV (27 May 1871),
      492-96.
         An anecdotal history of Irving's life and works, by his
      publisher.

1873 A   BOOKS - NONE

1873 B   SHORTER WRITINGS

1   COOKE, JOHN ESTEN. "A Morning at Sunnyside with Washington
      Irving." Southern Magazine, XII (June 1873), 710-16.
         Reminiscences of a visit with Irving in the summer before
      his death.

1875 A   BOOKS - NONE

1875 B   SHORTER WRITINGS

1   J., R. J. "Irving's English Sketches." Yale Literary Maga-
      zine, XL (March 1875), 311-16.
         Appreciative commentary on some of the English pieces in
      The Sketch Book, pronouncing the Christmas sketches and
      "Westminster Abbey" the best.

1876 A   BOOKS - NONE

1876 B   SHORTER WRITINGS

1   LATHROP, GEORGE P. A Study of Hawthorne. Boston: J. R.
      Osgood & Co., 1876.
         On page 304 Lathrop observes that Irving lacks the great
      touchstone of humor, pathos. For that reason Joseph Jef-
      ferson's stage version of "Rip Van Winkle" is superior to

(LATHROP, GEORGE P.)
Irving's original. He also deals with Irving's position in Anglo-American literary relations.

2 _____. "Poe, Irving, Hawthorne." Scribner's Monthly, XI (April 1876), 799-808.
Comparison of the three authors, chiefly in terms of their contribution to a uniquely American literature, ranking Irving at the bottom of the list: "Irving's superficial treatment of theme and acquired style operate against the originality of his few American fictions." Discusses The Sketch Book, A History of New York, and mentions other works, admitting that "for simple surface execution" he is unrivalled but that "at times the minute atom of real emotion or definite incident . . . is almost stifled by his insatiable desire of words."

3 *SEDLEY, E. "Notice." Vie et Voyages de Christophe Colombe. Paris: J. Delalain et fils, 1876.
Unobtainable. Cited in Morris (1916.B3), p. 12.

1879 A BOOKS

1 HILL, DAVID J. Washington Irving. New York: Sheldon and Company, 1879.
A full-length, laudatory literary biography of "the beloved Father of American Letters."

1879 B SHORTER WRITINGS

1 BRIGHTWELL, D. B. "Tennyson and Washington Irving." Notes and Queries, 5th Ser., XII (26 July 1879), 65.
Draws parallels which suggest the influence of Irving's "The Pride of the Village" (The Sketch Book) on Tennyson's "May Queen."

2 TOWNSEND, WALTER. "Washington Irving's Old Christmas." Canadian Monthly and National Review, II (January 1879), 20-29.
Irving's Christmas stories present an ideal Christmas; as such, the characters and scenes are all types rather than being drawn from life. As an essayist, Irving compares favorably with Steele, Goldsmith, and Lamb. He is "unrivalled" as a story-teller, despite weaknesses of plot and character, because of his "charm of manner" and the "direct simplicity" of his narration.

Washington Irving: A Reference Guide

1880

1880 A   BOOKS

1   WARNER, C. D., W. C. BRYANT, G. P. PUTNAM. Studies of Irving.
New York: G. P. Putnam's Sons, 1880.
Reprinted essays. Warner's is an approbatory, though not
effusive, piece of literary biography, emphasizing Irving's
fine character. This essay also appeared as the introduction to the Geoffrey Crayon Edition of Irving's works
(1880). For Bryant See 1860.B6, and for Putnam, 1860.B16.

1880 B   SHORTER WRITINGS

1   WARNER, CHARLES DUDLEY. "Washington Irving." Atlantic Monthly, XLV (March 1880), 396-408.
A biographical essay and an inquiry into the permanence
of Irving's work. His writings lack intellectual force
and do not address great human problems. On the other
hand, because of the calm beauty and morality in his work
he may still be well regarded when the more spectacular intellectual achievements of the age have passed away.

1881 A   BOOKS

1   WARNER, C. D. Washington Irving. Boston: Houghton Mifflin
and Company, 1881.
Attempts to be impartial. Finds Irving to have had a
"broad and eclectic genius," and sees his intellectual
shortcomings as more than balanced by the qualities in his
writings which reflect his own fine character. A full literary biography with extensive quotation from Irving's
works.

1881 B   SHORTER WRITINGS - NONE

1882 A   BOOKS - NONE

1882 B   SHORTER WRITINGS

1   HAWEIS, H. R. "Washington Irving." American Humorists. New
York: Funk and Wagnalls, 1882, pp. 7-36.
Witty commentary on Irving's career and some of his hu-
morous writings.

2   NICHOL, JOHN. American Literature: An Historical Sketch.
Edinburgh: Adam and Charles Black, 1882, pp. 170-75.
Irving belonged equally to the Old World and to the New.
He had great versatility and he started "the vein of

66

(NICHOL, JOHN)
burlesque that has run through his country's literature."
A History of New York, "in point of pure originality, [is]
Irving's masterpiece."

3   QUESNEL, LÉO. "La Littérature aux États-Unis." Nouvelle
revue, XVI (1 May 1882), 121-53.
The commentary on Irving is on pp. 123-26.

1883 A   BOOKS - NONE

1883 B   SHORTER WRITINGS

1   ANON. "A Bibliography of Irving." Critic, III (31 March
1883), 143-45.
Bibliography of Irving's works, and of biographies and
reviews. Incomplete. An appendix to the group of commemorative articles in this issue.

2   ANON. "Editor's Easy Chair." Harper's New Monthly Magazine,
LXVI (April 1883), 790-91.
Eulogistic tribute to Irving on the centenary of his
birth. Portrait, p. 650.

3   CURTIS, GEORGE W. "Irving's 'Knickerbocker.'" Critic, III
(31 March 1883), 139-40.
"Irving was the embodiment of the cosmopolitan character
of New York as distinguished from New England" with its
somber puritanism. Irving's treatment of the Hudson Valley
has given the whole region a magical charm.

4   FOSTER, W. E. "Washington Irving." Providence Public Library
Monthly Reference Lists, III (April 1883), 13-14.
Bibliographical reference guide to secondary sources.
Quotes from reviews.

5   GAY, S. H. "Irving the Historian." Critic, III (31 March
1883), 141-42.
Though Irving is not generally considered as an historian, he properly belongs among "the first of American historical scholars." Both Columbus and Life of Washington
are comprehensive and useful products of historical research.

6   GOSSE, EDMUND W. "Irving's 'Sketch-book.'" Critic, III (31
March 1883), 140-41.
With The Sketch Book Irving became "a finished and clas-
sic writer, bowing to the great tradition of English

1883

(GOSSE, EDMUND W.)
prose. . . ." He stands with the great essayists of the time--Hazlitt, Lamb, and Hunt, though he is more romantic than they. Cobbett is a source of his style.

7   G., W. E. "One of Irving's Old Cronies." Critic, III (31 March 1883), 142.
Anecdotal sketch of Irving and Capt. Jacob Storm, a friend and neighbor at Tarrytown.

8   HOLMES, OLIVER W. "Irving's Power of Idealization." Critic, III (31 March 1883), 138-39.
Personal reminiscence, and tribute to Irving. Comments on the joy of finding familiar American scenes and experiences turned into literature.

9   MORSE, JAMES H. "Washington Irving." Critic, III (31 March 1883), 137-38.
Biographical sketch, highlighting Irving's major works and the events in his life which influenced them. Appreciative tribute, the first of a group of articles in this issue commemorating the centennial of Irving's birth.

10   [SEDGWICK, A. G.] "Washington Irving." Nation, XXXVI (5 April 1883), 291-92.
An evaluation of Irving's reputation and work. Irving not only showed that Americans could write, but he made local traditions and customs proper material for literature. As an essayist and historian he lacked originality, but in A History of New York the device of ridicule helped New York realize "a proper perspective for its past." "In this respect he may be regarded as the father of a long line of American humorists who have persisted in exhibiting the reverse of the heroic view of American history."

11   *STODDARD, R. H. The Life of Washington Irving. New York: J. B. Alden, 1883.
Unlocatable; cited in Williams and Edge (1936.A1). Also printed as the introduction to several undated late nineteenth-century editions of Irving's works. An unexceptional, short literary biography.

12   [THOMPSON, J. B.] "The Genesis of the Rip Van Winkle Legend." Harper's Monthly Magazine, LXVII (September 1883), 617-22.
A discussion of the sources and analogues of "Rip Van Winkle." Retells the legends of the sleeping monarchs, Peter Klaus, and other narratives with the long sleep motif.

13 WARNER, C. D. "Irving's Humor." Critic, III (31 March 1883), 139.
    Irving is still highly regarded because his humor is always coupled with a warm sympathy for humanity. He has a gift for making us love the very characters he causes us to laugh at.

14 WISE, DANIEL. Washington Irving. Home College Series, No. 8. New York: Phillips and Hunt, 1883.
    A fifteen-page pamphlet which surveys Irving's life and works from a Christian perspective.

15 W., J. V. "Washington Irving and His Friends." Leisure Hour, XXXII (1883), 29-33.
    Irving's genius was the "cornerstone" of American literature. An overview of Irving's literary life and comments on his "literary friends"--those depicted in the well-known group painting of Irving and other writers at Sunnyside.

1884 A BOOKS

1   Washington Irving: Commemoration of the 100th Anniversary of His Birth by the Washington Irving Association. New York: G. P. Putnam's Sons, 1884.
    An account of the activities at the commemoration of Irving's birth, held at Tarrytown, N. Y. on April 3, 1883. The addresses delivered, including one by Irving's pastor and another by Charles Dudley Warner, are printed. Illustrated.

1884 B SHORTER WRITINGS

1   HULBERT, H. W. "Historic Homes: Washington Irving and Sunnyside." Magazine of American History, XII (August 1884), 153-61.
    Description of Sunnyside as Irving knew it, the history of its construction, the legends associated with its locale, etc. Illustration and portrait.

2   MITCHELL, D. G. Bound Together: A Sheaf of Papers. New York: Charles Scribner's Sons, 1884.
    Includes the text of an address at the Irving Centennial Celebration, 3 April 1883. Personal reminiscences about Irving. "There was no episode in his life of which he was more prone to talk" than of his years in Spain. See item 1884.A1.

1884

3   RODRIGUEZ PINILLA, TOMÁS. Colón en España. Madrid: Estable-
     cimiento Tip. de los Sucesores de Rivadeneyra, 1884.
         Scattered comments on Irving. See particularly Chap. VI,
     pp. 206-12.

1885 A BOOKS - NONE

1885 B SHORTER WRITINGS

1   BRAINARD, C. H. John Howard Payne, a Biographical Sketch of
     the Author of "Home Sweet Home." Washington, D. C.:
     G. A. Coolidge, 1885.
         Details the collaboration of Payne and Irving in writing
     and translating dramas.

1886 A BOOKS - NONE

1886 B SHORTER WRITINGS

1   BEERS, HENRY A. An Outline Sketch of American Literature.
     New York: Phillips & Hunt, 1886.
         A complimentary, six-page overview of Irving's work.
     Sees his gifts as sentiment and humor, supported by imagi-
     nation and powers of observation; his weaknesses as those
     inherent in a literature of leisure and retrospection.
     Praises him for bringing American literature to the atten-
     tion of Europe.

2   LANMAN, CHARLES. Haphazard Personalities; Chiefly of Noted
     Americans. Boston: Lee and Shepard, 1886.
         The comments on Irving were printed several times pre-
     viously. See 1859.B9.

3   *MILNE, R. "Notice." Vie et Voyages de Colombe. Paris:
     Garnier frères, 1886.
         Unobtainable. Cited in Morris (1916.B3), p. 12.

4   WILSON, JAMES GRANT. "Washington Irving." Bryant and His
     Friends: Some Reminiscences of the Knickerbocker Writers.
     New York: Fords, Howard, & Hulbert, 1886, pp. 157-78.
         An adulatory, anecdotal chapter, which deals largely with
     Irving in his old age at Sunnyside, particularly with a
     visit there by the author.

1887 A BOOKS - NONE

1887 B SHORTER WRITINGS

    1   CABOT, JAMES E. A Memoir of Ralph Waldo Emerson. Boston:
            Houghton Mifflin and Co., 1887, I, 92.
              On Bracebridge Hall, Emerson said in 1822: "The extracts
            which I have met with have disappointed me much, as
            [Irving] has left his fine 'Sketch Book' style for the de-
            plorable Dutch wit of 'Knickerbocker,' which to me is very
            tedious. . . ."

    2   GOURMONT, REMY de. "Etudes de Littérature américaine.
            L'humour et les Humoristes." Bibliothèque universelle et
            Revue suisse, XXXIV (1887), 5-24.
              The comments on Irving in this essay occur on pages 8-12.

    3   *ROSENZWEIG, L. G. "Notice." The Sketch Book. Paris: A.
            Fouraut, 1887.

    4   WHIPPLE, EDWIN P. American Literature and Other Papers.
            Boston: Ticknor and Co., 1887.
              Briefly (pp. 42-45) praises Irving's originality, dis-
            putes the notion of his having imitated eighteenth-century
            models, and emphasizes his admirable personality.

1888 A BOOKS - NONE

1888 B SHORTER WRITINGS

    1   Gaedertz, Karl T. "Zu Washington Irvings Skizzenbuch
            (Stratford am Avon)." Zur Kenntnis der altenglischen
            Buhne. Bremen: Verlag von C. Ed. Müller, 1888, pp. 33-48.

    2   *HAUSSAIRE, E. "Notice." The Sketch Book. Paris: C. Dela-
            grave, 1888.

1889 A BOOKS - NONE

1889 B SHORTER WRITINGS

    1   HODGKINS, LOUISE M. A Guide to the Study of Nineteenth Cen-
            tury Authors. Boston: D. C. Heath and Co., 1889.
              Notes originally written to accompany lectures at Wel-
            lesley College. For Irving, as for others included, these
            consist of very brief biographical and bibliographical
            data, recommended readings by and about the author, and
            other, peripheral material.

1889

2   RICHARDSON, CHARLES F. American Literature, 1607-1885, II.
     New York: G. P. Putnam's Sons, 1889.
        A general view of Irving, which praises his charm, humor,
     and novelistic abilities, but does not claim greatness for
     this "true beginner of American fiction."

1890 A BOOKS - NONE

1890 B SHORTER WRITINGS

1   RANDOLPH, A. D. F. "Leaves from the Journal of Frederick S.
     Cozzens." Lippincott's Monthly Magazine, XLV (May 1890),
     739-48.
        Extracts from the journal. Accounts of visits and con-
     versations with Irving, including a visit to Sunnyside
     with Thackeray.

2   UNDERWOOD, F. H. Washington Irving. Philadelphia: J. B.
     Lippincott Company, 1890.
        Very brief, factual account of Irving's life and work.

1891 A BOOKS

1   CURTIS, GEORGE W. Washington Irving. A Sketch. New York:
     The Grolier Club, 1891.
        An appreciative literary biography, focusing on Irving's
     early works and comparing him to his contemporaries,
     mainly Cooper and Bryant.

1891 B SHORTER WRITINGS

1   *FIÉVET, P. "Notice biographique." Le Livre d'esquisses.
     Paris: Hachette, 1891.

2   JAMESON, J. F. The History of Historical Writing in America.
     Boston: Houghton Mifflin and Company, 1891.
        Irving's greatest impact as a historian came, ironi-
     cally, from his burlesque History of New York. The book
     sparked important research into the Dutch period of New
     York history, largely as a result of descendants defend-
     ing their ancestors against Irving's barbs. Columbus was
     "an excellent piece of historical work," though Irving did
     not always rely on original research. Index.

3   KNORTZ, KARL. Geschichte der nordamerikanischen Literatur.
     2 vols. Berlin: Verlag von Hans Lüstenöder, 1891.
        Pages 146-67 in Vol. I deal with Irving.

4   SMILES, SAMUEL. A Publisher and His Friends: Memoir and Cor-
      respondence of the Late John Murray. 2 vols. London:
      John Murray, 1891.
         Details Irving's relations with his English publisher,
      including his financial maneuverings. Prints correspon-
      dence between Irving and Murray. Murray solicited outside
      opinions as to the merit of the works he was about to pub-
      lish. Prints letters to Murray from Robert Southey and
      Sharon Turner warning him about investing in Life of Colum-
      bus and from John Lockhart castigating Conquest of Granada.
      Points out the commercial failure of these works, though
      Murray continued to publish Irving's writings. Index.

5   WINSOR, JUSTIN. Christopher Columbus and How He Received and
      Imparted the Spirit of Discovery. Boston: Houghton,
      Mifflin and Co., 1891.
         Attacks Life of Columbus. Irving was out to create a
      hero; the book is "seductive," and its "insidious charms"
      distort the real history.

1892 A   BOOKS - NONE

1892 B   SHORTER WRITINGS

1   ANON. "Washington Irving's 'Alhambra.'" Spectator, LXIX (9
      July 1892), 66-67.
         Review of the Darro edition of The Alhambra. Irving's
      imagination fused history, travel, antiquarianism, and
      fiction into a unique work of art. Unlike most other de
      luxe editions, The Alhambra is enhanced by its sumptuous
      format.

2   ANON. "Washington Irving." Temple Bar, A London Magazine for
      Town and Country Readers, XCVI (November 1892), 321-41.
         Summarizes Irving's life by way of reviewing Pierre
      Irving's biography.

3   ANON. "Washington Irving." Littell's Living Age, CXCV (24
      December 1892), 791-805.
         Reprinted from Temple Bar, See item 1892.B2.

1893 A   BOOKS - NONE

1893 B   SHORTER WRITINGS

1   ANON. "Mr. Warner on Washington Irving." Critic, XXII (8
      April 1893), 220-21.

1893

(ANON.)
A description of Charles Dudley Warner's speech to the Brooklyn Institute on the 110th anniversary of Irving's birth, as reported by the Brooklyn Eagle. Warner surveys Irving's life and urges that a statue be erected in his honor.

2   GIST, W. W. "Washington Irving." The Chautauquan, XVIII (October 1893), 48-52.
Biographical sketch; appreciation of Irving's personal characteristics and literary genius. Much quotation.

3   NICHOLS, ROBERT H. "Washington Irving." Yale Literary Magazine, LVIII (February 1893), 178-86.
General essay on Irving as man and author, in which his weaknesses as a literary artist are seen as minor compared to his excellences. The man and his writings are judged of a piece--warm, sympathetic, moral, thoroughly human. The values he embodied in his life and works may well prove more durable than the brilliance of more modern authors.

1894 A   BOOKS - NONE

1894 B   SHORTER WRITINGS

1   [ADAMS, G. F.] "Study of Irving." School Review, II (January 1894), 29-35.
Suggests the value of and various approaches to the study of Irving in secondary school.

2   ANON. "An American Classic." Saturday Review, LXXVII (20 January 1894), 70.
Review of a new edition of A History of New York illustrated by Edward Kemble. Praises Irving's satire, his "burlesque of the grand historical style," and his own style of writing, which is "limpid yet nervous." Notes a falling off in Irving after he stopped using Diedrich Knickerbocker.

3   CURTIS, GEORGE W. "Washington Irving." Literary and Social Essays. New York: Harper and Brothers, 1894, pp. 239-93.
The essay on Irving in this volume is a reprint of Washington Irving. A Sketch (1891). See item 1891.A1.

4   SAUNDERS, FREDERICK. Character Studies, With Some Personal Recollections. New York: Thomas Whittaker, 1894.
One of the book's six chapters is an appreciative essay on Irving, man and writer, popular in tone.

5   STEVENSON, ROBERT LOUIS. "My First Book. Treasure Island."
       Idler, VI (August 1894), 3-11.
         Stevenson confesses Treasure Island's great debt to
       Tales of a Traveller: "Billy Bones, his chest, the company
       in the parlour, the whole inner spirit, and a good deal of
       the material detail of the first chapters--all were
       there. . . ."

1895 A BOOKS - NONE

1895 B SHORTER WRITINGS

1   HOWELLS, W. D. "Irving." My Literary Passions. New York:
       Harper and Brothers Publishers, 1895, pp. 23-27.
         Howells describes his early love of things Spanish, and
       of The Conquest of Granada in particular. He calls it "a
       study of history which, in unique measure, conveys not
       only the pathos, but the humour of one of the most splendid
       and impressive situations in the experience of the race."
       His reactions to Irving's other writings are mixed.

2   MENENDEZ Y PELAYO, MARCELINO. De los historiadores de Colón.
       Estudios de critica literaria, segunda serie. Madrid:
       Est. Tipografico, 1895.
         Discusses Irving's Columbus on pp. 270-72.

1896 A BOOKS - NONE

1896 B SHORTER WRITINGS

1   MORRIS, JOHN. "Personal Reminiscences of Washington Irving."
       Catholic World, LXII (February 1896), 627-42.
         The "reminiscences" are all public knowledge, and make
       up a rambling biographical essay, popular in tone.

2   TUCKERMAN, H. T. "Washington Irving." Little Journeys to the
       Homes of American Authors. Ed. E. Hubbard. New York and
       London: G. P. Putnam's Sons, 1896, pp. 263-96.
       Reprinted essay. See item 1853.B4.

1897 A BOOKS - NONE

1897 B SHORTER WRITINGS

1   ANON. "Irving's Astoria." Nation, LXV (23 December 1897),
       499-501.

1897

(ANON.)
Review of the Tacoma edition of Astoria. "No one can be proof against the charm of 'Astoria.'" But recently discovered documents do reveal some historical inaccuracies in the book. List of specific errors, such as dates, keyed to the Tacoma edition.

2   BURTON, RICHARD. "Washington Irving's Services to American History." New England Magazine, XVI (August 1897), 641-53.
Even in his imaginative writings, Irving was always brooding on the past. In his more serious historical works, he used literary devices to recreate scene and character, making history come alive. "There is no harm in the history writer giving pleasure--especially if he have thoroughness and be conscientious." Illustrations.

3   FETTEROLF, ADAM H. Washington Irving: Traveller, Diplomat, Author. Philadelphia: J. B. Lippincott Co., 1897.
An inspirational address to Girard College students on Irving's life and works. Derivative and simplistic. Concludes with an exhortation to read and imitate Irving for the moral effect of so doing.

4   HOWE, M. A. D. "American Bookmen: Washington Irving." Bookman, IV (February 1897), 516-28.
An account of Irving's life and career told mainly through anecdotes. Illustrated with portraits, paintings, and facsimiles of Irvingiana. Includes a sonnet on his death by Longfellow.

5   MITCHELL, D. G. American Lands and Letters: the Mayflower to Rip-Van-Winkle. New York: Charles Scribner's Sons, 1897.
Includes a thirty-page survey of Irving's life and career. Facsimile of a letter from Irving to Mitchell dated 31 December 1851. Illustrations.

1898 A   BOOKS - NONE

1898 B   SHORTER WRITINGS

1   LIVINGSTON, L. S. "The First Books of Some American Authors: III.--Irving, Poe and Whitman." Bookman, VIII (November 1898), 230-35.
Account of the circumstances of Irving's first publication, a translation from French entitled A Voyage to the Eastern Part of Terra Firma (1806). Title page facsimiles of this work and A History of New York.

1900 A   BOOKS - NONE

1900 B   SHORTER WRITINGS

1   SWIFT, L. "Our Literary Diplomats, Part II: From the 'Era
     of Good Feeling' to the Ashburton Treaty. Washington
     Irving." Book Buyer, XX (July 1900), 440-41.
          Irving avoided public life in America, but served well
     in a difficult time as American Ambassador at Madrid. His
     "greatest cross was that he had to publish his books."

2   WENDELL, BARRETT. "Washington Irving." A Literary History
     of America. New York: Charles Scribner's Sons, 1900,
     pp. 169-80.
          Surveys Irving's writings, crediting his sense of form
     as being even better than that of his English contempo-
     raries. Irving expressed the feelings of Romanticism in
     thoroughly classical modes, but unfortunately had nothing
     profound, no "sense of the mystery of existence," to com-
     municate.

1901 A   BOOKS

1   BOYNTON, H. W. Washington Irving. Boston: Houghton Mifflin
     and Co., 1901.
          A slim, flattering literary biography.

2   *SPRENGER, R. Über die Quelle von Washington Irvings Rip Van
     Winkle. Northeim, 1901.
          Unlocatable. Cited in Williams and Edge (1936.A1), p. 190.

1901 B   SHORTER WRITINGS

1   FORD, JAMES L. "A Century of American Humor." Munsey's Mag-
     azine, XXV (July 1901), 482-90.
          A survey in which Irving gets a paragraph and a portrait.
     He began "what may be called the scholarly school of Amer-
     ican humor," but his satires have not stood the test of
     time.

2   TRENT, W. P. "A Retrospect of American Humor." Century Mag-
     azine, LXIII (November 1901), 45-64.
          An overview. Irving only briefly mentioned as an "aca-
     demic humorist" whose humor is not "distinctively and orig-
     inally American," and who therefore lies beyond the scope
     of the article. Portrait.

1902

1902 A   BOOKS

1   *GROSSKUNZ, R. Die Natur in den Werken und Briefen des
         amerikanischen Schriftstellers Washington Irving. Leipzig:
         Pöschel und Trepte, 1902.

1902 B   SHORTER WRITINGS

1   CUYLER, T. L. "Memories of Famous Men." Current Literature,
         XXXIII (October 1902), 420-23.
             Excerpt from Cuyler's Recollections of a Long Life.
         Tells how he met Irving and how Irving showed him Sunny-
         side, telling him that it is "the original of Baltus Van
         Tassel's homestead in the Legend of Sleepy Hollow."

2   HALE, EDWARD EVERETT. "Memories of a Hundred Years." Out-
         look, LXXI (5 July 1902), 620-30.
             Reminiscences on historians Hale had known, including
         Irving. Recounts their first meeting and conversations.
         Irving had the power "of giving to diplomacy and matters
         of state the interest which is supposed to belong to adven-
         ture and to battle."

3   LARNED, J. N., ed. The Literature of American History: a
         Bibliographical Guide. Boston: Houghton Mifflin and Com-
         pany, 1902.
             Annotated bibliography evaluating works on American his-
         tory. Comments on Life and Voyages of Christopher Colum-
         bus, Life of George Washington, Astoria, and The Rocky
         Mountains (Adventures of Captain Bonneville). Irving re-
         ceives high marks as a historian. Astoria is called "in-
         dispensable" to the study of early Oregon--despite the
         fact that Irving's "mental equipment for historical inves-
         tigation would not now be called an ideal one."

4   LOUGHLIN, CLARA. "Two Famous Bachelors and Their Love Sto-
         ries." Book Buyer, XXV (October 1902), 241-47.
             Irving and Thoreau. The Irving section is essentially a
         sentimental retelling of the Matilda Hoffman story.

5   MABIE, HAMILTON WRIGHT. "The Washington Irving Country."
         Outlook, LXXII (6 December 1902), 821-29.
             Finds "a certain congruity between Irving's work and his
         country." Treats Irving and Longfellow as liberating the
         young nation from provincialism and tying the New World to
         the culture of the Old.

6   VAN ARKEL, G. "House of the Four Chimneys." New England Mag-
         azine, XXVII (September 1902), 59-66.

(VAN ARKEL, G.)
Account of a trip made by Irving and Martin Van Buren to
the Van Horne mansion in Communipaw. History and traditions of the house. Illustrated.

7   WOODBERRY, G. E. "Knickerbocker Era of American Letters."
     Harper's, CV (October 1902), 677-83.
          Essay on the early American literature that emanated from
     New York. Treats Cooper, Bryant, and lesser figures, but
     focuses mainly on Irving. Notes a great difference between
     The Scarlet Letter and "The Legend of Sleepy Hollow," in
     the latter of which the moral element is missing, and phys-
     ical comfort, shallow superstition, human warmth, and so-
     cietal pleasure are prominent. These characteristics de-
     rive from the New York milieu. In addition, Irving dealt
     with America, but in European terms. Despite his travels
     on the frontier, his imagination was not suited for the
     "western mystery."

1903 A BOOKS

     *SANDELL, GEORGE W. A Short Sketch of W. Irving and His Writ-
          ings. Southampton, 1903.
               Unobtainable. Cited in the British Museum Catalogue.

1903 B SHORTER WRITINGS

1   BURTON, RICHARD. "Irving." Literary Leaders of America.
     New York: The Chautauqua Press, 1903, pp. 12-41.
          This chapter on Irving recognizes his limitations, but
     calls him "so much an artist, and so wholesomely good a
     man, that however literary fashions may change, he cannot
     be ignored." Despite his debt to English writers, he is
     truly an American author.

2   GUERRA, ANGEL. "Washington Irving." Literatos extranjeros
     (impresiones criticas). Valencia: F. Sempere y compania,
     editores, 1903, pp. 61-67.
          Essentially on "Rip Van Winkle."

3   HEMSTREET, CHARLES. "The City That Irving Knew." Literary
     New York, its Landmarks and Associations. New York:
     G. P. Putnam's Sons, 1903, pp. 87-105.
          A popularized account.

4   JANVIER, THOMAS A. The Dutch Founding of New York. New York:
     Harper & Brothers, 1903.
          Scattered comments on A History of New York. It is de-
     lightful, but "subtly mendacious" because its historical

1903

(JANVIER, THOMAS A.)
accuracy is combined with "untruth to the spirit" of the
Dutch colony.

1904 A BOOKS - NONE

1904 B SHORTER WRITINGS

1   MABIE, HAMILTON WRIGHT. "The Washington Irving Country."
     Backgrounds of Literature. New York: The Macmillan Com-
     pany, 1904. pp. 98-131.
     Reprinted from Outlook; See item 1902.B5.

2   PEMBERTON, T. E. "Washington Irving in England." Munsey's
     Magazine, XXX (January 1904), 552-58.
     An account of the years Irving spent in the English mid-
     lands. Photographs.

1906 A BOOKS - NONE

1906 B SHORTER WRITINGS

1   BOWEN, E. W. "Washington Irving's Place in American Litera-
     ture." Sewanee Review, XIV (April 1906), 171-83.
     "Irving is properly accorded the first place among the
     pioneers in American literature." His fame and continued
     popularity are not due to intellectual force or literary
     acumen, but rather to "the free play of his romantic fancy,
     his pervading sentiment, his unfailing, delightful humor
     and his charming style."

2   McBRYDE, J. M. "Washington Irving Once More." Sewanee Re-
     view, XIV (July 1906), 358-60.
     Reply to Edwin Bowen's "Washington Irving's Place in Amer-
     ican Literature," Sewanee Review, XIV (April 1906). Quar-
     rels with Bowen's ranking of "The Wife" with such works as
     "Rip Van Winkle" and "The Legend of Sleepy Hollow," and sug-
     gests other Irving sketches that are superior. Other com-
     ments on Irving's works and Bowen's article. See item 1906.B1.

3   VINCENT, L. H. American Literary Masters. Boston: Houghton
     Mifflin and Company, 1906.
     Sections on Irving treating his life, character, style,
     early work, historical writings, the Spanish romances, and
     American history and travel. Covers all of Irving's works
     with varying degrees of description and critical commenta-
     ry, but finds fault with none of them. Discusses A History
     of New York as "one of the most extraordinary books of hu-
     mor in the English language" and credits Irving with per-
     fecting the short story. Notes Irving's balance and lack

80

(VINCENT, L. H.)
of prejudice in his histories and his helping to counteract
the trend towards needlessly abstruse and specialized ·his-
torical works.

1907 A   BOOKS - NONE

1907 B   SHORTER WRITINGS

1   DUNN, N. P. "An Artist of the Past: William Edward West and
His Friends at Home and Abroad." Putnam's Magazine, II
(September 1907), 658-69.
Includes letter from Irving to Leslie Patterson dated
7 May 1825 and quotes from an Irving letter to West.
Quotes from Irving's diary. Portrait.

1909 A   BOOKS - NONE

1909 B   SHORTER WRITINGS

1   CANBY, HENRY S. The Short Story in English. New York: Henry
Holt and Company, 1909.
Irving's better stories, such as "Rip Van Winkle" and
"The Legend of Sleepy Hollow," are far superior to other
short fiction before Poe. His forte was the "exquisitely
simple, perfectly balanced tale." In his interests a ro-
manticist, he was in his manner Augustan. Index.

2   *KNORTZ, KARL. "Washington Irving in Tarrytown." Ein Beitrag
zur Geschichte der nordamerikanischen Literatur. Nurnberg:
C. J. Koch, 1909.
Unobtainable. Cited in Williams and Edge (1936.A1).

3   *SCHALCK DE LA FAVERIE, A. Les premiers interprètes de la
pensée américaine. Essai d'histoire et de littérature sur
l'évolution du puritanisme aux États-Unis. Paris: E.
Sansot, 1909.
According to Williams and Edge (1936.A1), Irving is
treated on pp. 201-18.

4   WILLIAMS, LAWRENCE. "A Ghost in Irving Place." Bookman, XXX
(September 1909), 53-55.
A recollection of Irving in New York, occasioned by the
planned razing of the Irving family house.

1910 A   BOOKS - NONE

1910

1910 B   SHORTER WRITINGS

1   LUQUER, T. T. P., ed. "Correspondence of Washington Irving
        and John Howard Payne." Scribner's, XLVIII (October 1910),
        461-82; (November), 597-616.
           Letters, mostly from Irving to Payne, with introduction,
        notes, and illustrations.

2   PAYNE, W. M. "Washington Irving." Leading American Essay-
        ists. New York: Henry Holt and Co., 1910, pp. 43-134.
           A biographical essay, including details of Irving's trav-
        els and accounts of his social and political alignments.

3   SAMPSON, F. A. "Washington Irving. Travels in Missouri and
        the South." Missouri Historical Review, V (October 1910),
        15-33.
           Passages from Astoria and various Irving letters giving
        his impressions of Missouri and the adjacent territory.
        Sampson contributes notes and transitions.

1911 A   BOOKS

1   *KUNZIG, FERDINAND. Washington Irving und seine Beziehungen
        zur englischen Literatur des 18. Jahrhunderts. Heidelberg,
        1911.
           A dissertation.

1911 B   SHORTER WRITINGS

1   BALSTON, T. "Washington Irving's 'Sketch Book.'" Notes and
        Queries, IV (5 August 1911), 109; (12 August), 129; (19
        August), 148.
           Queries on a number of unidentified quotations and allu-
        sions in The Sketch Book.

2   BENSLY, EDWARD. "Washington Irving's 'Sketch Book.'" Notes
        and Queries, IV (30 September 1911), 275.
           Identifies a quotation in The Sketch Book.

3   B., W. "Washington Irving's 'Sketch Book.'" Notes and Que-
        ries, IV (2 September 1911), 196.
           Identifies a reference in The Sketch Book.

4   POLLARD, MATILDA. "Washington Irving's 'Sketch Book.'" Notes
        and Queries, IV (9 September 1911), 217.
           Identifies an allusion in The Sketch Book.

1912 A   BOOKS - NONE

1912 B   SHORTER WRITINGS

1   DeVRIES, TIEMEN. Dutch History, Art and Literature for Americans; Lectures Given in the University of Chicago. Grand Rapids, Mich.: Eerdmans-Sevensma Co., 1912.
 The chapter entitled "Washington Irving and the Dutch People of New York" is an attack on Irving's depiction of the Dutch in A History of New York and "Rip Van Winkle," with extended comments on "Rip" as an "imitation" of Erasmus' version of the fable of Epimenides.

2   MABIE, HAMILTON WRIGHT. The Writers of Knickerbocker New York. New York: The Grolier Club, 1912.
 On Irving and his contemporaries. Sketches New York as it was then and places Salmagundi and A History of New York in a topical context. Account of Irving's life in New York.

3   S., W. S. "Washington Irving's 'Sketch Book.'" Notes and Queries, V (6 January 1912), 14.
 Identifies a number of quotations and allusions in The Sketch Book.

4   TRENT, WILLIAM P. and JOHN ERSKINE. "Literary Work of Irving." Great American Writers. New York: Henry Holt and Co., 1912, pp. 20-27.
 Contains a survey of Irving's life and writings, including a judgment of his importance. The Sketch Book is Irving's chief claim to fame; with "The Spectre Bridegroom," he became the father of America's own genre, the short story, though he remained primarily an essayist rather than a fiction writer. He was also a pioneer in the writing of history and biography. Irving's most important achievement was in introducing the culture of the Old World to the developing culture of the New.

1913 A   BOOKS - NONE

1913 B   SHORTER WRITINGS

1   BRUCE, WALLACE. Along the Hudson with Washington Irving. Poughkeepsie, N. Y.: Press of the A. V. Haight Co., 1913.
 Extracts from Irving's works involving the Hudson valley, augmented by an appreciative essay focusing on The Sketch Book, and other commentary by the editor.

2   FURST, CLYDE. "A Century of Washington Irving." Sewanee Review, XXI (October 1913), 402-20.

1913

    (FURST, CLYDE)
       This article classifies the separate pieces in The Sketch
Book in six groups and discusses each one. They are "autobiographical, notes of racial and of national traits, ex-
cursions into literary criticism, descriptions of places
and things, studies of manners and customs, and experiments
in fiction." The comments, though specific, are appreciative rather than analytical.

3   MACY, JOHN. "Irving." The Spirit of American Literature.
    New York: Doubleday, Page and Company, 1913, pp. 18-34.
       A chapter on Irving as a man of genial imagination who
was almost as aloof from the great American social and intellectual struggles as was Poe. Discusses Irving's relation to the eighteenth century and notes his blend of sentiment and common sense. The Life of Goldsmith is "one of
the masterpieces of literary biography," and the influence
of Irving's histories may account for the "readability" of
subsequent American historians. For all his genius, however, Irving was not one of our greatest writers.

4   PLATH, OTTO. "Washington Irvings Einfluss auf Wilhelm Hauff."
    Euphorion, XX (1913), 459-71.

1914 A BOOKS - NONE

1914 B SHORTER WRITINGS

1   ANON. "Washington Irving Manuscripts." Columbia University
    Quarterly, XVI (September 1914), 448-49.
       Mrs. Cortlandt Irving has given Columbia University about
one-half the holograph manuscript of Bracebridge Hall and
a large "portion of the manuscript of the Spanish Legends"
[Legends of the Conquest of Spain?].

2   ANON. "Washington Irving Exhibition." Bulletin of the New
    York Public Library, XVIII (November 1914), 1255.
       A notice of an exhibition of books and manuscripts owned
by Isaac N. Seligman.

3   *APETZ, P. "Washington Irvings Aufenthalt in Dresden."
    Jahresbericht des Königlichen Gymnasiums zu Dresden-
    Neustadt, XL (1914), 1-11.
       Unlocatable. Cited in Williams and Edge (1936.A1).

4   PALM, ADA. "The Teaching of The Sketch Book." English Jour-
    nal, III (September 1914), 437-40.

(PALM, ADA)
Suggestions for teaching the book on the high school level.

1915 A BOOKS - NONE

1915 B SHORTER WRITINGS

1   HELLMAN, GEORGE S., ed. The Letters of Washington Irving to Henry Brevoort. 2 vols. New York: G. P. Putnam's Sons, 1915.
Historical introduction by the editor, and a preface by G. H. Putnam on Irving's relations with the Putnam publishing house. Table of contents includes a brief abstract of each letter.

2   TAYLOR, J. F. "Washington Irving's Mexico: A Lost Fragment." Bookman, XLI (August 1915), 665-69.
Discusses a manuscript fragment from Irving's proposed History of the Conquest of Mexico. Irving gave up the project in deference to Prescott. Includes a facsimile of the manuscript and quotes an Irving letter dated 24 March 1844.

1916 A BOOKS - NONE

1916 B SHORTER WRITINGS

1   FERGUSON, J. de L. "Washington Irving." American Literature in Spain. New York: Columbia University Press, 1916, pp. 8-31.
Examines his critical reception in Spain and the history of his works published in Spanish there. Irving generally received superficial attention, and the critical commentary is characterized by clichés and frequent ignorance.

2   GREENLAW, EDWIN. "Washington Irving's Comedy of Politics." Texas Review, I (April 1916), 291-306.
The History of New York, a fine literary work, was also a perceptive commentary on contemporary politics and Thomas Jefferson. Irving's comedy of politics "provokes thoughtful laughter."

3   MORRIS, G. D. Washington Irving's Fiction in the Light of French Criticism. Indiana Univ. Studies, No. 30. Bloomington, Ind.: Indiana Univ., 1916.

1916

(MORRIS, G. D.)
    A study of Irving's contemporary reception in France,
    with many quotations from critical articles and reviews.
    Also compares the French view with the British and Amer-
    ican. Bibliography.

4   WILKINS, W. G. "Charles Dickens and Washington Irving."
        Dickensian, XII (August 1916), 216-21; (September), 46-49;
        (October), 274-77.
        Series of comments on Dickens' friendship with Irving.
        Prints their correspondence.

1917 A   BOOKS - NONE

1917 B   SHORTER WRITINGS

1   CAMPBELL, KILLIS. "The Kennedy Papers: A Sheaf of Unpub-
        lished Letters from Washington Irving." Sewanee Review,
        XXV (January 1917), 1-19.
        Discussion of Irving's connection with John Pendleton
        Kennedy, followed by eighteen previously unpublished let-
        ters from Irving to Kennedy and his family, and some other
        related documents.

2   MANTZ, H. E. French Criticism of American Literature Before
        1850. New York: Columbia University Press, 1917.
        Scattered remarks on Irving. An overview, not a de-
        tailed study of contemporary reception. Relatively few
        French comments on Irving are cited.

1918 A   BOOKS - NONE

1918 B   SHORTER WRITINGS

1   CAIRNS, WILLIAM B. British Criticisms of American Writings,
        1783-1815. University of Wisconsin Studies in Language
        and Literature, No. 1. Madison, 1918.
        Contains brief comments on Scott's early knowledge of
        Irving's work, and on the 1811 review of Salmagundi in the
        Monthly Review. See item 1811.B1

2   WHITE, T. W. "Reparaciones de la historia de España:
        Fernandez de Navarrete y Washington Irving." Boletín de
        la Real Academia de la Historia, LXXIII (1918), 258-81.

1919 A BOOKS - NONE

1919 B SHORTER WRITINGS

1   ANON. "Geoffrey Crayon." Nation, CIX (6 December 1919), 710.
        Appreciative review of The Sketch Book on its centennial.
        Geoffrey Crayon created American legends, and stands at the
        source of the modern short story, which properly begins
        with "Rip Van Winkle."

1920 A BOOKS - NONE

1920 B SHORTER WRITINGS

1   HELLMAN, GEORGE S. "The Washington Irving Collection Formed
        by Isaac N. Seligman." Bulletin of the New York Public Li-
        brary, XXIV (May 1920), 275-79.
        Description of the contents of the Seligman Collection,
        on indefinite loan to the New York Public Library.

1921 A BOOKS - NONE

1921 B SHORTER WRITINGS

1   TRENT, W. P., ed. Notes and Journal of Travel in Europe 1804-
        1805. 3 vols. New York: The Grolier Club, 1921.
        Irving's journal, kept during his first trip to Europe,
        with notes, index, and an introduction summarizing the
        journal and Irving's travels. Trent suggests that even
        apart from its biographical significance, this account of
        a young man in Europe is interesting and entertaining.

1922 A BOOKS - NONE

1922 B SHORTER WRITINGS

1   CAIRNS, W. B. British Criticisms of American Writings, 1815-
        1833. University of Wisconsin Studies in Language and
        Literature, No. 14. Madison, Wisconsin: Univ. of Wiscon-
        sin Press, 1922.
        Chapter on Irving is a detailed essay on the critical re-
        ception of his works. Quotes extensively; accurate and
        scholarly. Valuable appendix of British periodicals.
        Index.

1922

2   INGRAHAM, CHARLES A. Washington Irving, and Other Essays,
     Biographical, Historical and Philosophical. Cambridge,
     N. Y.: C. A. Ingraham, 1922.
          A literary-biographical essay which finds the durable
     element in Irving and his works to be his goodness and
     nobility.

1923 A   BOOKS - NONE

1923 B   SHORTER WRITINGS

1   LOW, MILDRED. "A Lover of Good Company." Canadian Magazine,
     LX (January 1923), 230-32.
          Three letters to Joseph Gratz (two dated 8 July 1806 and
     the other 30 March 1808) are printed with commentary.

2   O'BRIEN, EDWARD J. "The Forerunners." The Advance of the
     American Short Story. New York: Dodd, Mead and Co., 1923,
     pp. 21-34.
          A favorable overview of Irving as progenitor of the Amer-
     ican short story. Comparisons to Defoe, Goldsmith, Addison,
     and Steele.

3   PATTEE, FRED LEWIS. The Development of the American Short
     Story. New York: Harper & Brothers, 1923.
          Study of the short story in America must begin with
     Irving and The Sketch Book. His contributions: he made
     short fiction popular, stripped away moral and didactic
     elements, added richness of atmosphere and unity of tone,
     added defined American locale, added humor, was original
     in manner, created individualized characters, used a fin-
     ished and beautiful style. Yet he lacked robustness, had
     no deep concern for plot, was weak on dialogue, and avoided
     the sinister. Pattee's treatment is historical-critical,
     and includes a chronology of Irving's "short stories."

1925 A   BOOKS

1   HELLMAN, GEORGE S. Washington Irving Esquire, Ambassador at
     Large from the New World to the Old. New York: A. A.
     Knopf, 1925.
          A full-length, romantic biography, making use of recently
     discovered materials to support a "new visualization of
     that talented, lazy, pleasure-loving, charming man. . . ."
     No literary criticism, per se.

1925 B   SHORTER WRITINGS

1   COAD, O. S. "The Gothic Element in American Literature Be-
      fore 1835." Journal of English and Germanic Philology,
      XXIV (January 1925), 72-93.
          Stresses the importance of Irving: "Of all our weavers
      of legends of fear prior to Poe, by far the most skilful,
      the most artistic, the most eery is Washington Irving. In
      his hands the story of terror for the first time becomes
      unmistakably literature." Traces the Gothic element
      through The Sketch Book, Bracebridge Hall, Tales of a
      Traveller, and The Alhambra.

2   MABBOTT, THOMAS OLLIVE. "An Unwritten Drama." Americana
      Collector, I (October 1925), 64-66.
          Prints Irving's uncollected sketch, "An Unwritten Drama
      of Lord Byron," with a brief introduction in which Mabbott
      argues that it is the source for Poe's "William Wilson."

3   PERRIN, P. G. The Life and Works of Thomas Green Fessenden.
      University of Maine Studies, 2nd series, No. 4 (Orono,
      Maine: University Press, 1925).
          On pp. 117-20 is an account of a controversy between
      Fessenden's magazine, Inspector, and Salmagundi. Prints
      extracts from the two magazine's satiric jabs at each
      other.

4   RUSK, R. L. The Literature of the Middle Western Frontier.
      2 vols. New York: Columbia University Press, 1925.
          Occasional mention of Irving, but not as a major con-
      tributor to the literature of the West. Westerners' opin-
      ions of Irving varied: though some praised his writings,
      others condemned their lack of force and virility. Index.

1926 A   BOOKS - NONE

1926 B   SHORTER WRITINGS

1   ANON. "How Irving Kept Warm." Literary Digest, XCI (9 Octo-
      ber 1926), 56.
          Reminiscence of Irving's activities with his parish
      church at Tarrytown. The article is occasioned by the re-
      placing of the furnace he donated.

2   CANBY, HENRY S. "Irving the Federalist." Saturday Review of
      Literature, III (25 December 1926), 461-63.
          "If any outside influence is to account for Washington
      Irving's really remarkable success [in belles lettres]

1926

(CANBY, HENRY S.)
with only a humorous temperament and a sensitive soul to
go on, then that influence will be found in [the spirit
of] American Federalism."

3   HEROLD, A. L. <u>James Kirke Paulding, Versatile American</u>. New
York: Columbia Univ. Press, 1926.
Scattered comments on Irving in relation to Paulding's
life and writings.

4   KELLEY, LEON. "England and America." <u>Bookman</u>, LXIV (October
1926), 133-37.
An answer to recent British condescension to American
art. Irving's position is cited, and his "English Writers
on America" is quoted extensively.

5   McDOWELL, GEORGE TREMAINE. "General James Wilkinson in the
Knickerbocker <u>History of New York</u>." <u>Modern Language Notes</u>,
XLI (June 1926), 353-59.
General Jacobus Von Poffenburgh is a strongly satirical
portrait of the American general, James Wilkinson.

6   PENNEY, CLARA LOUISE, ed. <u>Washington Irving Diary: Spain,
1828-1829</u>. New York: Hispanic Society of America, 1926.
This diary is edited with notes, index, facsimiles, and
an introduction detailing Irving's life in Spain.

7   PUTNAM, G. H. "Washington Irving." <u>Forum</u>, LXXV (March 1926),
397-409.
Biographical sketch by the son of Irving's publisher.
Deals especially with the relations of Irving and the
Putnam publishing house. Irving was ready to take up law
again at the age of 65 when Putnam agreed to re-issue his
books and to subsidize further writing.

8   SPILLER, ROBERT E. <u>The American in England During the First
Half Century of Independence</u>. New York: Henry Holt and
Company, 1926.
Study of Americans living or travelling in England from
the Revolution to 1835. Recounts Irving's life in England,
noting his cultural "detachment" and his primary association with Americans despite his being accepted into English
social life. Discusses the "Irving Circle"--the group of
American expatriates surrounding Irving--and his role as
an intermediary between the two cultures. Index.

9   WILLIAMS, STANLEY T. "Washington Irving and Matilda Hoffman."
<u>American Speech</u>, I (June 1926), 463-69.
The relationship has been too often oversentimentalized.

90

10   WILLIAMS, STANLEY T. "Washington Irving's Religion." Yale
      Review, XV (January 1926), 414-16.
          Prints letter to Emily Foster dated 23 August 1825.
      Brief introduction. The letter deals with the oppressive-
      ness of Irving's early religious training.

1927 A BOOKS - NONE

1927 B SHORTER WRITINGS

1   ARENS, E. "Washington Irving im Rheinland (1822). Ein
      Beitrag zur Geschichte der Rhein-Romantik." Eichendorff-
      Kalender, 1927/28. Ein Romantisches Jahrbuch (1927), pp.
      93-120.

2   BARRY, J. N. "Washington Irving and Astoria." Washington
      Historical Quarterly, XVIII (April 1927), 132-39.
          Extracts from Irving's letters to Pierre Irving on the
      compilation of Astoria. Introduction points out Pierre's
      large contribution to the project and attests to the his-
      torical accuracy of the book.

3   BENSON, ADOLPH B. "Scandinavians in the Works of Washington
      Irving." Scandinavian Studies and Notes, IX (1927),
      207-23.
          Studies Irving's treatment of the Swedes in A History of
      New York, and examines his handling of the Norse discovery
      of America in Columbus. Quotes from a review of Henry
      Wheaton's History of the Northmen, by Irving, in the North
      American Review (1832). Irving was an important figure in
      the "literary relations" between the United States and
      Scandinavia.

4   DAVENPORT, WALTER. "Was There a Real Rip Van Winkle?" Men-
      tor, XV (May 1927), 41-48.
          A popularized look into the origins of the character,
      the story, and the stage adaptations of Irving's tale,
      with comments on Joseph Jefferson's stage career as Rip.
      Illustrated.

5   HESPELT, E. HERMAN. "Irving's Version of Byron's The Isles
      of Greece." Modern Language Notes, XLII (February 1927),
      111.
          In one of Irving's notebooks is an inferior version of
      Byron's poem. Irving's source for it is unknown.

6   *McGEE, S. L. La littérature américaine dans la "Revue des
      deux mondes" (1831-1900). Montpellier, 1927.
          A dissertation.

91

1927

7   PARRINGTON, VERNON L. "Two Knickerbocker Romantics." Main
     Currents in American Thought. New York: Harcourt, Brace
     and Company, 1927, II, 203-21.
          Characterizes Irving as a "genial loiterer" who detached
     himself from the "immediate and actual" in favor of the
     romantic past, adapting just as easily to capitalism as to
     feudalism. Irving's early work is superior because "sober-
     ing experience" tends to dissipate romance, so Irving
     turned more and more to pure sentiment.

8   WILLIAMS, STANLEY T., ed. Notes While Preparing Sketch Book
     &c. New Haven: Yale Univ. Press, 1927.
          Irving's notebook of 1817 and earlier. Forty-three page
     critical introduction places the notebook in the context
     of Irving's life and his stylistic development. Prints
     parallel texts of a passage in the notebook and a finished
     essay ("The Wife") to show his methods of composition.
     Long discussion of Matilda Hoffman, including transcrip-
     tions of letters she wrote to members of her family. In-
     cludes a long meditation by Irving on her death, "by far
     the most important entry in the notebook." Footnotes, fac-
     similes, and index.

9   _____. Tour in Scotland 1817 and Other Manuscript Notes.
     New Haven: Yale Univ. Press, 1927.
          Irving's journal and notes written "at the very turning
     point of his career," when he was being influenced by Scott
     and by English literary circles, and when he was conceiving
     ideas for The Sketch Book. These writings have "a bio-
     graphical and literary importance not possessed by his
     other journals of travel." Introduction includes an itin-
     erary of Irving's travels, and critical and biographical
     commentary.

10   _____. "Letters of Washington Irving: Spanish Fetes and
     Ceremonies." Yale Review, XVII (October 1927), 99-117.
          Introduction remarking on Irving's "romantic appreciation
     towards the ceremonial of old Europe" and his astuteness as
     an observer of Spanish political intrigues. These five
     letters to his sister and Sarah Storrow, written between
     1842 and 1845, amount to "a series of informal, vivid es-
     says on the Spain of Espartero, Maria Christina, and Isa-
     bella the Second."

11   _____. "Unpublished Letters of Washington Irving: Sunnyside
     and New York Chronicles." Yale Review, XVI (April 1927),
     459-84.
          Biographical introduction. Letter "To my Six Nieces"

(WILLIAMS, STANLEY T.)
dated 4 February 1840; eight letters to Sarah Storrow written in 1841.

12   WILLIAMS, STANLEY T. and TREMAINE McDOWELL, eds. A History
of New York. New York: Harcourt, Brace and Co., 1927.
The long introduction deals with biographical, historical, textual, and critical matters, and comments on the
book's later reputation.

1928 A   BOOKS - NONE

1928 B   SHORTER WRITINGS

1   ELLIS, A. M. "What Does Irving Say?" English Journal, XVII
(September 1928), 576-78.
"Rip Van Winkle" provides an interesting test of reading
accuracy. Most people believe that Rip encountered dwarfs,
not the ghosts of Henry Hudson's crew.

2   *POCHMANN, HENRY A. The Influence of the German Tale on the
Short Stories of Washington Irving, Hawthorne, and Poe.
Univ. of North Carolina, 1928.
A dissertation.

3   WILLIAMS, STANLEY T., ed. Letters from Sunnyside and Spain.
New Haven: Yale Univ. Press, 1928.
Prints Irving letters from 1840-45, some of which appeared earlier in Yale Review. Brief preface; no other
apparatus.

1929 A   BOOKS - NONE

1929 B   SHORTER WRITINGS

1   ANON. "Catalogue of the Hellman Collection of Irvingiana."
Bulletin of the New York Public Library, XXXIII (April
1929), 209-19.
Descriptive list of manuscripts and other materials by
or about Irving, given to the Library by George S. Hellman; also other Irvingiana owned by the Library.

2   BROOKS, VAN WYCK. "Foreword." Voyages and Discoveries of the
Companions of Christopher Columbus. New York: Rimington
and Hooper, 1929, pp. vii-xii.
Foreword summarizes the book and describes its composition. Irving conducted his Spanish research in a spirit of

1929

(BROOKS, VAN WYCK)
nationalistic fervor. He had a "romantic enthusiasm" for
his subjects and he gave to his book a "distinguished
charm."

3   HASTINGS, G. E. "John Bull and His American Descendants."
American Literature, I (March 1929), 40-68.
The outline of Irving's portrait of John Bull in The
Sketch Book was borrowed from Arbuthnot's The History of
John Bull. Irving shows a rare sympathy, and greatly hu-
manizes the character. James Kirke Paulding's The Divert-
ing History of John Bull and Brother Jonathan (revised ed.,
1835), in turn shows the influence of Irving's sketch.

4   HUBBELL, J. B. "Introduction." Swallow Barn. New York:
Harcourt, Brace & Co., 1929, pp. ix-xxx.
Notes the resemblance of John Pendleton Kennedy's book
to The Sketch Book and Bracebridge Hall on p. xxviii.

5   LOPEZ NUÑEZ, JUAN. Romanticos y Bohemios. Un Hispanofilo
Ilustre. Madrid: Editorial Ibero-americana, 1929.
Irving is treated on pp. 121-24.

6   VAIL, R. W. G. "The Hellman Collection of Irvingiana." Bulletin of the New York Public Library, XXXIII (April 1929),
207-19.
Lists literary manuscripts, letters, books, and other
Irving materials donated to the Library by George S. Hellman. Brief introduction and annotations. Also lists other
Irvingiana held by the Library but not in the Hellman collection.

1930 A   BOOKS - NONE

1930 B   SHORTER WRITINGS

1   ADKINS, N. F. Fitz-Greene Halleck. New Haven: Yale Univ.
Press, 1930.
The mock scholarship and heroism of A History of New
York "set the tone of New York literature for the next
twenty years." Many other references to Irving in the con-
text of Halleck's life.

2   ALVAREZ AGUILAR, M. "Prologo." Washington Irving. Apuntes
literarios. Las Cien mejores obras de la literatura
universal. Madrid: Compania ibero-americana de publica-
ciones, 1930. VI, 7-12.

3   BARNES, H. F. Charles Fenno Hoffman. New York: Columbia
     Univ. Press, 1930.
          A number of brief comments on Irving, in relation to the
     life of Hoffman.

4   GOGGIO, EMILIO. "Washington Irving and Italy." Romanic Re-
     view, XXI (January-March 1930), 26-33.
          Traces Irving's contact with Italian literature and cul-
     ture, and their effect in his works.

5   HELLMAN, GEORGE S. "Irving's Washington and an Episode in
     Courtesy." Colophon, Part I (1930), n. p.
          Touches on some bibliographical aspects of The Life of
     George Washington. Irving was helped in his project by
     several well-wishers, such as Eliza Quincy's daughter and
     William H. Prescott, who sent him pertinent manuscript
     material.

6   LANGFELD, WILLIAM R. "The Poems of Washington Irving." Bul-
     letin of the New York Public Library, XXXIV (November
     1930), 763-79.
          A collection of Irving's poetry with a one-page introduc-
     tion. The poems are in the fashionable sentimental mode of
     the day, and Irving evidently did not take them very seri-
     ously. Most of them were written for friends or for spe-
     cial occasions. Also published separately by the New York
     Public Library, 1931.

7   MORRIS, MURIEL. "Mary Shelley and John Howard Payne." Lon-
     don Mercury, XXII (September 1930), 443-50.
          Describes a sort of love triangle involving Mary Shelley,
     John Howard Payne, and Irving. Payne was attracted to Mary
     and Mary was attracted to Irving, who was "indifferent to,
     and largely unaware of, the whole proceeding." Quotes
     correspondence.

8   NOLAN, OLIVE. "The Influence of Geography and History on
     Washington Irving's Writings." Education, L (June 1930),
     598-605.
          Little more than a survey of Irving's career, pointing
     out how important travel and history were to him. Sees
     "beneath all the charm, a ruggedness that seems to bespeak
     an author in a new country of vast expanse and full of
     promise."

9   POCHMANN, HENRY A. "Irving's German Sources in The Sketch
     Book." Studies in Philology, XXVII (July 1930), 477-507.
          Suggests that Irving's Romanticism derived partially from
     his contact with German culture. Prints parallel texts of

1930

(POCHMANN, HENRY A.)
Otmar's "Peter Klaus" and "Rip Van Winkle" and compares in detail several German tales with "The Legend of Sleepy Hollow." Discusses Bürger's ballad "Lenore" as the source of "The Spectre Bridegroom." Credits German tales as being the ultimate source of the American short story.

10 _____. "Irving's German Tour and Its Influence on His Tales." Publications of the Modern Language Association, XLV (December 1930), 1150-87.
Traces Irving's progress in Germany and examines the tales in The Sketch Book and Tales of a Traveller for German influence, which is strong and repeated.

11 SMALL, M. R. "A Possible Ancestor of Diedrich Knickerbocker." American Literature, II (March 1930), 21-24.
Irving may possibly have taken hints for his character from the ostensible author of Richard Graves' The Spiritual Quixote.

12 WILLIAMS, STANLEY T. "The First Version of the Writings of Washington Irving in Spanish." Modern Philology, XXVIII (November 1930), 185-201.
Bibliography of adaptations and translations of Irving's works into Spanish. Extensive comment on the first of these, Tareas de un solitario, and its author, George Washington Montgomery, a friend of Irving's.

13 _____. "Washington Irving and Fernán Caballero." Journal of English and Germanic Philology, XXIX (1930), 352-66.
Traces Irving's friendship in Spain with Cecilia Böhl Von Faber (Fernán Caballero). Suggests mutual influences and their connections with Spanish literature. Quotes unpublished letters.

14 _____. "Washington Irving's First Stay in Paris." American Literature, II (March 1930), 15-20.
A blank in Irving's diaries and journals during his first stay in Paris can now be partially filled. His notes of May 24-June 19, 1805, printed here, show him intimately involved in "the world of Parisian boulevards and theatres."

15 YARBOROUGH, M. C. "Rambles with Washington Irving: Quotations From an Unpublished Autobiography of William C. Preston." South Atlantic Quarterly, XXIX (October 1930), 423-39.

(YARBOROUGH, M. C.)
Quotations from Preston's autobiography interspersed with comments on the relationship between Preston and Irving. Focuses on the tour of Scotland Irving made with Preston in 1817. See also item 1933.B6.

1931 A BOOKS - NONE

1931 B SHORTER WRITINGS

1   BOYNTON, H. W. "Irving." American Writers on American Literature, by Thirty-Seven Contemporary Writers. Ed. John Macy. New York: Horace Liveright, 1931, pp. 58-71.
    A biographical essay, popular in tone.

2   CANBY, H. S. Classic Americans. A Study of Eminent American Writers from Irving to Whitman. New York: Harcourt, Brace and Company, 1931.
    Irving, the first real American man of letters, won respect at home and abroad largely because of his polished style and gentle, romantic temperament. At heart he remained always a Federalist, and clung to a romantic idea of the European past. His work lacks originality, depth, and concern with great ideas, but is successful as graceful, suave belles lettres.

3   GOGGIO, EMILIO. "Washington Irving's Works in Italy." Romanic Review, XXII (October-December 1931), 301-303.
    The reception of Irving's works in Italy. Mentions translations, and quotes from Italian reviews. The Italians were among Irving's "sincerest admirers and most appreciative readers."

4   GWATHMEY, E. M. John Pendleton Kennedy. New York: Thomas Nelson and Sons, 1931.
    On pp. 91-92 are brief comments on Irving's influence on Kennedy's Swallow Barn.

5   RUDWIN, MAXIMILIAN. The Devil in Legend and Literature. Chicago: Open Court Publishing Co., 1931.
    "The Devil and Tom Walker" is "redolent of the American soil" because Irving depicts the Devil and Walker as types of American businessmen (pp. 218-19).

6   RUSSELL, JASON ALMUS. "Irving: Recorder of Indian Life." Journal of American History, XXV, No. 4 (1931), 185-95.
    Summarizes and quotes from Irving's work dealing with Indians. Irving presented the Indians as human beings,

1931

(RUSSELL, JASON ALMUS)
acting as their "literary defender, interpreter, and recording historian."

7   WILLIAMS, STANLEY T., ed. The Journal of Washington Irving
(1823-1824). Cambridge, Mass.: Harvard Univ. Press, 1931.
Footnotes, index, introduction. Though this journal is
not as introspective as Irving's other notebooks, "it is
an encyclopedic narrative of his external life during thir-
teen months" and details the inception of Tales of a Traveller. Also prints a previously unpublished sketch,
"William the Conqueror."

8   ZEYDEL, E. H. "Washington Irving and Ludwig Tieck." Publications of the Modern Language Association of America, XLVI
(1931), 946-47.
A note commenting on Henry Pochmann's supposition, in
PMLA XLV (1930), that Irving knew Ludwig Tieck. Documen-
tary evidence proves the two were acquainted. See item
1930.B10.

1932 A   BOOKS - NONE

1932 B   SHORTER WRITINGS

1   BIRSS, J. H. "New Verses by Washington Irving." American
Literature, IV (November 1932), 296.
A draft and a final version, in Irving's hand, of a
quatrain on Shakespeare, are exhibited in the house in
which Shakespeare was born. See item 1938.B1.

2   BLACKBURN, P. C. "Irving's Biography of James Lawrence--and
a New Discovery." Bulletin of the New York Public Library,
XXXVI (November 1932), 742-43.
A unique copy is bibliographically described and com-
mented on.

3   KNIGHT, GRANT C. American Literature and Culture. New York:
Ray Long & Richard R. Smith, Inc., 1932.
Evaluative literary history. "Irving belongs to the
number of Eighteenth Century writers who can still be read
by all who admire a combination of elegance, sentiment,
and wit."

4   LANGFELD, WILLIAM R. "Washington Irving--A Bibliography."
Bulletin of the New York Public Library, XXXVI (1932).
A complete, annotated, descriptive bibliography. Printed
in monthly installments in this vol. as follows: (June),

(LANGFELD, WILLIAM R.)
415-22; (July), 487-94; (August), 561-71; (September),
627-36; (October), 683-89; (November), 755-78; (December),
828-41.

5   LEWISOHN, LUDWIG. Expression in America. New York and London: Harper and Brothers, 1932.
Irving "sedulously" avoided thinking on fundamental subjects. He wrote elegantly and conventionally, and was not
really a creator. He was class-conscious, the "root and
core" of the genteel tradition; and he indulged, like most
American Romantic writers, in escapism. He did have, however, ability in delineating actual scenes.

6   P[ALTSITS], V. H. "Washington Irving and Frederick Saunders."
Bulletin of the New York Public Library, XXXVI (April
1932), 218-19.
Prints two letters from Irving to Saunders, an author,
with brief commentary.

7   THOBURN, JOSEPH B. "Centennial of the Tour of the Prairies
by Washington Irving (1832-1932)." Chronicles of Oklahoma,
X (September 1932), 426-33.
Merely recounts the book's main incidents and mentions
plans for a centennial celebration.

8   WADEPUHL, WALTER. "Amerika, du hast es besser." Germanic
Review, VII (April 1932), 186-91.
Discussion of Goethe's interest in America. Goethe had
little regard for Irving, who turned his back on the great
possibilities of American themes to imitate European modes.

9   WEBSTER, CLARENCE M. "Irving's Expurgation of the 1809 History of New York." American Literature, IV (November
1932), 293-95.
Although Irving, in the interest of good taste, expur-
gated a number of passages which appeared in the 1809 ed.,
he retained a scatological Dutch invective--probably real-
izing that the few who knew its meaning would laugh in
private and keep the secret.

10   WELLER, ARTHUR. "Irving--Writer and Patriot." National Re-
public, XX (August 1932), 22-23.
A brief overview of Irving's life, containing some sentimental inaccuracies.

1933

1933 A BOOKS

1   LANGFELD, WILLIAM R. and PHILIP C. BLACKBURN, comps. <u>Washing-ton Irving: A Bibliography</u>. New York: The New York Pub-lic Library, 1933.
      A revised and augmented reprinting of the Irving bibliog-raphy published in the <u>Bulletin of the New York Public Li-brary</u>, June-December 1932. The best analytical and de-scriptive bibliography. Contains lists of translations, illustrated editions, and other associated items.

1933 B SHORTER WRITINGS

1   ADKINS, NELSON F. "Irving's 'Wolfert's Roost': A Biblio-graphical Note." <u>Notes and Queries</u>, CLXIV (21 January 1933), 42.
      Two additions to Langfeld's bibliographical description, and details on the original publication of the sketch "The Contented Man."

2   A[DKINS], N[ELSON] F. "Irving's 'Wolfert's Roost.'" <u>Notes and Queries</u>, CLXIV (6 May 1933), 323.
      Reply to query by Southam (<u>N&Q</u>, 18 March 1933). <u>Wol-fert's Roost</u> was first published by Bohn in 1855. <u>See</u> item 1933.B7.

3   AXSON, STOCKTON. "Washington Irving and the Knickerbocker Group." <u>Rice Institute Pamphlet</u>, XX (April 1933), 178-95.
      Almost entirely on Irving, who was "our first complete artist in words." He was also, as a person, "finer than anything he wrote." The Knickerbocker group (Irving, Cooper, Bryant, Halleck, Drake, Paulding, <u>et al</u>.) "prac-tically originated artistic literature of pleasure" in America.

4   GARDNER, JAMES H. "One Hundred Years Ago in the Region of Tulsa." <u>Chronicles of Oklahoma</u>, XI (June 1933), 765-85.
      In part, identifies one of the spots mentioned in <u>A Tour on the Prairies</u>, at which Irving's party camped.

5   KEISER, ALBERT. "The Natives Through the Eyes of an Opti-mist." <u>The Indian in American Literature</u>. New York: Oxford Univ. Press, 1933, pp. 52-64.
      On Irving's treatment of Indians in <u>The Sketch Book</u>, <u>A Tour on the Prairies</u>, <u>Astoria</u>, and <u>Adventures of Captain Bonneville</u>.

6   PRESTON, W. C. <u>The Reminiscences of William C. Preston</u>. Ed. M. C. Yarborough. Chapel Hill: Univ. of North Carolina Press, 1933.

(PRESTON, W. C.)
The reminiscences include those on his friendship with Irving.

7   SOUTHAM, HERBERT. "Irving's 'Wolfert's Roost.'" Notes and Queries, CLXIV (18 March 1933), 194.
Comments and a query on Henry Bohn's publication of Wolfert's Roost and other works by Irving.

8   WILLIAMS, STANLEY T., ed. Washington Irving and the Storrows: Letters from England and the Continent, 1821-1828. Cambridge, Mass.: Harvard Univ. Press, 1933.
The editor provides annotations and a brief historical preface.

9   _____. "Washington Irving, Matilda Hoffman, and Emily Foster." Modern Language Notes, XLVIII (March 1933), 182-86.
Contrary to the contentions of G. S. Hellman, there is not "conclusive evidence" either that Irving proposed marriage to Emily Foster, or that her rejection of him affected his writing.

1934 A   BOOKS - NONE

1934 B   SHORTER WRITINGS

1   ADKINS, NELSON F. "An Uncollected Tale by Washington Irving." American Literature, V (January 1934), 364-67.
Reprints "The Haunted Ship," which appeared in Friendship's Offering: A Christmas, New Year and Birthday Present for MDCCCXLIX, an annual. See items 1935.B5, 1935.B6, and 1939.B2.

2   BENNETT, S. S. "The Cheves Family of South Carolina." South Carolina Historical and Genealogical Magazine, XXXV (October 1934), 130-52.
Includes Irving letter to James Renwick dated 8 December 1812.

3   HESPELT, E. H. "The Genesis of La Familia de Alvareda." Hispanic Review, II (July 1934), 179-201.
Uses letters and notes of Irving to establish the first version of Fernán Caballero's novel La familia de Alvareda and to determine the date of its composition. "It is not at all incredible that [La familia de Alvareda] may have come into existence as a result of Irving's interest and enthusiasm; . . . that he is, therefore, directly respon-

1934

(HESPELT, E. H.)
sible for it and indirectly responsible for the regenera-
tion of the Spanish novel in the nineteenth century."

4   HESPELT, E. HERMAN and STANLEY T. WILLIAMS. "Two Unpublished
Anecdotes by Fernán Caballero Preserved by Washington
Irving." Modern Language Notes, XLIX (January 1934),
25-31.
A letter from Irving to Johann Nikolaus Böhl von Faber,
previously published only in part, refers to a manuscript
which can be identified as by Fernán Caballero and is here
printed with commentary.

5   _____. "Washington Irving's Notes on Fernán Caballero's Stories." Publications of the Modern Language Association of
America, XLIX (1934), 1129-39.
Notes in Irving's diary, recording anecdotes and tales
told him by Fernán Caballero, parallel in most instances
the stories that she later published. Irving no doubt intended to use the notes for his own writings, but never
did so.

6   POCHMANN, HENRY A., ed. Washington Irving: Representative
Selections. New York: American Book Co., 1934.
Selections from Irving's works with notes, a selected
bibliography, and a chronological table. Introduction
treats Irving's life in terms of his social milieu, his
politics, his literary development, and his non-intellec-
tual approach to philosophy and religion. His popularity
is due essentially to his temperament, which would vary
"from pure sentiment and romance to wit and urbanity," and
to his style, which was "graciously suave" and engaging.

7   TOYNBEE, ARNOLD J. A Study of History. London: Oxford Univ.
Press, 1934, III, 137.
Mentions "Rip Van Winkle" as a myth embodying "the es-
sence of the overseas experience"--geographical expansion
creating social regression.

8   WEBSTER, CLARENCE M. "Washington Irving as Imitator of
Swift." Notes and Queries, CLXVI (April 1934), 295.
In the last chapter of Book I of A History of New York,
Irving experimented with a social satire obviously influenced by Swift. But he never again attempted satire, and
in later editions of the History he omitted his previous
harsh remarks.

9   WILLIAMS, STANLEY T. and ERNEST E. LEISY, eds. "Polly
     Holman's Wedding: Notes by Washington Irving." Southwest
     Review, XIX (July 1934), 449-54.
          An unpublished sketch by Irving, written on his trip to
     the Southwest. Editorial comments on the manuscript and
     on Irving as "an inexact romantic historian of the fron-
     tier."

10   ____ and LEONARD B. BEACH. "Washington Irving's Letters to
     Mary Kennedy." American Literature, VI (March 1934),
     45-65.
          Reprints ten letters (1853-56) to the niece of John
     Pendleton Kennedy, revealing Irving's love of children and
     details of his life at age seventy.

11   WILLIAMS, STANLEY T. "Authorship in Irving's Day." Saturday
     Review of Literature, XI (29 December 1934), 400.
          Ostensibly a review of Irving and Cooper bibliographies,
     but mainly an article on the hindrance to American litera-
     ture--exemplified by Irving's case--created by the lack of
     an international copyright law.

12   ____., ed. Journal, 1803. London: Oxford Univ. Press,
     1934.
          An edition of Irving's first journal with preface and
     notes. Though purely juvenilia, this diary "reflects his
     most permanent impulses, those of observing and of writ-
     ing."

13   WINTERICH, J. T. "Early American Books and Printing: Enter
     the Professional Author." Publishers' Weekly, CXXV (17
     March 1934), 1148-50; (21 April), 1547-50.
          Chapter IX in a series on the history of publishing in
     the United States. Survey of Irving's career as America's
     first truly professional author, with emphasis on the pub-
     lication history of his works.

1935 A BOOKS

1   WILLIAMS, STANLEY T. The Life of Washington Irving. 2 vols.
     New York: Oxford Univ. Press, 1935.
          The definitive scholarly biography; critical as well as
     historical.

1935 B SHORTER WRITINGS

1   MOWAT, R. B. "The England of Washington Irving." Americans
     in England. Cambridge, Mass.: Houghton Mifflin Co., 1935,
     pp. 103-22.

1935

(MOWAT, R. B.)
An account of Irving's life, travels, and reception in England. He was gracious and popular, but he remained distinctly American in loyalties and outlook. The Sketch Book is judged "one of the best things ever written on England." Portrait.

2 OSTERWEIS, ROLLIN G. Rebecca Gratz: A Study in Charm. New York: G. P. Putnam's Sons, 1935.
A biography which mentions Irving repeatedly in the context of Miss Gratz's life.

3 PARSONS, COLEMAN O. "Washington Irving Writes from Granada." American Literature, VI (January 1935), 439-43.
Prints and comments on a letter from Irving to his brother Peter, dated "Granada, April 9, 1829."

4 REICHART, WALTER A. "Washington Irving, the Fosters, and the Forsters." Modern Language Notes, L (January 1935), 35-39.
Irving knew two families, the Fosters and the Forsters, who have sometimes been confused by scholars.

5 STARKE, AUBREY. "Irving's 'Haunted Ship'--A Correction." American Literature, VI (January 1935), 444-45.
The tale is probably not by Irving. It had been reprinted in the New York Mirror, 9 January 1836, from some English annual. See items 1934.B1, 1935.B6, and 1939.B2.

6 THOMPSON, RALPH. "Irving's 'Haunted Ship.'" American Literature, VI (January 1935), 443-44.
The "uncollected story" printed in American Literature for January 1934 and attributed to Irving by Mr. N. F. Adkins, may very well not be by Irving because the compilers of the annual in which it appeared in 1849 were demonstrably unscrupulous. See items 1934.B1, 1935.B5, and 1939.B2.

1936 A BOOKS

1 WILLIAMS, STANLEY T. and MARY ALLEN EDGE, comps. A Bibliography of the Writings of Washington Irving: A Check List. New York: Oxford Univ. Press, 1936.
Supplements the Langfeld and Blackburn bibliography (1933). Lists all known printings of Irving's writings, in all languages, individually, in collected editions, or as selections. Also includes contributions, journals, collections of printed letters, ascriptions, Irvingiana, and a list of Irving scholarship and criticism, as well as all

(WILLIAMS, STANLEY T. and MARY ALLEN EDGE)
editions of P. M. Irving's Life and Letters of Washington
Irving.

1936 B   SHORTER WRITINGS

1   ANON. "A Master of the Obsolete: Washington Irving in the
     Shadows." Times Literary Supplement (21 March 1936), pp.
     229-30.
         An overview of Irving's literary life, ostensibly a re-
     view of Williams' Life. Treats Irving as basically an
     imitative, shallow scribbler. Only "Rip Van Winkle" has
     the reviewer's genuine admiration.

2   BLANCK, JACOB. "The Authorship of 'Salmagundi.'" Publishers'
     Weekly, CXXX (28 November 1936), 2101.
         Announces the discovery of what was apparently James K.
     Paulding's own copy of Salmagundi, Vol. I (N. Y., 1814).
     It includes, after most of the articles, the name of the
     author in Paulding's hand. Lists the articles with a
     transcription of Paulding's notations.

3   LEISY, ERNEST E. "Irving and the Genteel Tradition." South-
     west Review, XXI (January 1936), 223-27.
         Suggests that American literature can be classified in
     terms of a "robust" and a "genteel" tradition. Irving,
     who exemplified urbane civilization and Old-World manners,
     had a tremendous hold on his generation. Traces Irving's
     influence on American writers and sympathetically discusses
     some of his "genteel" qualities.

4   O'NEILL, E. H. Review of The Life of Washington Irving by
     Stanley Williams. North American Review, CCXLI (March
     1936), 161-70.
         Mostly summary and praise of Williams' biography. Sug-
     gests that Williams neglected Irving's connection with
     Dickens and maintains that Dickens was indebted to Irving
     for his Christmas stories and for some of his characters.

5   REICHART, WALTER A. "Washington Irving as a Source for Borel
     and Dumas." Modern Language Notes, LI (June 1936), 388-89.
         Dumas père plagiarized a story from Pétrus Borel, whose
     own tale was also a plagiarism--an exact translation of
     Irving's "Adventure of the German Student."

6   RICHARDS, IRVING T. "John Neal's Gleanings in Irvingiana."
     American Literature, VIII (May 1936), 170-79.
         Some comments by Neal in a letter and an 1843 periodical
     piece bear on Irving, his character, and some of the people
     about whom he wrote.

1937

1937 A BOOKS - NONE

1937 B SHORTER WRITINGS

1 ELLSWORTH, HENRY L. Washington Irving on the Prairie, or A
     Narrative of a Tour of the Southwest in the Year 1832.
     Ed. Stanley T. Williams and Barbara D. Simison. New York:
     American Book Co., 1937.
        Ellsworth's journal adds to our knowledge of Irving, his
     trip, and A Tour on the Prairies itself.

2 SMITH, FRANCES P. "Washington Irving on French Romanticism."
     Revue de littérature comparée, XVII (October 1937), 715-32.
        Collation of two versions of an essay by Irving on French
     Romanticism.

3 _____. "Washington Irving, the Fosters, and Some Poetry."
     American Literature, IX (May 1937), 228-32.
        The sonnet "Echo and Silence," included in Langfeld's
     Poems of Washington Irving, is not by Irving as the Foster
     sisters said it was, but by Sir Egerton Brydges.

4 SPILLER, ROBERT E. "War with the Book Pirates." Publishers'
     Weekly, CXXXII (30 October 1937), 1736-38.
        Describes how Irving and Cooper "outwitted the book pi-
     rates" and exploited the adverse copyright laws so they
     could receive royalties both in England and America. "The
     story of how these two astute business men overcame ob-
     stacles and made writing a lucrative profession is the
     first chapter in the history of our national literature."

5 WILLIAMS, STANLEY T., ed. Journal of Washington Irving, 1828,
     and Miscellaneous Notes on Moorish Legend and History.
     New York: American Book Co., 1937.
        One of Irving's Spanish journals, which fills a gap in
     our previous knowledge of his stay in Spain. Includes in-
     formation on Irving's sources for Alhambra and Conquest of
     Granada. Introduction, explanatory footnotes, and fac-
     similes of Irving's drawings.

6 WOLFE, J. W. "Did Rip Van Winkle Ever Live?" Scholastic,
     XXIX (9 January 1937), 11-12.
        A survey of Rip Van Winkle legends and folklore.

7 *ZIRKLE, MARY. "Meeting the West." Christian Science Monitor,
     XXIX (20 March 1937), 4.
        Unlocatable. Cited in Lewis Leary, Articles on American
     Literature, 1900-1950.

1938 A   BOOKS

1   *SMITH, FRANCÈS P.   Washington Irving and France.   Harvard
      Univ., 1938.
         A dissertation.

1938 B   SHORTER WRITINGS

1   LANGFELD, WILLIAM R.   "A Letter to the Editors."   American
      Literature, X (November 1938), 351.
         Explains that "new verses" published in AL, IV (November
      1932) had actually been published previously elsewhere.
      See item 1932.B1.

2   SMITH, F. PRESCOTT.   "Un Conte Fantastique Chez Irving, Borel
      et Dumas Père."   Revue de littérature comparée, XVIII
      (April 1938), 334–46.
         Shows how Irving's "Adventure of the German Student" was
      used by Pétrus Borel in "Gottfried Wolfgang" and by Dumas
      père in "La Femme au Collier de Velours."   Compares the
      three treatments and examines the sources of the story.

3   WILLIAMS, STANLEY T. and LEONARD B. BEACH, eds.   The Journal
      of Emily Foster.   New York: Oxford Univ. Press, 1938.
         "This Journal will remain significant for students of
      American literature because it offers an authoritative ac-
      count of an important and puzzling episode in the life of
      Washington Irving; and because it recreates so completely
      the character of a woman with whom he was, apparently, in
      love."   Introduction and footnotes.

1939 A   BOOKS – NONE

1939 B   SHORTER WRITINGS

1   LEE, FRANK.   "Washington Irving and the Battle of Waterloo."
      Notes and Queries, CLXXVI (25 March 1939), 207.
         A query about where Irving's description of the arrival
      in Liverpool of the news of Waterloo can be found.

2   McCARTER, PETE KYLE.   "The Authorship and Date of 'The
      Haunted Ship.'"   American Literature, XI (May 1939),
      294–95.
         A letter by Irving proves "The Haunted Ship" to be his,
      and to have been written as early as 1835.   Thus the doubts
      expressed in the Thompson and Starke articles in American
      Literature, VI (January 1935) are now resolved.   See items
      1935.B5–B6.

1939

3   MATHEWS, J. C. "Washington Irving's Knowledge of Dante."
     American Literature, X (January 1939), 480-83.
          Irving read the *Inferno* in Italian, and may also have
     read the rest of the *Divina Commedia*.

1940 A BOOKS

1   BOWERS, CLAUDE G. *The Spanish Adventures of Washington Ir-
     ving*. Boston: Houghton Mifflin Co., 1940.
          A popular biography of Irving during his years in Spain,
     containing new facts about some of his friends and ac-
     quaintances.

2   *McCARTER, PETE K. *The Literary, Political and Social Theo-
     ries of Washington Irving*. Univ. of Wisconsin, 1940.
          A dissertation.

1940 B SHORTER WRITINGS

1   FORREST, REX. "Irving and 'The Almighty Dollar.'" *American
     Speech*, XV (December 1940), 443-44.
          Irving did indeed coin the phrase, as he claimed.

2   LAIRD, CHARLTON G. "Tragedy and Irony in *Knickerbocker's
     History*." *American Literature*, XII (May 1940), 157-72.
          Elements of irony and tragedy in the Peter Stuyvesant
     section of *Knickerbocker* affect our sense of Irving's per-
     sonality and creative power, as well as our interpretation
     of the book. They also suggest a means of more precisely
     dating its composition.

1941 A BOOKS - NONE

1941 B SHORTER WRITINGS

1   DAVIS, RICHARD B. "James Ogilvie and Washington Irving."
     Americana, XXXV (July 1941), 435-58.
          Traces "one of the most interesting of Irving's early
     friendships." Ogilvie was a rather eccentric New Yorker
     who gave Irving crucial emotional support and who served
     as a model for some of Irving's characters. Discusses the
     notes for *Rosalie*, Irving's projected novel.

2   REICHART, WALTER A. "Washington Irving's Friend and Collabo-
     rator: Barham John Livius, Esq." *Publications of the
     Modern Language Association of America*, LVI (June 1941),
     513-31.

(REICHART, WALTER A.)
Livius was a minor English dramatist whom Irving met
through the Fosters. Irving became involved with him in a
few amateur theatricals, for which Irving did not publicly
claim any credit.

3   WILLIAMS, STANLEY T. "Introduction." Letters of Jonathan
Oldstyle. Facsimile Text Society, No. 52. New York:
Columbia Univ. Press, 1941.
Williams notes that though "ephemeral" as literature,
these letters provide valuable insights into American culture of the time and into Irving's development as an essayist and satirist. Historical and textual comments.

1942 A   BOOKS - NONE

1942 B   SHORTER WRITINGS

1   FRANCIS, F. C. "Washington Irving." Times Literary Supplement (7 February 1942), p. 72.
Adds an Icelandic translation of "The Pride of the Village" (The Sketch Book) to the other translations listed
in Williams and Edge (1936.A1).

1943 A   BOOKS - NONE

1943 B   SHORTER WRITINGS

1   GATES, WILLIAM B. "Washington Irving in Mississippi." Modern Language Notes, LVIII (February 1943), 130-31.
Irving stopped in Vicksburg in November 1832.

1944 A   BOOKS

1   BENÉT, LAURA. Washington Irving, Explorer of American Legend.
New York: Dodd, Mead & Company, 1944.
A fictionalized, romantic account of Irving's early life.

1944 B   SHORTER WRITINGS

1   BOLL, ERNEST. "Charles Dickens and Washington Irving." Modern Language Quarterly, V (December 1944), 453-67.
Irving's work had a strong, positive influence on Dickens' writing, and many parallels can be seen in the subjects and techniques of the two writers.

1944

2   BROOKS, VAN WYCK. The World of Washington Irving. New York:
     E. P. Dutton and Company, Inc., 1944.
         An appreciative, popular history of American literature
     from 1800 to ca. 1840, with a number of extended passages
     on Irving. Discursive and wide-ranging. Treats Irving's
     life and character, themes and style, reputation, with em-
     phasis on his connections with the writers, artists, and
     other public figures of his day. No critical analyses of
     the works.

3   GOHDES, CLARENCE. American Literature in Nineteenth-Century
     England. New York: Columbia Univ. Press, 1944.
         A study of the English interest in American literature,
     with scattered references to Irving's popularity, critical
     success, and influence upon such writers as Dickens. In-
     dex, and list of representative articles on American lit-
     erature in British periodicals, 1833-1901.

4   McDERMOTT, JOHN F., ed. The Western Journals of Washington
     Irving. Norman: Univ. of Oklahoma Press, 1944.
         The five extant Irving journals of 1832 are reproduced
     "as faithfully as possible." The editor contributes a
     long introduction, in which he comments on Irving's methods
     in taking material from his journals for A Tour on the
     Prairies, and numerous notes.

5   ZABRISKIE, G. A. "A Little About Washington Irving." New
     York Historical Society Quarterly Bulletin, XXIX (January
     1944), 5-15.
         A light overview of Irving's life and work.

1945 A BOOKS - NONE

1945 B SHORTER WRITINGS

1   COMMINS, SAXE. "America's First Man of Letters." Saturday
     Review of Literature, XXVIII (1 September 1945), 5-7.
         An overview of Irving's career. "In the life and travels
     and works of Washington Irving, it is possible to read the
     cycle of [our] nation. . . ."

2   HOFFMAN, LOUISE M. "Irving's Use of Spanish Sources in The
     Conquest of Granada." Hispania, XXVIII (November 1945),
     483-98.
         Places side by side excerpts from Granada and the his-
     torical sources Irving drew from. "Irving takes the his-
     torical facts as he finds them, then adds to them the color
     he deems worthy of such deeds." Defends Irving against the

(HOFFMAN, LOUISE M.)
charges of repetition and exaggeration, showing that he kept close to his sources. Defends the point-of-view character, Fray Antonio Agapida, as essential to preserve the tone of the sixteenth-century historians.

3   KIRK, CLARA and RUDOLPH KIRK, eds. "Seven Letters of Washington Irving." Journal of the Rutgers University Library, IX (December 1945), 1-22; X (June 1946), 36-58; (December 1946), 20-27.
This three-part article prints, with editorial commentary, letters to Peter and William Irving and to Andrew Hicks, written during Irving's first trip to Europe.

4   MORRIS, ROBERT L. "Three Arkansas Travelers." Arkansas Historical Quarterly, IV (Autumn 1945), 215-30.
Summarizes the early accounts of Arkansas territory as given by Timothy Flint, Frederick Gerstaecker, and Irving in A Tour on the Prairies. Shows how Irving "allowed his senses to be impressed by the shifting scenes of his voyage down the Arkansas."

5   PACEY, W. C. DESMOND. "Washington Irving and Charles Dickens." American Literature, XVI (January 1945), 332-39.
Virtually all the evidence shows Irving and Dickens to have been great friends and mutual admirers. But Irving was later critical of Dickens' aspersions on the United States.

6   REICHART, WALTER A. "Baron Von Gumppenberg, Emily Foster, and Washington Irving." Modern Language Notes, LX (May 1945), 333-35.
Identifies and gives a brief biographical sketch of Baron von Gumppenberg, Irving's chief rival for the affections of Emily Foster in Dresden.

7   TROP, SYLVIA. "An Italian Rip Van Winkle." New York Folklore Quarterly, I (May 1945), 101-105.
Merely an Italian story with the long sleep motif.

8   WILLIAMS, STANLEY T. "Washington Irving and Andrew Jackson." Yale University Library Gazette, XIX (April 1945), 67-69.
A letter to Andrew Jackson dated 10 October 1830 and a letter to William M. Blackford dated 27 October 1833, printed with a brief introduction.

1946 A BOOKS - NONE

1946

1946 B   SHORTER WRITINGS

1   LE FEVRE, LOUIS. "Paul Bunyan and Rip Van Winkle." Yale Re-
     view, XXXVI (September 1946), 66-76.
          Essay arguing that "American life may be symbolized as a
     continuing debate between Paul Bunyan and Rip Van Winkle."
     Bunyan represents the desire to get things done on a vast
     scale; Rip symbolizes the desire for indolent leisure.
     The motifs are traced through American culture--Huck Finn
     and labor saving appliances are all seen as types of Rip
     Van Winkle and the impulse to escape drudgery. No literary
     criticism.

2   LLOYD, F. V., JR. "Irving's Rip Van Winkle." Explicator, IV
     (February 1946), 26.
          An answer to a query in the October 1945 Explicator as
     to whether there is a theme in "Rip Van Winkle." Asserts
     that it is a satire on the small town mind.

3   SNELL, GEORGE. "Washington Irving: A Revaluation." Modern
     Language Quarterly, VII (September 1946), 303-309.
          An attempt to put Irving's works in perspective. Snell
     says that we owe respect to him not primarily for what he
     achieved, but for the directions his works gave to his more
     gifted successors. The Sketch Book is his only lasting
     achievement.

4   WEGELIN, CHRISTOF. "Dickens and Irving: The Problem of In-
     fluence." Modern Language Quarterly, VII (March 1946),
     83-91.
          Contrary to Ernest Boll's opinion in MLQ, V (December
     1944), the demonstrable influence of Irving on Dickens is
     limited to the latter's early work, including Sketches by
     Boz and some short periodical pieces. See item 1944.B1.

5   WILSON, JAMES L. "Washington Irving's 'Celebrated English
     Poet.'" American Literature, XVIII (November 1946),
     247-49.
          The poet alluded to in "Philip of Pokanoket" in The
     Sketch Book is Robert Southey, and the poem he was writing
     but never finished is Oliver Newman: A Tale of New
     England.

1947 A   BOOKS

1   *OSBORNE, ROBERT S. A Study of Washington Irving's Development
     as a Man of Letters to 1825. Univ. of North Carolina,
     1947.
          A dissertation.

2   *YOUNG, JOHN P. <u>Washington Irving à Bordeaux</u>. Univ. of
        Bordeaux, 1947.
            A dissertation.

<u>1947 B   SHORTER WRITINGS</u>

1   BLANCK, JACOB. "<u>Salmagundi</u> and Its Publisher." <u>Papers of
        the Bibliographical Society of America</u>, XLI (First Quarter
        1947), 1-32.
            A discussion of David Longworth prefaces detailed biblio-
        graphical description.

2   KIRBY, THOMAS. "Irving and Moore: A Note on Anglo-American
        Literary Relations." <u>Modern Language Notes</u>, LXII (April
        1947), 251-55.
            Despite <u>Salmagundi</u>'s attack on Moore, and his aspersions
        on America, Irving and Moore became good friends, and
        Irving was instrumental in getting the <u>Life of Byron</u> pub-
        lished in America.

3   LAMB, G. F. "Some Anglo-American Literary Contacts." <u>Quar-
        terly Review</u>, CCLXXXV (April 1947), 247-58.
            On early American men of letters in England. Discusses
        Irving's publishing ventures and his friendship with Scott.
        Praises <u>Abbotsford</u> as "one of the most graceful tributes
        . . . ever paid by . . . a guest to his host."

4   *NARITA, NARIHISA. "Irving's 'Rip Van Winkle.'" <u>Senior
        English</u> (Japan), No. 7 (1947).
            Cited in the Modern Humanities Research Association
        <u>Annual Bibliography of English Language and Literature</u>.
        Unobtainable.

5   SEIGLER, MILLEDGE B. "Washington Irving to William C. Pres-
        ton: An Unpublished Letter." <u>American Literature</u>, XIX
        (November 1947), 256-59.
            Prints the 1852 letter, with brief commentary.

6   SNELL, GEORGE. "Washington Irving: A Revaluation." <u>The
        Shapers of American Fiction, 1798-1947</u>. New York: E. P.
        Dutton & Co., 1947, pp. 105-17.
            Reprinted. <u>See</u> item 1946.B3.

7   *WEGELIN, CHRISTOF A. <u>The Concept of European American Fiction
        from Irving to Hawthorne</u>. The Johns Hopkins Univ., 1947.
            A dissertation.

1948

1948 A   BOOKS - NONE

1948 B   SHORTER WRITINGS

1   BEACH, LEONARD. "Washington Irving: The Artist in a Changing
      World." University of Kansas City Review, XIV (Summer
      1948), 259-66.
          Focuses on Irving's "deliberate realism" which was to
      find its sequels in Hawthorne and James. Discusses
      Irving's "journalistic method," his artistic detachment,
      and his search for native themes. Notes occasional artis-
      tic similarities to Hawthorne and Mark Twain. Also notes
      Irving as America's "first great myth-maker" and as a seri-
      ous student of folklore.

2   EATON, V. L. "The Leonard Kebler Gift of Washington Irving
      First Editions." Library of Congress Quarterly Journal, V
      (February 1948), 9-13.
          Describes the contents and physical characteristics of
      the books, with related comments on Irving's career and
      the Library's other Irving holdings.

3   PRICE, GEORGE R. "Washington Irving's Librettos." Music and
      Letters, XXIX (October 1948), 348-55.
          A biographical and historical essay exploring Irving's
      connection with the London theatre of the early 1820s.
      Irving "played a major part" in translating and introducing
      Weber's operas, "The Wild Huntsman" and "Abu Hassan." See
      item 1950.B2.

1949 A   BOOKS - NONE

1949 B   SHORTER WRITINGS

1   OLIVE, W. J. "Davenant and Davenport." Notes and Queries,
      CXLIV (23 July 1949), 320.
          Irving quotes, in Bracebridge Hall, from a play by Robert
      Davenport, who has been at times confused with his better-
      known contemporary William Davenant.

2   SIMISON, BARBARA D. "Washington Irving's Notebook of 1810."
      Yale University Library Gazette, XXIV (July 1949), 1-16;
      (October), 74-94.
          Irving's 1810 Notebook printed in its entirety. Bio-
      graphical, bibliographical, and critical introduction.
      "The notebook not only serves as a commonplace book for
      quotations, but it also becomes a kind of exercise book
      for the young author," revealing "his growing enthusiasm

(SIMISON, BARBARD D.)
and talent for writing." It shows him revising and polish-
ing unwieldy sentences. Words, descriptions, and thoughts
jotted down will later be incorporated into his works.

3   VAN WART, R. B. "Washington Irving and Scotland." Blackwood's Magazine, CCLXVI (September 1949), 257-63.
Traces Irving's genealogy to "one of the most noteworthy
families in Scotland" and discusses Irving's association
with Scottish literary circles. Details on Irving's
friendship with Sir Walter Scott.

1950 A   BOOKS - NONE

1950 B   SHORTER WRITINGS

1   *BINDER, SISTER M. CLAUDIA. Studien zur Charakterisierungstechnik in Kurzgeschichten Washington Irvings, E. A. Poes,
und Nathaniel Hawthornes. Graz, 1950.
A dissertation.

2   KIRBY, P. R. "Washington Irving, Barham Livius and Weber."
Music and Letters, XXXI (April 1950), 133-47.
A rejoinder to the article by George Price, Music and
Letters, XXIX (October 1948), 348-55. Irving did not play
"'a major part'" in translating Weber's operas; and what
he did contribute had to be rewritten. See item 1948.B3.

3   SPAULDING, K. A. "A Note on Astoria: Irving's Use of the
Robert Stuart Manuscript." American Literature, XXII (May
1950), 150-57.
His various alterations of the story told in Stuart's
account show that "the artist in Irving was steadily
triumphant over the geographer, the historian, or the
biographer."

4   WILLIAMS, STANLEY T. "Cosmopolitanism in American Literature
Before 1880." The American Writer and the European Tradition. Eds. Margaret Denny and William H. Gilman. New
York: McGraw-Hill Book Co., 1950, pp. 45-62.
Study of the tendency of American writers to look to
Europe for cultural enrichment, with emphasis on Irving,
Longfellow, and James. Irving craved Romance, while America offered only the "'commonplace.'" Longfellow was primarily interested in the books of the Old World, James in
the society, and Irving in the places, the scenes that he
could minutely observe.

1950

5   WILLIAMS, STANLEY T. "Introduction." Washington Irving:
      Selected Prose. New York: Holt, Rinehart and Winston,
      1950, pp. v-xx.
          Discusses Irving's major themes, his treatment of nature,
      the European elements in his work (such as the influence
      of Dutch painting), and stylistic matters such as rhythm
      and sound. Special attention to "Rip Van Winkle," the
      "epitome of Irving the writer."

1951 A BOOKS - NONE

1951 B SHORTER WRITINGS

1   DAVIS, RICHARD BEALE. "Washington Irving and Joseph C.
      Cabell." English Studies in Honor of James Southall
      Wilson. University of Virginia Studies, V (1951), pp.
      7-22.
          Account of Irving's friendship with Joseph C. Cabell who
      "assisted, at least, in initiating Irving to Europe."
      Prints extracts from journals, letters, and notebooks of
      both men, and reconstructs their travels and Cabell's pos-
      sible influence.

2   RABSON, BARRIE. "Irving's Sunnyside." New York Folklore
      Quarterly, VII (Fall 1951), 205-16.
          Irving's home, its history and lore.

3   *SPAULDING, KENNETH A. Robert Stuart's Traveling Memoranda:
      A Source for Washington Irving's Astoria. Univ. of Iowa,
      1951.
          A dissertation.

1952 A BOOKS - NONE

1952 B SHORTER WRITINGS

1   HORSFORD, HOWARD C. "Illustration to the Legend of Prince
      Ahmed: An Unpublished Sketch by Washington Irving."
      Princeton University Library Chronicle, XIV (Autumn 1952),
      30-36.
          Description and transcription of a previously unpublished
      manuscript. Prints Irving's source for the sketch. Photo-
      graph of the manuscript.

2   LYDENBERG, HARRY MILLER. "Irving's Knickerbocker and Some of
      Its Sources." Bulletin of the New York Public Library,
      LVI (November 1952), 544-53; (December), 596-619.

(LYDENBERG, HARRY MILLER)
A discursive, rambling, detailed essay on the sources of A History of New York's burlesque erudition and its historical detail.

3   LYNCH, JAMES J. "The Devil in the Writings of Irving, Hawthorne, and Poe." New York Folklore Quarterly, VIII (Summer 1952), 111-31.
Irving's devil, in "The Devil and Tom Walker," "is of the pure New England variety."

4   WETZEL, GEORGE. "Irving's Rip Van Winkle." Explicator, X (June 1952), 54.
An explication of Rip Van Winkle's name. "Rip" is the common abbreviation of "Rest in Peace"; "Winkle" suggests "forty winks."

1953 A   BOOKS - NONE

1953 B   SHORTER WRITINGS

1   ADAMS, THOMAS R. "Washington Irving--Another Letter from Spain." American Literature, XXV (November 1953), 354-58.
A previously unpublished 1845 letter from Irving to Sarah Storrow recounts some experiences in Spain.

2   BERGHOLZ, HARRY. "Was Washington Irving Stendhal's first American critic?" Revue de littérature comparée, XXVII (July-September 1953), 328-39.
Speculates that Irving may have been the anonymous reviewer of Stendahl's Rome, Naples et Florence in the Analectic Magazine for July 1818.

3   BROOKS, E. L. "A Note on Irving's Sources." American Literature, XXV (May 1953), 229-30.
One of Irving's recognized sources for "The Legend of Sleepy Hollow" appeared in English in 1791.

4   HOFFMAN, DANIEL G. "Irving's Use of American Folklore in 'The Legend of Sleepy Hollow.'" Publications of the Modern Language Association of America, LXVIII (June 1953), 425-35.
Irving is the "first important American author to put to literary use the comic mythology and popular traditions of American character." He did so mainly in his depiction of Ichabod Crane, the Yankee, vs. Brom Bones, the backwoodsman. When Irving "found archetypal figures already half-created by the popular imagination" and when his "milieu

1953

(HOFFMAN, DANIEL G.)
was the fabulous," he had tremendous power. Reprinted with slight alterations in Form and Fable in American Fiction; see item 1961.B3.

5   REICHART, WALTER A. "Impromptu by Washington Irving." Notes and Queries, CXCVIII (December 1953), 531.
Irving's quatrain on Shakespeare actually appeared first in the English magazine Portfolio (June 1825).

1954 A   BOOKS

1   *HEDGES, WILLIAM L. The Fiction of History: Washington Irving Against a Romantic Transition. Harvard Univ., 1954.
A dissertation.

1954 B   SHORTER WRITINGS

1   BROOKS, ELMER L. "A Note on the Source of 'Rip Van Winkle.'" American Literature, XXV (January 1954), 495-96.
Another German version, and an 1822 English translation, of "Peter Klaus" are noted.

2   JONES, CHARLES W. "Knickerbocker Santa Claus." New York Historical Society Quarterly, XXXVIII (October 1954), 357-83.
Article on the development of the idea of Santa Claus in America. Details Irving's contributions to the myth in A History of New York and Salmagundi, concluding that "without Irving there would be no Santa Claus."

3   WALKER, R. J. "Geoffrey Crayon." Hobbies, LIX (March 1954), 133-34, 138.
Adulatory praise of Irving and his work.

1955 A   BOOKS - NONE

1955 B   SHORTER WRITINGS

1   ANON. "Irvingiana." Hobbies, LX (December 1955), 42.
A notice of the Commander Edward Walker Hardin Collection of Irvingiana, on exhibit at Sunnyside, which includes a textually rare first edition of The Sketch Book.

2   FISKE, JOHN C. "The Soviet Controversy Over Pushkin and Washington Irving." Comparative Literature, VII (Winter 1955), 25-31.
Describes the literary-political controversy over whether

(FISKE, JOHN C.)
or not Pushkin took his "Tale of the Golden Cockerel" from
Irving's "Legend of the Arabian Astrologer" in The Alhambra. Describes Irving's early popularity in Russia and
his probable influence on Pushkin.

3   KRUMPELMANN, JOHN T.   "Revealing the Source of Irving's 'Rip
     Van Winkle.'"   Monatshefte, XLVII (November 1955), 361-62.
       Bayard Taylor, in Atlantic Monthly (May 1868), was the
     first to point to the story of ·Peter Klaus as the source
     of "Rip Van Winkle." He did a more thorough analysis than
     did J. B. Thompson in Harper's Magazine (September 1883).
     See items 1868.B1 and 1883.B12.

4   TEICHMANN, ELIZABETH. "Deux Adaptations Inconnues du Conte
     de Washington Irving: The Adventure of the German Stu-
     dent." Modern Philology, LIII (August 1955), 8-16.
       A discussion of two French works, a poem by H. de La-
     touche, "Une Nuit de 1793," and an anonymous story, "L'
     Inconnue," and their relation to Irving's tale.

5   THOBURN, JOSEPH B. and GEORGE C. WELLS, eds. A Tour on the
     Prairies. Oklahoma City: Harlow Publishing Co., 1955.
       Includes extracts from Irving's journals and Latrobe's
     account of their journey, and exhaustive historical foot-
     notes. Very brief critical introduction.

6   WATTS, CHARLES H., II. "Poe, Irving and The Southern Literary
     Messenger." American Literature, XXVII (May 1955), 249-51.
       Irving apparently did not respond to an 1836 letter from
     Poe (previously unpublished) asking that Irving contribute
     a piece of writing to The Southern Literary Messenger.
     This article also appeared in an expanded version; see
     item 1956.B12.

7   WILLIAMS, STANLEY T. "Washington Irving." The Spanish Back-
     ground of American Literature. New Haven: Yale Univ.
     Press, 1955, II, 3-45.
       Details Irving's early interest in things Spanish, his
     years in Spain, its influence on his thinking, and the
     works he produced as a result. "His interpretation of
     Spanish legends, and of all phases of Spain, was often
     shrewdly humorous--and altogether it was just." Many other
     comments on Irving throughout the two volumes.

1956 A BOOKS - NONE

1956

1956 B   SHORTER WRITINGS

1   FATOUT, PAUL. "Mark Twain's First Lecture: A Parallel."
    Pacific Historical Review, XXV (November 1956), 347-54.
         Compares a passage from Roughing It with an account in
    Irving's Life of Goldsmith. Speculates on Irving's pos-
    sible influence on Twain.

2   HEDGES, WILLIAM L. "Irving's Columbus: The Problem of Ro-
    mantic Biography." The Americas, XIII (October 1956),
    127-40.
         Examines the genre of the book. To Irving, among others,
    history was closer to epic romance than anything else.

3   KRUMPELMANN, JOHN T. "Revealing the Source of Irving's 'Rip
    Van Winkle.'" Archiv für das Studium der neueren Sprachen
    und Literaturen, CXCIII (1956), 39-40.
         Same article as in Monatshefte (November 1955). See item
    1955.B3.

4   LAMBERTS, J. J. "Knickerbocker." Names, IV (June 1956), 70-
    74.
         Irving's use of the name made it a synonym for "Dutch."
    It was probably derived from a nickname, contrary to the
    etymological explanation of a member of the Knickerbocker
    family.

5   McDERMOTT, JOHN F., ed. A Tour on the Prairies. Norman:
    Univ. of Oklahoma Press, 1956.
         The editor's introduction deals with literary and his-
    torical considerations, but not incisively.

6   _____. "Washington Irving and the Journal of Captain Bonne-
    ville." Mississippi Valley Historical Review, XLIII (De-
    cember 1956), 459-67.
         Sketches the life and career of Bonneville. Prints a
    previously unpublished letter from Irving to J. H. Hook
    and quotes from other correspondence. Speculates as to
    the location of Bonneville's journal from which Irving
    drew his narrative.

7   REICHART, WALTER A. "Concerning the Source of Irving's 'Rip
    Van Winkle.'" Monatshefte, XLVIII (February 1956), 94-95.
         A rejoinder to Krumpelmann's article, Monatshefte (No-
    vember 1955). Irving's German borrowing had been acknowl-
    edged from the first and was well-known at the time. He
    took the story not from Otmar, but from Büsching.

8   REICHART, WALTER A. "The Early Reception of Washington Ir-
     ving's Works in Germany." Anglia, LXXIV (1956), 345-63.
        A survey of German reviews and translations of Irving's
     works through Tales of a Traveller. Irving was both a pop-
     ular and a critical success in Germany. "Particularly the
     younger generation of Germans came in their formative years
     under the spell of Irving's narratives and acknowledged or
     reflected in their own work--as in the cases of Hauff,
     Heine, Droste-Hülshoff, Immermann, and others--Irving's
     literary influence."

9   _____. "Washington Irvings Quelle für seinen 'Rip Van
     Winkle.'" Archiv für das Studium der neueren Sprachen,
     CXCIII (April 1956), 291.

10   RODES, SARA P. "Washington Irving's Use of Traditional Folk-
     lore." Southern Folklore Quarterly, XX (September 1956),
     143-53.
        Irving used "authentic settings and local characters,
     folk materials," and his imagination, in his tales. He
     used traditional folk motifs but did not merely copy.
     "The Legend of Sleepy Hollow" and "Rip Van Winkle" in par-
     ticular are distinctly Americanized tales.

11   SORIA, ANDRÉS. "Hispanismo y romanticismo en Washington Ir-
     ving (1859-1959)." Arbor, XLIV (December 1956), 144-62.

12   WATTS, CHARLES H., II. "Washington Irving and E. A. Poe."
     Books at Brown, XVIII (May 1956), 10-13.
        Though Irving expressed interest in the new Southern
     Literary Messenger in 1834, he ignored a request from Poe
     for a contribution of a piece of his writing to the jour-
     nal, and did not respond to a later Poe request in the name
     of another journal. For a shorter version of this article,
     See item 1955.B6.

1957 A   BOOKS

1   REICHART, WALTER A. Washington Irving and Germany. Ann
     Arbor: Univ. of Michigan Press, 1957.
        Traces Irving's connections with German culture. Dis-
     cusses his early contact with German Romanticism, his trav-
     els in Germany (including a chapter on his six months in
     Dresden), his attempts to be a dramatist, and the German
     sources for his works. Chapter on Tales of a Traveller
     detailing its sources, composition, and considerable in-
     fluence on the Continent, despite its poor critical recep-
     tion in England and America. Appendix listing German plays

1957

(REICHART, WALTER A.)
and books mentioned by Irving or known to have been in his
library.

1957 B   SHORTER WRITINGS

1   CATER, HAROLD DEAN. "Washington Irving and Sunnyside." New
          York History, XXXVIII (April 1957), 123-66.
             The history of the estate and its importance to Irving.
          Description of his life there, with quotations from several
          Irving letters. Illustrated.

2   GRIFFITH, BEN W. "An Experiment on the American Bookseller:
          Two Letters from Irving to Godwin." Nineteenth-Century
          Fiction, XII (December 1957), 237-39.
             Two previously unpublished letters to William Godwin
          dated 30 January 1830 and 16 January 1830. They contain
          asides on the American publishing scene and Irving's crit-
          icism of Godwin's Cloudesly.

3   REICHART, WALTER A. "The Earliest German Translations of
          Washington Irving's Writings: A Bibliography." Bulletin
          of the New York Public Library, LXI (October 1957), 491-98.
             A chronological list, with commentary.

4   _____. "Washington Irving's Influence on German Literature."
          Modern Language Review, LII (October 1957), 537-53.
             Traces Irving's influence on Heine, Hauff, Droste-
          Hülshoff, Raabe, and other German writers. Mentions
          Goethe's acquaintance with Irving's work and discusses
          Irving's general popularity in Germany.

5   _____. "Washington Irving's Interest in German Folklore."
          New York Folklore Quarterly, XIII (Autumn 1957), 181-92.
             Deals with Irving's travels in Germany, his interest in
          German tales and superstitions, and the dependence of "Rip
          Van Winkle," "The Legend of Sleepy Hollow," and other tales
          on German materials.

6   RODES, SARA P. "Washington Irving's Use of Traditional Folk-
          lore." New York Folklore Quarterly, XIII (Spring 1957),
          3-15.
             Same article as in Southern Folklore Quarterly; See item
          1956.B10.

7   SPENCER, BENJAMIN T. The Quest for Nationality. Syracuse:
          Syracuse Univ. Press, 1957.

(SPENCER, BENJAMIN T.)
Study of the attempt to create a uniquely American literature, with scattered references to Irving. Though he was
committed to European modes of writing, he still actively
promoted an indigenous American literature. Index.

8   TODD, EDGELEY W. "Washington Irving Discovers the Frontier."
Western Humanities Review, XI (Winter 1957), 29-39.
A study of Irving's contact with the West and its hold
upon his imagination. Summarizes his experiences. A Tour
on the Prairies, Astoria, and The Adventures of Captain
Bonneville "show us a writer whose artistic orientation
had always been European now discovering the West for the
first time." Relates the works to the Turner thesis and
urges that they be re-evaluated.

9   TROUGHTON, MARION. "Americans in Britain." Contemporary Re-
view, CXCII (December 1957), 338-42.
Famous Americans' impressions of England. Treats Irving,
Harriet Beecher Stowe, Hawthorne, and Lowell. Quotes from
The Sketch Book.

10   WILLIAMS, RUTH S. "Irving's Stories in Quidor's Paintings."
Antiques, LXXII (November 1957), 443-45.
Irving's writings are highly pictorial, and Quidor
"translated Irving's words into paintings of weird beauty"
which share certain technical and stylistic traits with
Irving's work. Illustrated.

1958 A   BOOKS - NONE

1958 B   SHORTER WRITINGS

1   BROOKS, VAN WYCK. "Washington Irving and Washington Allston."
The Dream of Arcadia: American Writers and Artists in
Italy, 1760-1915. New York: E. P. Dutton and Company,
Inc., 1958, pp. 13-25.
A light, popularizing account of Irving's experiences in
Italy, and his depiction of things Italian in his stories.

2   GERDTS, W. H. "Inman and Irving: Derivations from Sleepy
Hollow." Antiques, LXXIV (November 1958), 420-23.
A study of Henry Inman's paintings derived from Irving's
stories. Survey of Inman's career and the influence of
Irving's romanticism. Illustrated.

3   HEWETT-THAYER, HARVEY. "The First Literary Invasion: Irving
and Cooper." American Literature as Viewed in Germany,

(HEWETT-THAYER, HARVEY)
1818-1861. Univ. of North Carolina Studies in Comparative
Literature, No. 22. Chapel Hill: Univ. of North Carolina
Press, 1958, pp. 18-37.
Focuses on articles in the Blätter für literarische
Unterhaltung and the Magazin für die Literatur des Aus-
lands, with some references to other journals. Summarizes
the articles cited.

4   JOHNSON, H. EARLE. "Young American Abroad." Musical Quarterly, XLIV (January 1958), 65-75.
Irving enthusiastically attended the theater, concerts,
and opera in Europe. Describes his musical experience and
his own attempts to write librettos. Includes a list of
operas he attended, compiled from his notes.

5   LARRABEE, STEPHEN A. "Some Printings of Irving in Finland
before 1900." American Literature, XXX (November 1958),
358-59.
Lists and comments on five items not included in the
Williams and Edge bibliography (1936.A1).

6   MYERS, ANDREW BREEN, ed. "Washington Irving's Madrid Journal
1827-1828 and Related Letters." Bulletin of the New York
Public Library, LXII (May 1958), 217-27; (June), 300-11;
(August), 407-19; (September), 463-71.
Myers provides annotations and an introduction to the
materials.

7   MYERS, ANDREW B. "Washington Irving's Moorish Manuscript; A
Columbia Rediscovery." Columbia Library Columns, VIII
(November 1958), 22-29.
Description of the unpublished manuscript, "Chronicle of
the Ommiades," an account of the Moorish dynasty in Spain,
not included in the Spanish Papers, now in the Columbia
Univ. library.

8   PENNEY, CLARA L. "Washington Irving in Spain: Unpublished
Letters Chiefly to Mrs. Henry O'Shea, 1844-1854." Bulletin of the New York Public Library, LXII (December 1958),
615-31; LXIII (January 1959), 23-39.
The letters are accompanied by a brief introduction and
detailed annotations.

9   RIESE, TEUT. Das englische Erbe in der amerikanischen
Literatur: Studien zur Entstehungsgeschichte des amerikan-
ischen Selbstbewusstseins im Zeitalter Washingtons und
Jeffersons. Bochum-Langendreer: Heinrich Pöppinghaus,
1958.
Irving is treated on pp. 53-68.

10   WAINSTEIN, LIA. "Washington Irving alla ricerca del passato."
      Studi Americani, IV (1958), 57-84.

1959 A BOOKS - NONE

1959 B SHORTER WRITINGS

1   BLANCK, JACOB. "Washington Irving's 'Life of Capt. James
     Lawrence.'" Papers of the Bibliographical Society of Amer-
     ica, LIII (Fourth Quarter 1959), 338-40.
          Corrects the Langfeld-Blackburn bibliography's mistaken
     identification of the New Brunswick, N. J. printing, 1813,
     as a first edition.

2   BOWDEN, EDWIN T. "American First Editions at Tx U: XII.
     Washington Irving (1783-1859)." Library Chronicle of the
     University of Texas, VI (Spring 1959), 20-23.
          This collection of Irving material, based on the library
     of Stanley Williams, is "a good collection, a useful col-
     lection, and a nearly complete collection that offers the
     scholar all of the material that he might need for his im-
     mediate use in working on Irving." Prints a list of edi-
     tions that the library would still like to acquire.

3   EDWARDS, TUDOR. "Washington Irving." Contemporary Review,
     CXCVI (December 1959), 308-10.
          Lively sketch of Irving's career, emphasizing the time
     he spent in Europe and the popularity of his works among
     European artists. He was an ambassador to Europe in a way
     Henry James was not.

4   FREEMAN, JOHN F. "Pirated Editions of Schoolcraft's Oneóta."
     Papers of the Bibliographical Society of America, LIII
     (Third Quarter 1959), 252-61.
          Quotes with brief comment a letter by Irving supporting
     Schoolcraft's rights as an author.

5   GATES, WILLIAM B. "Shakespearean Elements in Irving's Sketch
     Book." American Literature, XXX (January 1959), 450-58.
          Throughout The Sketch Book, as in no other work by Ir-
     ving, the diverse influence of Shakespeare is apparent.

6   GREEN, DAVID BONNELL. "Irving and Moore Again." Notes and
     Queries, VI (July-August 1959), 288-89.
          Two new letters from Moore to Irving further reveal the
     close relationship between the two.

1959

7   HEDGES, WILLIAM L. "Knickerbocker, Bolingbroke, and the Fic-
     tion of History." Journal of the History of Ideas, XX
     (June-September 1959), 317-28.
          Though Irving is usually seen as a genial humorist, A
     History of New York is "essentially negative." It is Ir-
     ving's "final onslaught on neo-classicism" which "asserts
     through irony and humor the virtual meaninglessness of
     history." Irving both parodies and accepts Bolingbroke's
     reduction of history. He was a transitional figure who
     gradually turned from neo-classicism to a positive roman-
     ticism. In his later histories, Irving "was to give al-
     most free rein to the impulse to view history aesthetical-
     ly, to organize it into a series of reenactments of arche-
     typal mythic dramas," and to read supposedly objective
     truths symbolically.

8   HEIMAN, MARCEL. "Rip Van Winkle: A Psychoanalytic Note on
     the Story and Its Author." American Imago, XVI (Spring
     1959), 3-47.
          Psychoanalytic study of Irving. Correlates the events
     of his life with elements in "Rip Van Winkle," concluding
     that Irving "used this story to find a solution for his
     particular oedipal and general neurotic conflicts." Also
     discusses the oedipal significance of Irving's pen names
     and the psychological implications of Abu Hassan. De-
     tailed analyses of Irving's relationships with the members
     of his family, Matilda Hoffman, and Emily Foster.

9   HUDSON, RUTH. "A Literary 'Area of Freedom' Between Irving
     and Twain." Western Humanities Review, XIII (Winter 1959),
     46-60.
          Mainly concerned with the minor writers of the frontier
     and their contribution to a distinctly American literature.
     Irving, with A Tour on the Prairies, "became the initial
     sponsor of the Western story as a reputable literary ven-
     ture and the first writer of national and international
     reputation to discover a literary bonanza in the trans-
     Mississippi West." Irving also helped make Western excur-
     sions fashionable for young, genteel Americans.

10   MARTIN, TERENCE. "Rip, Ichabod, and the American Imagina-
     tion." American Literature, XXXI (May 1959), 137-49.
          "Rip Van Winkle" and "The Legend of Sleepy Hollow" are
     considered in the context of American culture, and are
     shown to suggest that the American concept of reality is
     circumscribed and that imaginative endeavor is inadequate
     to the living of an American life. The tales ultimately
     say more about the culture than it says about them.

11   PRADES, JUANA DE JOSÉ. "'Cuentos de la Alhambra' y otros
      temas hispánicos de Washington Irving." Libro Español, II
      (August-September 1959), 509-14.

12   REICHART, WALTER A. "Some Sources of Irving's 'Italian Ban-
      ditti' Stories." Festschrift für Walther Fischer. Heidel-
      berg: Carl Winter, 1959, pp. 181-86.
          Irving used specific sources, in manuscript and in print,
      for the "banditti" stories in Tales of a Traveller.

13   _____. "Washington Irving (1783-1859) und Friedrich Schiller
      (1759-1805)." Jahrbuch der Deutschen Schiller-Gesellschaft,
      III (1959), 210-17.

14   WOODWARD, ROBERT H. "Dating the Action of 'Rip Van Winkle.'"
      New York Folklore Quarterly, XV (Spring 1959), 70.
          The election day on which Rip returned to his village
      was in 1789, the year of the first presidential election
      and ratification of the Constitution.

15   _____. "Moore's St. Nick: Model and Motif." New York Folk-
      lore Quarterly, XV (Winter 1959), 251-54.
          One literary source for the picture of St. Nick in
      Clement Clarke Moore's well-known poem, "A Visit From St.
      Nicholas," is probably A History of New York (the dream of
      Oloffe Van Kortlandt, II, v, and the description of Wouter
      Van Twiller, III, i).

16   WRIGHT, NATHALIA. "Irving's Use of His Italian Experiences
      in Tales of a Traveller: The Beginning of an American Tra-
      dition." American Literature, XXXI (May 1959), 191-96.
          Irving's Italian tales, based on life as well as on lit-
      erary tradition, anticipate Italian novels by Cooper, Haw-
      thorne, Howells and James.

1960 A BOOKS - NONE

1960 B SHORTER WRITINGS

1   CAMERON, K. W. "The Long-Sleep-and-Changed-World Motif in
      'Rip Van Winkle.'" Emerson Society Quarterly, No. 19 (Sec-
      ond Quarter 1960), pp. 35-36.
          A distinct motif, with possible "relevance to neurotic
      components of the Romantic Movement."

2   EMRICH, DUNCAN. "A Certain Nicholas of Patara." American
      Heritage, XII (December 1960), 22-27.

1960

(EMRICH, DUNCAN)
Briefly comments on Irving's contribution to the American
version of St. Nicholas.

3   HERRON, I. H. "Our Incomparable Jefferson." Eleusis of Chi
Omega, LXII (May 1960), 269-75.
Detailed analysis of Joseph Jefferson's adaptation and
interpretation of "Rip Van Winkle."

4   HOWARD, LEON. Literature and the American Tradition. New
York: Doubleday & Co., Inc., 1960.
Irving was basically not a humorist. He was a conven-
tional Romantic who found in Europe his real literary inspiration. Index.

5   MYERS, ANDREW B. "Alma Mater to 'Geoffrey Crayon.'" Columbia
Library Columns, IX (February 1960), 28-31.
Circumstances of Columbia's awarding Irving an honorary
degree. Prints Irving's letter of acceptance, dated 6
August 1821.

6   STEEGMULLER, FRANCIS. "Washington Irving's 'Snuggery.'"
Holiday, XXVII (May 1960), 120-23, 217.
Article on Sunnyside, on the occasion of its restoration.
Surveys Irving's character and career, crediting him with
introducing "Gotham," "knickerbocker," and "the almighty
dollar" to the national vocabulary.

7   TILLETT, A. S. "Washington Irving in the Revue Encyclopédique." Revue de littérature comparée, XXXIV (July-
September 1960), 442-47.
Some of the earliest criticism of Irving's work in France
appeared in the Revue Encyclopédique. These opinions are
quite similar to those of later, better-known critics.
The article summarizes these critical views.

8   YOUNG, PHILIP. "Fallen From Time: The Mythic Rip Van
Winkle." Kenyon Review, XXII (Autumn 1960), 547-73.
Explores Irving's tale, "the richest in our literature,"
as a primeval myth. Examines its analogues in other my-
thologies and analyzes Irving's version in its mythological
elements. Also interprets the story psychologically as
dream. "On the 'prehistoric' level we are dimly aware of
immemorial ritual significance, on the psychological of an
extraordinary picture of the self arrested in a timeless
infancy." Rip is able to pass "from childhood to second
childhood with next to nothing in between."

1961 A   BOOKS - NONE

1961 B   SHORTER WRITINGS

1   CONDON, THOMAS J. "New York's Dutch Period: An Interpretive
    Problem." de Halve Maen, XXXVI, iii (1961), 7-8, 14-15.
        Though A History of New York did contribute to creating
    an inaccurate image of New Netherland, it has received far
    more blame than it deserves.

2   DAHL, CURTIS. "The Sunny Master of Sunnyside." American
    Heritage, XIII (December 1961), 36-55, 92-93.
        An overview of Irving's literary life and accomplish-
    ments, emphasizing his optimism.

3   HOFFMAN, DANIEL G. "Prefigurations: 'The Legend of Sleepy
    Hollow.'" Form and Fable in American Fiction. New York:
    Oxford Univ. Press, 1961, pp. 83-96.
        Contains a chapter on "The Legend of Sleepy Hollow" re-
    printed with slight alterations from PMLA; See item
    1953.B4.

4   KHOURSHEED, MARIAM. "Washington Irving's Alhambra." Arab
    World, VIII (September 1961), 5-7.
        Describes Irving's understanding and admiration of Mos-
    lem civilization as expressed in The Alhambra.

5   LEARY, LEWIS. "Washington Irving." Six Classic American
    Writers: An Introduction. Ed. Sherman Paul. Minneapolis:
    Univ. of Minnesota Press, 1961, pp. 50-85.
        Judicious overview of Irving's career. "Few writers have
    successfully stretched a small talent farther than . . .
    Irving." He was "an exotic local colorist before Flau-
    bert," "a mildly boisterous . . . rural humorist, a comic
    realist before Thackeray, a caricaturist before Dickens,"
    and an eminently skillful writer. But he had "little of
    final importance to write about." Also published separate-
    ly. See item 1963.A1.

6   ROSS, DANFORTH. The American Short Story. Minnesota Pam-
    phlets on American Writers, No. 14. Minneapolis: Univ.
    of Minnesota Press, 1961.
        Pages 5-8 treat Irving as the first important American
    short story writer. Irving saw the "sketch" as a vehicle
    to depict characters, local color, and his own personality.
    In "Rip Van Winkle" and "The Legend of Sleepy Hollow," he
    captured aspects of the national character. Shows how
    Irving "mediates between his materials and the reader."

1961

7   TODD, EDGELEY W., ed. <u>The Adventures of Captain Bonneville,</u>
<u>U.S.A., in the Rocky Mountains and the Far West</u>. Norman:
Univ. of Oklahoma Press, 1961.
    The editor provides extensive notes, commentary, appendices, and a bibliography.

1962 A BOOKS

1   WAGENKNECHT, EDWARD. <u>Washington Irving: Moderation Dis-</u>
<u>played</u>. New York: Oxford Univ. Press, 1962.
    Biography and literary criticism. Asserts that "Irving's
temperament was much less simple than has often been supposed." Accordingly, of the book's three divisions, "The
Life," "The Man," "The Work," the second is more than
twice as long as the others combined.

1962 B SHORTER WRITINGS

1   EBY, CECIL D., JR. "Ichabod Crane in Yoknapatawpha."
<u>Georgia Review</u>, XVI (Winter 1962), 465-69.
    Faulkner reworked "The Legend of Sleepy Hollow" in <u>The</u>
<u>Hamlet</u>. Parallels in plot, setting, characters, and theme
are apparent. Both works illustrate "the conflict between
the Yankee (or national) pattern of life and the frontier
(or regional) pattern. In portraying the defeat of the
Yankee within the region and in suggesting his success outside it, the authors show their sympathy with the threatened folk culture."

2   HAGOPIAN, JOHN V. and MARTIN DOLCH. <u>Insight I: Analyses of</u>
<u>American Literature</u>. Frankfurt am Main: Hirschgraben-
Verlag, 1962.
    Includes an analysis of "Rip Van Winkle" aimed at German
university students.

3   ISELLA RUSSELL, DORA. "Washington Irving y el alma española."
<u>Cuadernos hispano-americanos</u>, No. 152-53 (August-September
1962), pp. 312-16.

4   KLEINFIELD, HERBERT L. "Washington Irving at Newstead Abbey."
<u>Bulletin of the New York Public Library</u>, LXVI (1962),
244-49.
    Irving responded to the personal and literary associations of Byron's estate. His sentiments were shared by
many Americans who, like Irving, could not resist the lure
of Europe.

5   REICHART, WALTER A. "Washington Irvings Reise durch Öster-
    reich." Jahrbuch des Wiener Goethe-Vereins, LXVI (1962),
    120-26.

6   WEBB, JAMES W. "Irving and His 'Favorite Author.'" Univer-
    sity of Mississippi Studies in English, III (1962), 61-74.
        A study of the development of Irving's biography of Gold-
    smith and its reception by readers and critics. Refers to
    Irving's "remarkable ability for reworking old material."
    Discusses Goldsmith's influence on Irving. Points out
    that most of Irving's work is biographical and that even
    "in his best fictional material he employs biographical,
    or rather pseudo-biographical, method."

1963 A   BOOKS

1   LEARY, LEWIS. Washington Irving. University of Minnesota
    Pamphlets on American Writers, No. 25. Minneapolis: Univ.
    of Minnesota Press, 1963.
    Reprinted essay. See item 1961.B5.

1963 B   SHORTER WRITINGS

1   ABEL, DARREL. "Washington Irving. 1783-1859." American
    Literature. Volume I: Colonial and Early National Writ-
    ing. Great Neck, New York: Barron's Educational Series,
    1963, pp. 322-40.
        "The final impression of Irving's career is that he al-
    ways relished good things without much expense of mind or
    conscience." "His vestiges of reputation remain because
    of his delightful style and the seasoning of whimsy in his
    work."

2   BONE, ROBERT A. "Irving's Headless Hessian: Prosperity and
    the Inner Life." American Quarterly, XV (Summer 1963),
    167-75.
        Explication of "The Legend of Sleepy Hollow" as illus-
    trative of "a central theme in our national letters: the
    relentless pressure of commodities on the American imagina-
    tion." Ichabod is the "artist-intellectual" who is "over-
    whelmed by the new materialism, but at an awesome price to
    society. For in order to conquer, the Hessian must throw
    away his head. The next morning a shattered pumpkin is
    found in the vicinity of the bridge. The organ of intel-
    lect and imagination has become an edible. The forces of
    thought have yielded to the forces of digestion." The
    postscript emerges as "an ironic defense of the literary
    imagination."

1963

3   EMERSON, EVERETT H. and KATHERINE T. "Some Letters of Wash-
         ington Irving: 1833-1843." American Literature, XXXV
         (May 1963), 156-72.
             Fourteen letters to Gouverneur Kemble and one to Alexan-
         der Hamilton, Irving's secretary.

4   REED, HERBERT B. "Ichabod Crane and Washington Irving."
         Staten Island Historian, XXIV (April-June 1963), 9-11.
             Argues that Irving got the name from Capt. Ichabod B.
         Crane who was stationed at Sackett's Harbor when Irving,
         aide-de-camp to Gov. Tompkins, was there in 1814 overseeing
         its fortification.

5   SIMISON, BARBARA D. "Some Autobiographical Notes of Washing-
         ton Irving." Yale University Library Gazette, XXXVIII
         (July 1963), 3-13.
             Transcription from one of Irving's notebooks. The notes
         were written in Spain and are dated either 1843 or 1845.
         Introduction.

6   *TAKEDA, KATSUHIKO. "Kanu and American Literature, Irving."
         Hiyoshi Ronbun Shu, No. 13 (May 1963), pp. 45-58.
             Cited in Leary, Articles on American Literature, 1950-
         1967 (1970).

7   WEST, ELSIE L. "Another Reprint of Irving's Biography of
         James Lawrence." Papers of the Bibliographical Society of
         America, LVII (Fourth Quarter 1963), 448-49.
             Examines bibliographical and textual details of an item
         omitted by Williams and Edge (1936.A1).

1964 A BOOKS - NONE

1964 B SHORTER WRITINGS

1   BOWDEN, EDWIN T., ed. A History of New York. New Haven:
         Twayne Publishers, 1964.
             Introduction summarizes Irving's early career and de-
         scribes the precedents, sources, and contemporary context
         of A History of New York. Examines Irving's peculiarly
         American humor and sees the whole work as a "deliberately
         conceived myth." A History of New York is Irving's
         "strongest sustained work" and the one most consistently
         readable today.

2   BRUNER, MARJORIE W. "The Legend of Sleepy Hollow: A Mytho-
         logical Parody." College English, XXV (January 1964),
         274, 279-83.
             Sees "The Legend of Sleepy Hollow" as "a rollicking

(BRUNER, MARJORIE W.)
parody of ancient Greek myths and rites of Greek fertility
cults, a comic story of death and rebirth, fertility and
immortality." Brom Bones is Hercules, Katrina is Demeter,
and Ichabod is both the river god Acheloos and "a burlesque
of a worshipper of one of the Greek Mysteries." Shows
other classical parallels and how Irving parodies them.

3   BUCCO, MARTIN. "Astoria." Alaska Review, I (Fall 1964),
52-53.
Review of the edition by Edgeley W. Todd. Astoria itself
"is a unique combination of historical fact and novelistic
technique." Although his reputation has declined, the review suggests, "Irving's potential awakening as a Rip Van
Winkle of American letters presumably will rest less on his
European romances than on his American histories."

4   CLENDENNING, JOHN. "Irving and the Gothic Tradition." Buck-
nell Review, XII (May 1964), 90-98.
Irving was interested in "the psychology of gothicism.
Turning the external gothic theme inward, he treated the
supernatural world as an expression of an excessively mor-
bid imagination." Treats Irving's "sportive" gothic in a
close reading of "The Legend of Sleepy Hollow." Suggests
the term inverted gothic for stories in which the hero
gives a supernatural explanation to hide what really hap-
pened. Besides "The Bold Dragoon" and "Dolph Heyliger,"
"Rip Van Winkle" is analyzed in this light, making Rip a
proto-artist figure who makes up a story to explain his
long absence. Analyzes "Adventure of the German Student"
as a study of "the derangement and the delusions that give
a horribly false view of the world."

5   GUTTMANN, ALLEN. "Washington Irving and the Conservative
Imagination." American Literature, XXXVI (May 1964),
165-73.
Irving sought a settled society with a sense of the past,
and chose Federalism in politics because of an instinctive
Burkean conservatism; but, like Cooper, he was "divided between the attractions of the new and the steady appeal of
the old," and so his best work implicitly celebrated the
American democrat.

6   KLEINFIELD, HERBERT L. "A Census of Washington Irving Manuscripts." Bulletin of the New York Public Library, LXVIII
(January 1964), 13-32.
Comprises journals, notebooks, literary manuscripts, letters, and miscellaneous pieces.

1964

7   MENGELING, MARVIN E. "Characterization in 'Rip Van Winkle.'" _English Journal_, LIII (December 1964), 643-46.
      Irving delineates Rip in relation to the landscape and to other characters, for whom he relies particularly on caricature. Individual characterizations are representative of the country in a period of transition.

8   SIMISON, BARBARA D. "Washington Irving's 'My Uncle.'" _Yale University Library Gazette_, XXXVIII (January 1964), 86-91.
      Transcription of a previously unpublished sketch, with introduction and notes.

9   TODD, EDGELEY W., ed. _Astoria, or Anecdotes of an Enterprise Beyond the Rocky Mountains_. Norman: Univ. of Oklahoma Press, 1964.
      A heavily annotated edition, with particular attention given to Irving's sources.

10   WHYTE, PETER. "Deux Emprunts de Gautier à Irving." _Revue de Littérature Comparée_, XXXVIII (October-December 1964), 572-77.

11   WOODWARD, ROBERT H. "Inn-Window Poetry." _New York Folklore Quarterly_, XX (March 1964), 59.
      Raises questions about the nature and possible survival of the sort of "inn-window poetry" mentioned in "The Stout Gentleman" (_Bracebridge Hall_).

1965 A BOOKS

1   HEDGES, WILLIAM L. _Washington Irving: An American Study, 1802-1832_. Baltimore: The Johns Hopkins Press, 1965.
      A revaluation of Irving's best work, challenging the older, yet still accepted view of him as a genteel, affable romanticist, minimally American in attitudes and style. Attempts to "define his major contributions as a writer and to work out . . . his relation to his intellectual environment." Sees in Irving motives, tensions, shadows, and uncertainties akin to those in the more distinctly "American" writers of the 19th Century, particularly Poe, Hawthorne, and Melville--whose works, in several ways, demonstrate the significance of Irving's.

2   MYERS, ANDREW BREEN. _Washington Irving, Fur Trade Chronicler: An Analysis of_ Astoria _With Notes for a Corrected Edition_. _Dissertation Abstracts_, XXV (1965), 7248.
      Surveys both the background and reception of _Astoria_. It faded after a brief popularity, though modern historical

(MYERS, ANDREW BREEN)
scholarship rates it more highly than did contemporary
commentators.

3   *ROTH, MARTIN. Satire, Humor, and Burlesque in the Early Works
    of Washington Irving. Univ. of Chicago, 1965.
        A dissertation.

1965 B   SHORTER WRITINGS

1   CAMERON, KENNETH W. "Irving's Prayerbook--and a Letter."
    Emerson Society Quarterly, No. 38 (First Quarter 1965),
    pp. 142-43.
        Two separate items: a prayer book with Irving's name
    and church stamped on it, and a letter to his friend, Col.
    Aspinwall, announcing his appointment as Secretary of Lega-
    tion at London.

2   COHEN, HENNIG. "Instinct for Misanthropy." Reporter, XXXIII
    (16 December 1965), 51-52.
        On John Quidor's paintings based on Irving's tales.
    Quidor is faithful to Irving's text while at the same time
    he follows "his own dark vision." Describes the paintings
    and compares them to the corresponding scenes in Irving.

3   DIETRICH, ROSALIA KRYSTYNA TOLCZYNSKA. American Literature
    in Poland: A Preliminary Check List, 1790-1940, With a
    Critical Introduction Concerning the Reputation of Barlow,
    Franklin and Irving. Dissertation Abstracts, XXVI (1965),
    2207.
        Reception of the first American writers known in Poland.
    Checklist includes American works translated into Polish,
    and Polish works about them.

4   HUDDLESTON, EUGENE L. "Washington Irving's 'On Passaic
    Falls.'" American Notes and Queries, IV (December 1965),
    51-52.
        The poem is one of many celebrating this New Jersey
    scenic attraction, whose popularity in poetry was probably
    due in part to a demand for native American nature verse.

5   McCLARY, BEN HARRIS. "Washington Irving to Walter Scott:
    Two Unpublished Letters." Studies in Scottish Literature,
    III (October 1965), 114-18.
        Two annotated letters to Scott dated 3 November 1819 and
    15 August 1820. Introduction comments on the significance
    of Irving's relationship with Scott.

1965

6   McDERMOTT, JOHN FRANCIS. "An Unpublished Washington Irving
      Manuscript." Papers on English Language and Literature, I
      (Autumn 1965), 369-73.
         Transcription of a piece of manuscript entitled "The Log
      House Hotel" dealing with Irving's travels in the West.
      Introduction.

7   MYERS, ANDREW B. "Washington Irving's First Academic Lau-
      rels." Columbia Library Columns, XIV (May 1965), 21-25.
         Columbia University awarded Irving an honorary Master of
      Arts degree in 1821. It was Irving's first academic award,
      and the first honorary degree for literature to be given
      by the college. Letter of announcement; facsimile of the
      diploma.

8   WRIGHT, NATHALIA. American Novelists in Italy. The Discover-
      ers: Allston to James. Philadelphia: Univ. of Pennsyl-
      vania Press, 1965.
         Irving's eight months in Italy were reflected twenty
      years later in ten stories in Tales of a Traveller which
      have Italian settings and characters. Eight of the ten are
      set in places Irving had visited, and otherwise reflect his
      own experiences. He had briefly considered becoming a
      painter, and the image of the artist's life in Italy is a
      major element in most of the tales.

1966 A BOOKS

1   BUELL, THOMAS COCHRAN. The Professional Idler: Washington
      Irving's European Years: The Sketch Book and Its Sequels.
      Dissertation Abstracts, XXVII (1966), 197A-98A.
         Irving was divided between an inner world of imagination
      and an outer one of worldly success. The Sketch Book is
      the result of both interests. Ultimately the latter became
      preëminent with him.

2   McCLARY, BEN H. Addressed to 50, Albemarle Street. The
      Letters of Washington Irving to the House of Murray, 1817-
      1856. Univ. of Sussex, 1966.
         A dissertation.

3   WEST, ELSIE LEE. Gentle Flute: Washington Irving as Biog-
      rapher. Dissertation Abstracts, XXVII (1966), 463A-64A.
         Irving's lives of Columbus, Goldsmith, and Washington
      deserve more praise than they have received. Two of his
      finest biographies were written after 1832, and thus belie
      the popular notion that his writing career was really over
      by that date.

1966 B   SHORTER WRITINGS

1   COLOMBO, ROSA MARIA. "Un inedito di Washington Irving."
     Studi Americani, XII (1966), 7-14.

2   LEE, HELEN. "Clue Patterns in 'Rip Van Winkle.'" English
     Journal, LV (February 1966), 192-94, 200.
         Various intricate patterns of language, plot, character-
     ization, and setting occur throughout the story. They
     provide a foreshadowing and consistent reinforcement of
     events.

3   LEE, ROBERT EDSON. "The Easterners: Washington Irving and
     Francis Parkman." From West to East: Studies in the Lit-
     erature of the American West. Urbana: Univ. of Illinois
     Press, 1966, pp. 58-81.
         A Tour on the Prairies is "a pale reflection" of Irving's
     lively journals because of its misguided attempt to be
     "literary."

4   LYON, T. J. "Washington Irving's Wilderness." Western Amer-
     ican Literature, I (Fall 1966), 167-74.
         Critical study of The Rocky Mountains (Adventures of Cap-
     tain Bonneville). Irving is romantic, but he is remark-
     ably restrained, judicious, and accurate. Discusses Ir-
     ving's handling of mountain climbing and his balanced but
     sympathetic view of Indians.

5   McCLARY, BEN HARRIS. "The Moore-Irving Letter File." Notes
     and Queries, XIII (May 1966), 181-82.
         The only seven letters of Thomas Moore to Irving known
     to exist are printed in various places.

6   _____. "Two of Washington Irving's Friends Identified."
     American Literature, XXXVII (January 1966), 471-73.
         The friends are William Willes, British landscape paint-
     er, and John Cockburn, son of James Pattison Cockburn.

7   _____. "Washington Irving's Amiable Scotch Friends: Three
     Unpublished Letters to the John Gibson Lockharts." Stud-
     ies in Scottish Literature, IV (October 1966), 101-104.
         Three annotated letters dated 26 October [1830], 1 Sep-
     tember 1831, and 8 April 1835 addressed to the often abra-
     sive Scotch critic. Introduction, which deals with Ir-
     ving's friendship with Lockhart, and Lockhart's ambivalent
     treatment of Irving.

8   MENGELING, MARVIN E. "Structure and Tone in 'Rip Van Winkle':
     The Irony of Silence." Discourse, IX (Autumn 1966),
     457-63.
          Contends that Irving ironically uses structure and tone
     to delineate the victory of practicality and defeat of the
     imagination in his story. The structure is one of ascent
     and descent: "from mountain to village to mountain, etc.,"
     paralleling the ascent and descent of the imagination. The
     tone is one of "tranquil, and for Rip, lonely silences. . .
     which Irving skillfully reenforces through his technique of
     echoing sounds." Touches on Irving's irony.

9   MYERS, ANDREW BREEN. "Washington Irving in London in 1846."
     Bulletin of the New York Public Library, LXX (January
     1966), 34-35.
          Background comments helping to explain the several refer-
     ences to Irving in Gansevoort Melville's London journal,
     published in the Bulletin in three installments, beginning
     December 1965 and concluding January 1966.

10   PICKERING, JAMES H. "Melville's 'Ducking' Duyckinck." Bul-
     letin of the New York Public Library, LXX (November 1966),
     551-52.
          Suggests A History of New York as the source of Mel-
     ville's pun on the name of Evert Duyckinck.

11   SIMISON, BARBARA D. "A Footnote to Washington Irving." Yale
     University Library Gazette, XL (April 1966), 194-96.
          Description of a newly acquired manuscript that was the
     printer's copy of a brief note by Irving published anony-
     mously in the Knickerbocker's "Editor's Table." Transcrip-
     tion of the manuscript.

12   _____. "A Second Footnote to Washington Irving." Yale Uni-
     versity Library Gazette, XLI (October 1966), 74-76.
          Facsimile of a fragment from the manuscript of Alhambra.
     Probably an early draft of the "Preface" to the Author's
     Revised Edition. The final preface is printed for com-
     parison.

13   STROBRIDGE, TRUMAN S. and EDWIN TURNBLADH. "Lieutenant Icha-
     bod Crane, United States Marine Corps." Proceedings of the
     New Jersey Historical Society, LXXXIV (July 1966), 170-73.
          The source of the name in "The Legend of Sleepy Hollow."
     Lieutenant Ichabod Crane served under Stephen Decatur who
     was a good friend of Irving's. One of Ichabod's descen-
     dants was Stephen Crane, the novelist.

1967 A   BOOKS

1   BLACK, MICHAEL L. Washington Irving's A History of New York
     with Emphasis on the 1848 Revision. Dissertation Ab-
     stracts, XXVIII (1967), 1386A-87A.
         The History was revised five times (1812, 1819, 1824,
     1829, 1848), each time with increased stress on narration,
     and diminution of digression and reflection. The original
     History of 1809 is still the best because of Irving's imag-
     inativeness and youthful enthusiasm.

2   TERRELL, DAHLIA J. A Textual Study of Washington Irving's
     A Tour on the Prairies. Dissertation Abstracts, XXVIII
     (1967), 245A.
         Compares the British and American manuscripts to their
     first printed editions (1835) to expose discrepancies
     which alter meaning. Both editions contain errors, but
     the American in particular varies significantly from the
     manuscript.

1967 B   SHORTER WRITINGS

1   BALLEW, HAL L. "Irving and Ticknor in Spain: Some Parallels
     and Contrasts." University of Mississippi Studies in
     English, VIII (1967), 57-66.
         Discusses Irving's interest in Spain. Compares him to
     George Ticknor, "the first American to become interested in
     Spanish literature." Survey of "their accomplishments,
     personalities, and general qualifications in the field of
     Hispanic studies." Notes Irving's popularity in Spain.

2   BARNES, DANIEL R. "Washington Irving: An Unrecorded Period-
     ical Publication." Studies in Bibliography: Papers of
     the Bibliographical Society of the University of Virginia,
     XX (1967), 260-61.
         Introduces and prints a previously unrecorded item by
     Irving in The Ladies' Repository (February 1852) entitled
     "Our Changing Sky and Climate." Suggests that the piece
     was written in response to a slight criticism in the July
     1848 issue, that Irving never attempted "sublime topics."
     See item 1848.B1.

3   KIME, WAYNE R. "Washington Irving and Frontier Speech."
     American Speech, XLII (February 1967), 5-18.
         Cites many examples from A Tour on the Prairies, Astoria,
     and Bonneville, of Irving's use of authentic vocabulary
     then current in the Far West.

1967

4   McCLARY, BEN H. "Irving's Literary Midwifery: Five Unpub-
      lished Letters from British Repositories." Philological
      Quarterly, XLVI (April 1967), 277-83.
         Suggests that Irving's greatest impact may have been
      through his activities as a literary agent. Prints letters
      to William Godwin, Thomas Moore, John Gibson Lockhart, Rob-
      ert Southey, and "Rosa," each with an introduction.

5   _____. "A Washington Irving Postscript." Notes and Queries,
      XIV (August 1967), 304.
         Irving's 1827 postscript to a copy of a letter by Sir
      Robert Peel recalls the pleasures of an 1804 trip to Genoa.

6   OLENJEVA, B. "Amerikans'ka novela epoxy romantyzmu."
      Radians'ke Literaturoznavstvo, XI, x (1967), 46-55.
         In Ukrainian.

7   OSBORNE, WILLIAM S. "A Note from Washington Irving to Eliza-
      beth Gray Kennedy." American Notes and Queries, V (March
      1967), 100-101.
         The note is further evidence of Irving's close, friendly
      relationship with the family of John Pendleton Kennedy.

8   PECK, RICHARD E. "An Unpublished Poem by Washington Irving."
      American Literature, XXXIX (May 1967), 204-207.
         Melancholy poem written in Spanish in 1830, beginning
      "¡Ay Dios de mi alma!"

9   POCHMANN, HENRY A. "Washington Irving: Amateur or Profes-
      sional?" Essays on American Literature in Honor of Jay B.
      Hubbell. Ed. Clarence Gohdes. Durham, N. C.: Duke Univ.
      Press, 1967, pp. 63-76.
         Though Irving began as a gentleman-scribbler, the details
      of his literary life show him to have been "less the ama-
      teur toying with esoteric aspirations beyond his reach
      than the canny professional gauging his grasp by his
      reach."

10 RINGE, DONALD A. "New York and New England: Irving's Criti-
      cism of American Society." American Literature, XXXVIII
      (January 1967), 455-67.
         The conflict between New York and New England, Yankee
      and Dutchman, appears not only in "The Legend of Sleepy
      Hollow," but in "Rip Van Winkle," A History of New York,
      and lesser works as well. It is "a significant element in
      any interpretation of his major writings."

11 WIMSATT, MARY A. "Simms and Irving." Mississippi Quarterly,
      XX (First Quarter 1967), 25-37.

(WIMSATT, MARY A.)
Traces Irving's influence on William Gilmore Simms.
Simms's opinion of Irving varied, especially in times of
virulent literary controversies, but parallels and borrowings occur throughout Simms's writings.

12   WOOD, JAMES PLAYSTED, ed. A Tour on the Prairies. New York:
Pantheon Books, Inc., 1967.
Preface places the book in the context of Irving's career
and notes the vividness of his account of frontier life,
especially notable in someone so used to "civilization."
Appendix contains extracts from the report prepared by
Ellsworth and the other commissioners of Indian affairs,
and notes their plea for Indian rights.

1968 A   BOOKS

1   KIME, WAYNE R. Washington Irving's Astoria: A Critical
Study. Dissertation Abstracts, XXIX (1968), 1869A-70A.
Astoria was the result of Irving's lifelong interest in
the frontier and not, as critics have claimed, mere hack
work. It integrates history, legend, and social commentary, the best features of his writing, and yet maintains
historical accuracy. It is one of his major achievements.

1968 B   SHORTER WRITINGS

1   BLACK, MICHAEL L. "Bibliographical Problems in Washington
Irving's Early Works." Early American Literature, III
(Winter 1968), 148-58.
A detailed examination of the distinct problems posed by
Letters of Jonathan Oldstyle, Gent., Salmagundi, and A His-
tory of New York.

2   CAMERON, KENNETH W. "Letters of Cooper, Irving and Others
Endorsing the Lyceum in Paris, France." Emerson Society
Quarterly, No. 52 (Third Quarter 1968), pp. 76-82.
This item merely reprints the pamphlet containing Ir-
ving's testimonial.

3   CONLEY, PATRICK T. "The Real Ichabod Crane." American Literature, XL (March 1968), 70-71.
It is probable that Irving used the name of Captain
Ichabod Crane (U. S. Army) in "The Legend of Sleepy Hollow."

4   HOLT, CHARLES C. Short Fiction in American Periodicals:
1775-1825. Dissertation Abstracts, XXVIII (1968), 4131A-32A.

1968

(HOLT, CHARLES C.)
The American short story originated in the desire to create a significant and distinctively American genre. Irving recognized the possibilities of the form, built on the efforts of earlier writers, and established the genre as we know it.

5   HOUGH, ROBERT L. "Washington Irving, Indians, and the West." South Dakota Review, VI (Winter 1968), 27-39.
Irving's books about the West strongly influenced the public's understanding of it and directly provoked important legislation. Irving vacillated between belief in the progress of civilization and the idea that nature should remain unspoiled. His view of the Indians was "realistic," he knew the diversity of their cultures, and he staunchly defended their rights.

6   KIME, WAYNE R. "Poe's Use of Irving's Astoria in 'The Journal of Julius Rodman.'" American Literature, XL (May 1968), 215-22.
Argues persuasively for Poe's use of specific detail from Astoria, to the point of accounting for Poe's not writing a conclusion to his work.

7   KIME, WAYNE R. "The Satiric Use of Names in Irving's History of New York." Names, XVI (1968), 380-89.
Irving used etymological and naming devices humorously, to mock some scholarship, satirize the Dutch and others, and reveal shortcomings of the new United States.

8   McCLARY, BEN H. "Ichabod Crane's Scottish Origin." Notes and Queries, XV (January 1968), 29.
A letter from Irving to Sir Walter Scott describes a "Lockie Longlegs" in a way echoed in his portrait of Ichabod Crane.

9   _____. "Mr. Irving of the Shakespeare Committee: Anglo-American Jealousy." American Notes and Queries, VII (October 1968), 19-21.
The same article as appears in American Literature, XLI (March 1969). See item 1969.B16.

10   McLENDON, WILL. "A Problem in Plagiarism: Washington Irving and Cousen de Courchamps." Comparative Literature, XX (Spring 1968), 157-69.
Irving took "The Grand Prior of Minorca" (Wolfert's Roost) from Courchamps' plagiarism of Jan Potocki's "Histoire du Commandeur de Toralva." Irving closely followed Courchamps in dramatically embellishing the original story.

11   MONTEIRO, GEORGE. "Washington Irving: A Grace Note on 'The
      Pride of the Village.'" Research Studies, XXXVI (December
      1968), 347-50.
          The tale is "more complex both in purpose and effect
      than is customarily acknowledged." Irving plays off his
      use of Ecclesiastes against other statements, and creates
      meanings which are veiled for the modern reader by the
      story's sentimentality.

12   MYERS, ANDREW. "Washington Irving and the Astor Library."
      Bulletin of the New York Public Library, LXXII (June 1968),
      378-99.
          Discusses the founding of the Astor library, and Irving's
      role as first president of its Board of Trustees.

13   PROFFER, CARL R. "Washington Irving in Russia: Pushkin,
      Gogol, Marlinsky." Comparative Literature, XX (Fall 1968),
      329-42.
          Irving clearly influenced Russian literature of the
      1830's. Though his effect on Gogol is not clear, Pushkin's
      narrative technique in his first stories was compared to
      Irving's by Russian critics; and a similarity between Mar-
      linsky and Irving, in structure and narration, was also
      noted by reviewers at the time.

14   REICHART, WALTER A. "Washington Irving and the Theatre."
      Maske und Kothurn, XIV (1968), 341-50.
          Biographical treatment of Irving's interest in the the-
      ater. Includes lists of plays he attended, his friends in
      theatrical circles, and his attempts to be a dramatist.
      Quotes from letters, giving Irving's impressions of actors
      and plays.

15   ROTH, MARTIN, ed. Washington Irving's Contributions to The
      Corrector. Minneapolis: Univ. of Minnesota Press, 1968.
          The first attempt to identify Irving's pieces in The Cor-
      rector, 1804. Roth analyzes these writings and places
      them in context with Salmagundi, A History of New York,
      and the literary concerns of the day.

16   SPAULDING, GEORGE F., ed. On the Western Tour With Washington
      Irving: The Journal and Letters of Count de Pourtalès.
      Norman: Univ. of Oklahoma Press, 1968.
          Count Albert-Alexandre de Pourtalès' account of his West-
      ern travels with Irving. Another side to A Tour on the
      Prairies. Notes, illustrations, and index.

17   ZUG, CHARLES G., III. "The Construction of The Devil and Tom
      Walker: A Study of Irving's Later Use of Folklore." New

(ZUG, CHARLES G., III)
York Folkore Quarterly, XXIV (December 1968), 243-60.
Irving was not a mere imitator of old legend, but "a
highly skilled manipulator of both American and German
folklore." He combined and reshaped folk motifs "into new
and significant forms."

1969 A BOOKS

1   McCLARY, BEN H., ed. Washington Irving and the House of Murray: Geoffrey Crayon Charms the British, 1817-1856. Knox-
ville: Univ. of Tennessee Press, 1969.
A study of the Irving-Murray relationship, built around
the surviving correspondence between author and publisher.

1969 B   SHORTER WRITINGS

1   ADERMAN, RALPH M. "A 'Most Negligent Man': Washington Irving's Opinion of John Murray." Center for Editions of
American Authors Newsletter, II (1969), 1-3.
Documents Irving's repeated exasperation at Murray's ne-
glect of his desires and specific requests concerning The
Life and Voyages of Christopher Columbus and The Conquest
of Granada.

2   ANDERSON, HILTON. "A Southern Sleepy Hollow." Mississippi
Folklore Register, III (1969), 85-88.
Analyzes Joseph B. Cobb's "The Legend of Black Creek"
(1851) as an obvious imitation of "The Legend of Sleepy
Hollow."

3   BLACK, MICHAEL L. "A History of New York: Significant Revisions in 1848." Washington Irving Reconsidered: A Symposium. Ed. Ralph M. Aderman. Hartford: Transcendental
Books, 1969, pp. 40-47.
Studies Irving's 1848 revision of A History of New York,
particularly his addition of Killian Van Rensellaer which
was an attempt to give the book greater unity. Suggests
that in revising the book Irving recovered much of his former "zest" and that the project helped him recover his
creative energy. Disputes the view that all the "hearty
humor" and satire had been revised out of the 1848 version.
This article also appeared in American Transcendental Quarterly, No. 5 (First Quarter 1970).

4   GLOWES, KATHERINE A. "Devices of Repetition in Irving's 'The
Wife.'" Washington Irving Reconsidered: A Symposium. Ed.

(GLOWES, KATHERINE A.)
Ralph M. Aderman. Hartford: Transcendental Books, 1969, pp. 60-66.
Analyzes Irving's style in terms of its "euphony." Tabulates the instances of alliteration and assonance in "The Wife" from notebook to finished sketch. Summarizes earlier criticism of his style. Also appeared in American Transcendental Quarterly, No. 5 (First Quarter 1970).

5   HAGENSICK, DONNA. "Irving--A Litterateur in Politics." Washington Irving Reconsidered: A Symposium. Ed. Ralph M. Aderman. Hartford: Transcendental Books, 1969, pp. 53-60.
Traces Irving's shifting political affiliations in terms of his "ardent nationalism" and his "inherent conservatism." Surveys Irving's interest in politics and his diplomatic appointments. Also appeared in American Transcendental Quarterly, No. 5 (First Quarter 1970).

6   HARBERT, EARL N. "Fray Antonio Agapida and Washington Irving's Romance With History." Tulane Studies in English, XVII (1969), 135-44.
Discusses Irving's fictional techniques in writing factual history. Focuses on his fictional narrative voice in Granada, Fray Antonio Agapida, who serves to unify the work and to bridge "the gap between the ancient past and the literary present." Account of the composition and reception of Granada and how Irving treated it as an "'experiment in literature.'"

7   ____. "Irving's Conquest of Granada: Authorial Intention and Untoward Accident." Washington Irving Reconsidered: A Symposium. Ed. Ralph M. Aderman. Hartford: Transcendental Books, 1969, pp. 26-31.
Deals with the mishaps Irving faced in publishing Conquest of Granada--"the crises of missing chapters, misdirected and miscarried manuscripts, and the vacillations of his publisher." Comments on the textual condition of the book and the problems caused by Irving's "abnegation of the editorial responsibilities." Also appeared in American Transcendental Quarterly, No. 5 (First Quarter 1970).

8   HEDGES, WILLIAM L. "Irving, Hawthorne, and the Image of the Wife." Washington Irving Reconsidered: A Symposium. Ed. Ralph M. Aderman. Hartford: Transcendental Books, 1969, pp. 22-26.
"Irving in The Sketch Book, and particularly in 'The Wife,' began a domestication of the sentimental heroine which was to become a hallmark of Hawthorne's fiction." Irving's idealized view of women and his ambivalent

1969

(HEDGES, WILLIAM L.)
attitude toward marriage are reflected throughout Hawthorne and help to elucidate "the American avidity for sentimentality." Also appeared in _American Transcendental Quarterly_, No. 5 (First Quarter 1970).

9 _____. "Washington Irving: _The Sketch Book of Geoffrey Crayon, Gent._" _Landmarks of American Writing_. Ed. Hennig Cohen. New York: Basic Books, Inc., 1969, pp. 56-65.
Discusses the character of Geoffrey Crayon as revealed in _The Sketch Book_ in terms of the conflict between English and American culture, and the author's own insecurity and uncertainty. Examines Crayon's preoccupation with mutability, his need for tradition, his simultaneous longing for marriage and fear of settling down, and his "self-mocking" sentimentalism.

10 INGRAM, FRANK L. "Puskin's Skazka o 'zolotom petuske' and Washington Irving's 'The Legend of the Arabian Astrologer.'" _Russian Language Journal_, XXIII (February 1969), 3-18.
Compares Irving's story in _The Alhambra_ with Pushkin's controversial satire. Tabular listing of similar and dissimilar motifs. Discusses the components of Pushkin's story, accepting the view that Irving was his basic source.

11 KIME, WAYNE R. "Washington Irving's Revision of the _Tonquin_ Episode in _Astoria_." _Western American Literature_, IV (Spring 1969), 51-59.
Irving successfully rewrote the episode for its drama, without compromising historical accuracy.

12 KLEINFIELD, HERBERT L. "Irving as a Journal Writer." _Washington Irving Reconsidered: A Symposium_. Ed. Ralph M. Aderman. Hartford: Transcendental Books, 1969, pp. 11-14.
Irving's journals parallel his literary development. They enable us to evaluate his literary accomplishment by "following the eye with which he saw his materials and watching him fashion them into literary form." He was a wanderer and an observer whose "historical perspective" steadily increased. Also appeared in _American Transcendental Quarterly_, No. 5 (First Quarter 1970).

13 LIBMAN, VALENTINA A., comp. _Russian Studies of American Literature, A Bibliography_. University of North Carolina Studies in Comparative Literature, No. 46. Chapel Hill: Univ. of North Carolina Press, 1969.
For Irving, an incomplete list with brief annotation.

14   LYNEN, JOHN F. "The Fiction in the Landscape: Irving and
Cooper." The Design of the Present: Essays on Time and
Form in American Literature. New Haven and London: Yale
Univ. Press, 1969, pp. 153–204.
American literature consistently is concerned with the
interplay between the present moment and eternity; this
temporal dimension also determines content and form. Irving carefully frames Rip Van Winkle's mythic story in
terms of an unchanging landscape and "a number of pasts
nested, like Chinese boxes, one within the other." Discusses Irving's only "tentative" acceptance of fiction and
his ambivalent view of nature.

15   McCLARY, BEN H. "Irving's Literary Borrowing." Notes and
Queries, XVI (February 1969), 57–58.
Irving borrowed a literary manuscript and, unbeknownst
to the author, sent it to John Howard Payne, encouraging
him to try to sell it to a publisher.

16   _____. "Mr. Irving of the Shakespeare Committee: A Bit of
Anglo-American Jealousy." American Literature, XLI (March
1969), 92–95.
Irving's appointment in 1820 to a committee to erect a
monument to Shakespeare at Stratford-on-Avon stirred up
some British opposition and one satire. See item 1968.B9.

17   _____. "Washington Irving's British Edition of Slidell's A
Year in Spain." Bulletin of the New York Public Library,
LXXIII (June 1969), 368–74.
Discusses Irving's work in successfully revising and
adapting Slidell's book for a British audience.

18   POCHMANN, HENRY A. "Copy-Editing of Irving's Journals." Center for Editions of American Authors Newsletter, II (1969),
15.
Explains that for proper and expeditious copy-editing,
the press should have two Xerox copies of the original
manuscript.

19   ROTH, MARTIN. "The Final Chapter of Knickerbocker's New
York." Modern Philology, LXVI (February 1969), 248–55.
"Rip Van Winkle" is an extension of the political satire
of A History of New York, including the theme of the transition from Dutch to Yankee and the consequent loss of
fertile ground for the artistic imagination.

20   SMITH, HERBERT F. "The Spell of Nature in Irving's Famous
Stories." Washington Irving Reconsidered: A Symposium."

1969

(SMITH, HERBERT F.)
Ed. Ralph M. Aderman. Hartford: Transcendental Books,
1969, pp. 18-21.
Studies the relationship between civilization and "wild
nature" in "Rip Van Winkle" and "The Legend of Sleepy Hollow," especially in regard to the conservation movement.
Rip is attuned to nature but alienated from civilization;
his sleep is a surrender to "organic" time in contrast to
the "mechanical" time of the village. "The Legend of
Sleepy Hollow" portrays a culture existing in close co-
operation with nature while Ichabod "counts nature only
as something to be raped and pillaged. . . ." Also appeared in American Transcendental Quarterly, No. 5 (First
Quarter 1970).

21   SPRINGER, HASKELL S. "Creative Contradictions in Irving."
Washington Irving Reconsidered: A Symposium. Ed. Ralph M.
Aderman. Hartford: Transcendental Books, 1969, pp. 14-18.
"The Legend of Sleepy Hollow" is a perfectly rational
tale, yet is called a "legend"; "Rip Van Winkle" is wholly
supernatural, yet its veracity is insisted on. This self-
contradiction suggests an imaginative middle ground (established by motifs of dream, sleep, and reverie) between
reality and fantasy, in which the stories exist. Rip becomes a storyteller, and a version of Irving, who, in shar-
ing his own imaginative experience, "offered what his time
evidently wanted--and needed." Also appeared in American
Transcendental Quarterly, No. 5 (First Quarter 1970).

22   _____. Washington Irving's Sketch Book: A Critical Edition.
Dissertation Abstracts, XXIX (1969), 3621A.
A corrected, ummodernized edition of The Sketch Book as
Irving originally conceived it, following the theory and
practice of the Center for Editions of American Authors.
Includes historical and textual essays, clear reading
text, and textual appendices.

23   SZLADITS, LOLA L. "New in the Berg Collection: 1962-1964."
Bulletin of the New York Public Library, LXXIII (April
1969), 227-52.
Includes a brief note on the manuscript of A Tour on the
Prairies, discovered in 1964.

24   TERRELL, DAHLIA. "Textual Errors in A Tour on the Prairies."
Washington Irving Reconsidered: A Symposium. Ed. Ralph M.
Aderman. Hartford: Transcendental Books, 1969, pp. 37-40.
Notes important substantive errors in the 1835 American
edition and the subsequent 1848 Author's Revised Edition

(TERRELL, DAHLIA)
    of A Tour on the Prairies. Compares the text with manu-
scripts and an earlier English edition, concluding that
Irving never proofread the American text. Also appeared
in American Transcendental Quarterly, No. 5 (First Quarter
1970).

25   WEATHERSPOON, MARY A. The Political Activities of Philip
Freneau and Washington Irving. Dissertation Abstracts,
XXIX (1969), 3591A.
    Irving's quiet involvement both in New York and national
politics. He supported Burr, Lewis, Jackson, Van Buren
(for a while), and Fremont.

26   WEST, ELSIE LEE. "Washington Irving, Biographer." Washington
Irving Reconsidered: A Symposium. Ed. Ralph M. Aderman.
Hartford: Transcendental Books, 1969, pp. 47-52.
    Emphasizes Irving's "remarkable" achievement in the field
of biography. Discusses Life of Columbus, praising Ir-
ving's "notable skill in using and evaluating his source
material," and Life of Washington, his "finest biography."
Examines the sources and artistry of Life of Goldsmith.
Also appeared in American Transcendental Quarterly, No. 5
(First Quarter 1970).

27   WHITFORD, KATHRYN. "Romantic Metamorphosis in Irving's Western Tour." Washington Irving Reconsidered: A Symposium.
Ed. Ralph M. Aderman. Hartford: Transcendental Books,
1969, pp. 31-36.
    In trying to romanticize his tour on the prairies, Irving
created serious problems with point of view and theme or
motif. He tried various literary devices but then abandoned them by the last quarter of the book. He was too
fastidious and self-conscious to truly exploit the expedi-
tion's comic possibilities, or to "treat realistically its
harsher details." Also appeared in American Transcendental
Quarterly, No. 5 (First Quarter 1970).

28   WRIGHT, NATHALIA, ed. Journals and Notebooks: Volume I,
1803-1806. The Complete Works of Washington Irving. Madison: Univ. of Wisconsin Press, 1969.
    The authoritative edition, with extensive annotations,
textual and historical.

29   _____. "Travel Books and Histories in Irving's European
Journal, 1804-1805." Washington Irving Reconsidered: A
Symposium. Ed. Ralph M. Aderman. Hartford: Transcenden-
tal Books, 1969, pp. 5-11.
    Shows Irving's dependence on travel books and histories

1969

(WRIGHT, NATHALIA)
in writing his first European journal. Traces his "unsystematic and even irresponsible" borrowings and suggests that "when Irving's own inspiration failed him, he tended to turn to history." Also appeared in American Transcendental Quarterly, No. 5 (First Quarter 1970).

30   YANOW, LILLI ANNE. Washington Irving as United States Minister to Spain: The Revolution of 1843. Dissertation Abstracts, XXX (1969), 3420A-21A.
Deals with events in Spain, including the revolution of 1843, while Irving was U. S. Minister in Madrid. Not much on Irving himself, apparently.

1970 A   BOOKS

1   CRACROFT, RICHARD H. The American West of Washington Irving: The Quest for a National Tradition. Dissertation Abstracts International, XXXI (1970), 1221A.
In 1832 Irving abandoned Federalism for Jacksonian democracy. His three Western narratives, distorted by his romantic imagination and his European experiences, are byproducts of this new enthusiasm and of his renewed desire to build a significant national literary tradition.

2   JENNEY, ADELE G. The Irvingesque Story in the United States: 1820-1860. Dissertation Abstracts International, XXXI (1970), 1760A-1761A.
Approximately 3400 short stories written from 1820 to 1860 are examined for Irving's influence. The fact that about one-third of these can be classified as "Irvingesque" because of several characteristics, tends to substantiate the common claim that Irving founded the American short story.

1970 B   SHORTER WRITINGS

1   ADERMAN, RALPH M. "The Editors' Intentions in the Washington Irving Letters." Center for Editions of American Authors Newsletter, III (1970), 23-24.
Fidelity to Irving's text and utility to the reader are the primary intentions of the editors.

2   BEEBE, RICHARD T. "Hunter's Syndrome: Gargoyles--Washington Irving--'Rip Van Winkle.'" Bulletin of the History of Medicine, XLIV (November-December 1970), 582-85.
Discussion of "gargoylism," a genetic disorder characterized by facial distortions and "dwarf-like" appearance,

(BEEBE, RICHARD T.)
found most notably in certain families of the Catskill region. Speculates that Irving saw them in his travels along
the Hudson because Hendrick Hudson and his crew in "Rip Van
Winkle" seem to be described as gargoyles.

3   CONDON, VESTA. "Washington Irving's Andalusia." Travel,
CXXXIV (October 1970), 52-56, 69-70.
Describes Irving's trip through Andalusia. A travelogue
with occasional quotations from Irving.

4   DURANT, DAVID. "Aeolism in Knickerbocker's A History of New
York." American Literature, XLI (January 1970), 493-506.
A unifying thread of satire in the whole work is "Irving's treatment of Aeolism--the inflation of empty subjects into false importance through idle words."

5   FINK, GUIDO. "Il 'corsivo vivente' di Washington Irving."
Studi Americani, XVI (1970), 25-56.

6   KIME, WAYNE R. "Alfred Seton's Journal: A Source for Irving's Tonquin Disaster Account." Oregon Historical Quarterly, LXXI (December 1970), 309-24.
Transcribes part of Alfred Seton's journal recently discovered to have been in Irving's possession. Analyzes Irving's use of this source, and others, in Astoria. Irving
did not merely make up incidents, as has been charged; instead, he carefully weighed evidence "according to the
criteria of consensus, consistency, and probability."
Praises Irving's careful historical method. As new evidence is gathered, "the solidity of his performance as a
historian becomes increasingly clear."

7   McCLARY, BEN H. "A Bracebridge-Hall Christmas for Van Buren:
An Unpublished Irving Letter." English Language Notes,
VIII (September 1970), 18-22.
Takes up the controversy over which manor was the original Bracebridge Hall. Favors Barlborough Hall, the home
of the Rev. Cornelius H. Reaston Rodes. Prints an 1833
description of the Hall, noting parallels in Irving.
Prints a previously unpublished Irving letter to Rodes
dated 5 December 1831 inviting himself and Van Buren over
for Christmas. Quotes letter from Irving to Catherine
Paris describing Rodes' Christmas customs.

8   NOBLE, DONALD R. "Washington Irving's 'Peter' Pun." American Notes and Queries, VIII (March 1970), 103-104.
Irving probably punned for humorous purposes on the name

1970

(NOBLE, DONALD R.)
"Peter" Stuyvesant in A History of New York. In several
passages he apparently intended to suggest "penis."

9   POCHMANN, HENRY A., and E. N. FELTSKOG, eds. Mahomet and His
Successors. The Complete Works of Washington Irving. Madison: Univ. of Wisconsin Press, 1970.
    The authoritative edition, with historical and textual
essays and extensive editorial apparatus.

10 POCHMANN, HENRY A. "An Example of Progressive Plate Deterioration." Center for Editions of American Authors Newsletter, III (1970), 16.
    The example is from Mahomet and His Successors.

11 REED, KENNETH T. "Oh These Women! These Women!: Irving's
Shrews and Coquettes." American Notes and Queries, VIII
(June 1970), 147-50.
    Irving's attitudes toward women are compounded of love,
puzzlement, and irritation. The two dominant types in his
work are the shrew and the coquette.

12 REED, KENNETH T. "Washington Irving and the Negro." Negro
American Literature Forum, IV (July 1970), 43-44.
    Quotes from Irving's books and journals, showing that he
was indifferent to the moral issue of slavery and that he
perpetuated Black stereotypes.

13 REICHART, WALTER, ed. Journals and Notebooks: Volume III,
1819-1827. The Complete Works of Washington Irving. Madison: Univ. of Wisconsin Press, 1970.
    The authoritative edition, with an introduction and ex-
tensive annotations.

14 SABBADINI, SILVANO. "La morte e le maschera: Note sullo
Sketch Book." Studi Americani, XVI (1970), 57-79.

15 WEATHERSPOON, M. A. "1815-1819: Prelude to Irving's Sketch
Book." American Literature, XLI (January 1970), 566-71.
    Serena Livingston, who is not mentioned in any of the
Irving biographies, influenced his mood in the years pre-
ceding the publication of The Sketch Book.

1971 A BOOKS

1   COHN, JILL WILSON. The Short Fiction of Washington Irving.
Dissertation Abstracts International, XXXII (1971), 5176A-
5177A.

(COHN, JILL WILSON)

The four major volumes of Irving's short works include four basic forms of fiction: the sketch, tale, short story, and framing story. Irving's only short stories appear in The Sketch Book, the framing stories dominate Tales of a Traveller, and Bracebridge Hall and The Alhambra are basically tales and sketches.

2 JOHNSTON, JOHANNA. The Heart That Would Not Hold. New York: M. Evans and Co., 1971.

A popular biography, rather sentimental in tone.

3 LOSCHKY, HELEN M. J. Washington Irving's Knickerbocker's History of New York: Folk History as a Literary Form. Dissertation Abstracts International, XXXI (1971), 6559A.

Irving uses the history of New Netherland (1609-1664) as the basis of a political allegory in which the four Dutch governors stand for the first four American presidents. Irving's moral: if Americans want to lose their country as the Dutch lost theirs, they need only betray Madison as the Dutch did Stuyvesant.

4 WESS, ROBERT C. The Image and Use of the Dutch in the Literary Works of Washington Irving. Dissertation Abstracts International, XXXI (1971), 4799A-4800A.

The Dutch suited Irving temperamentally, and provided him an intellectual vehicle for the expression of ideas about history, literature, and the uses of the imagination.

1971 B   SHORTER WRITINGS

1 ALBERT, BURTON, JR. "Alexander Robertson: Irving's drawing instructor." American Notes and Queries, IX (June 1971), 148-50.

Alexander and Archibald Robertson, brothers, were artists and teachers. It is most likely that Alexander was ving's drawing instructor.

2 GILMAN, WILLIAM H. "How Should Journals Be Edited?" Early American Literature, VI (Spring 1971), 73-83.

An essay review occasioned by the publication of Vol. I of Irving's Journals and Notebooks by the Univ. of Wisconsin Press. Gilman calls it one of the best editorial efforts involving private manuscripts that we have, but says that the editorial method has some flaws, the chief of which is that it results in a text of limited usefulness.

3 GRAY, JAMES L. The Development of the Early American Short Story to Washington Irving. Dissertation Abstracts Inter-

1971

(GRAY, JAMES L.)
national, XXXII (1971), 1471A.
Irving developed the prototypic short story which originated in 18th-century British and American periodicals,
and became the major initiator of the form in America. He
took up the author as entertainer or narrator (used by
American periodical essayists), and adapted the English
sentimental tradition.

4   KIME, WAYNE R. "Pierre M. Irving's Account of Peter Irving,
Washington Irving, and the Corrector." American Literature, XLIII (March 1971), 108-14.
P. M. Irving's fragmentary account, in a draft passage
omitted from his biography of his uncle, is still the best
we have.

5   KIME, WAYNE R. "Washington Irving and The Empire of the
West." Western American Literature, V (Winter 1971),
277-85.
An article in the Knickerbocker (March 1840), published
anonymously but written by Irving, shows how his aesthetic
interest in the West developed into a political concern
for the importance of the West to the welfare of the nation. Text of Irving's article included.

6   MARTINEAU, BARBARA J. Dramatized Narration in the Short Fiction of Irving, Poe, and Melville. Dissertation Abstracts
International, XXXI (1971), 4725A.
Irving, Poe, and Melville experimented with first-person
narration in short fiction, in ways revealing of their own
interpretations of experience. Irving's narrator is usu-
ally external--a storyteller, or preserver of cultural
tradition.

7   McDOUGAL, EDWARD D. "Lost New York." Times Literary Supplement (11 June 1971), p. 677.
A letter to the editor, explaining that a friend of Irving's reported that Irving found Charles Dickens in per-
son "outrageously vulgar."

8   PAULY, THOMAS H. The Travel Sketch-Book and the American Author: A Study of the European Travelogues of Irving,
Longfellow, Hawthorne, Howells, and James. Dissertation
Abstracts International, XXXII (1971), 928A.
Traces the origins of the literary sketch and examines
its influence on Irving and other American writers. The
Sketch Book was the first widely acclaimed book of the
type, and showed later writers the artistic value of the
form.

154

9   POCHMANN, HENRY A. "Washington Irving." Fifteen American
     Authors Before 1900: Bibliographic Essays on Research and
     Criticism. Eds. Robert A. Rees and Earl N. Harbert. Mad-
     ison: Univ. of Wisconsin Press, 1971, pp. 245-61.
          Survey of Irving bibliography, biography, and criticism.
     Discusses some of the controversies about Irving's life,
     and notes the influence of the biographies by Pierre Ir-
     ving and Stanley Williams on the whole field of American
     biography. Irving's works have not lent themselves to
     "new criticism" and most emphasis has been in the field of
     literary history.

10   RINGE, DONALD A. The Pictorial Mode: Space and Time in the
     Art of Bryant, Irving and Cooper. Lexington: Univ. Press
     of Kentucky, 1971.
          Explores the "strong emphasis on the visual" in the
     three authors. Analyzes their use of description and com-
     pares their sense of space with that of the Hudson River
     school of painters. Also discusses the sense of time, par-
     ticularly the theme of mutability and the continuity of
     change. Irving receives a full third of the author's at-
     tention.

11   SCHIK, BERTHOLD. "Washington Irving: Rip Van Winkle." In-
     terpretationen zu Irving, Melville und Poe. Ed. Hans
     Finger. Frankfort: Moritz Diesterweg, 1971, pp. 7-21.

12   SHAW, CATHERINE M. "The Dramatic View of Washington Irving."
     Texas Studies in Literature and Language, XIII (Fall 1971),
     461-74.
          Examines Irving as a devotee of the theater and as drama
     critic. Quotes from letters, journals, and Jonathan Old-
     style. In his taste for drama, as in his fiction and sat-
     ire, Irving is both a romantic dreamer and a neoclassical
     critic.

13   SHORT, JULEE. "Irving's Eden: Oklahoma, 1832." Journal of
     the West, X (October 1971), 700-12.
          Summarizes the accounts of Irving, Latrobe, Ellsworth,
     and Pourtalès, and defends A Tour on the Prairies. "[Ir-
     ving] wrote the earliest social and cultural history of
     the West. He wrote a travel account that recognizes the
     insistent tug of men to escape the complexities of urban
     living," anticipating Turner. The book is thoroughly Amer-
     ican.

14   SLOANE, DAVID E. E. "Washington Irving's 'Insuperable Diffi-
     dence.'" American Literature, XLIII (March 1971), 114-15.

1971

(SLOANE, DAVID E. E.)
Prints a letter in which Irving rejects a public speaking invitation.

1972 A BOOKS

1   MYERS, ANDREW B., ed. Washington Irving: A Tribute. Tarry-
    town: Sleepy Hollow Restorations, 1972.
        Brief papers delivered at the 1970 "Washington Irving
    Symposium" sponsored by Sleepy Hollow Restorations, Tarry-
    town, New York. Introduction is a survey of Irving's ca-
    reer by Andrew B. Myers. Papers include a discussion of
    the textual history and editorial problems of The Sketch
    Book by Haskell S. Springer, "The Theme of Americanism in
    Irving's Writing" by William L. Hedges, "The English Liter-
    ary Scene in the 1820s" by Carl H. Woodring, "American
    Nationalism Fifty Years After the Revolution" by Lorman A.
    Ratner, "Irving in Spain" by Andrew B. Myers, "Irving: As
    Seen Through His Letters" by Herbert L. Kleinfield, "Wash-
    ington Irving and His Home, Sunnyside" by Joseph T. Butler,
    and "The American Literary Scene, 1815-1860: by William M.
    Gibson. Illustrated.

1972 B SHORTER WRITINGS

1   BAIOCCO, C. N. "Washington Irving's Hispanic Literature."
    Americas, XXIV (April 1972), 2-11.
        ". . . there has been a failure to recognize properly
    the extent of Spain's influence on [Irving]. . . . the
    key to his imagination is Spain."

2   GRANGER, BRUCE. "The Whim-Whamsical Bachelors in Salmagundi."
    Costerus, II (1972), 63-69.
        Comments on the caricatured bachelors. Each one is ex-
    amined.

3   HUBBELL, JAY B. Who Are the Major American Writers? Durham:
    Duke Univ. Press, 1972.
        Irving's literary standing, as measured by various in-
    dicators, is dealt with. Index.

4   KIME, WAYNE R. "The First Locomotive to Cross the Rocky Moun-
    tains: An Unidentified Sketch in the Knickerbocker Maga-
    zine, May 1839, by Washington Irving." Bulletin of the
    New York Public Library, LXXVI (1972), 242-50.
        Irving wrote an anonymous "droll sequel" to a hoax which
    had appeared in Knickerbocker. It combines "his relish

(KIME, WAYNE R.)
for burlesque history and his enthusiasm for the West as a topic for literary exploitation.

5 _____. "Washington Irving and the 'Extension of the Empire of Freedom': An Unrecorded Contribution to the Evening Post, May 14, 1804." Bulletin of the New York Public Library, LXXVI (1972), 220-30.
Background and analysis of a witty Irving piece in the Evening Post, published anonymously.

6 LEARY, LEWIS. "The Two Voices of Washington Irving." From Irving to Steinbeck: Studies in American Literature in Honor of Harry R. Warfel. Eds. Motley Deakin and Peter Lisca. Gainesville: Univ. of Florida Press, 1972, pp. 13-26.
As Geoffrey Crayon, Irving became the American representative to the world of fashionable literature. Crayon was courteous, genteel, sophisticated, and smoothly polished, but is rather bland to many readers. Though Irving settled on Geoffrey Crayon, he would occasionally write a story through the voice of Diedrich Knickerbocker, and these have proved his best works. Knickerbocker is irreverent, ironic, and "lusty," anticipating the best in the American tradition of humor. Discusses A History of New York, "Rip Van Winkle," and "The Legend of Sleepy Hollow," as illustrations of the Knickerbocker persona. Suggests that yet a third voice can be detected in Irving's Spanish tales.

7 LEASE, BENJAMIN. "John Bull versus Washington Irving: More on the Shakespeare Committee Controversy." English Language Notes, IX (June 1972), 272-77.
Deals with the controversy in England over Irving, an American, being appointed to the committee in charge of planning a monument to Shakespeare. "These new evidences concerning the Shakespeare Committee controversy put into clearer perspective the difficulties inherent in Irving's literary situation at a time of acute Anglo-American distrust."

8 McCLARY, BEN HARRIS. "Irving, Lockhart, and the Quarterly Review." Bulletin of the New York Public Library, LXXVI (1972), 231-36.
Compares an article in the Quarterly Review with Irving's manuscript version of it.

9 McCLARY, BEN H. "Irving's Literary Pimpery." American Notes and Queries, X (June 1972), 150-51.

1972

(McCLARY, BEN H.)
Basically the same article as was published in Notes and Queries (February 1969). See item 1969.B15.

10   MYERS, ANDREW B. "Washington Irving and Gilbert Stuart Newton: A New-York Mirror Contribution Identified." Bulletin of the New York Public Library, LXXVI (1972), 237-41.
Identifies a three-page Irving manuscript in the Berg
Collection. Treats Irving's relationship with Newton.

11   SCHEICK, WILLIAM J., ed. "'The Seven Sons of Lara': A Washington Irving Manuscript." Resources for American Literary Study, II (Autumn 1972), 208-17.
Transcription of a hitherto unpublished manuscript. An
introduction analyzes it historically, bibliographically,
and critically. "Considered alone [it] is not a major contribution; but seen in the perspective of his entire literary corpus, [it] reveals not only Irving's perennial fas-
cination with Spain but also facets of his artistry."

12   SOKOL, D. M. "John Quidor and the Literary Sources for his
Paintings." Antiques, CII (October 1972), 675-79.
Quidor concentrated on subjects taken almost exclusively
from American literature. The article discusses Quidor's
pictorial interpretation of passages from Cooper and Irving. Illustrated.

1973 A   BOOKS - NONE

1973 B   SHORTER WRITINGS

1   CLARK, JAMES W., JR. "Washington Irving and New England
Witchlore." New York Folklore Quarterly, XXIX (December
1973), 304-13.
Irving was among the first to draw upon the New England
witchcraft trials for artistic purposes. He treated them
satirically in "The Legend of Sleepy Hollow," A History of
New York, and "The Devil and Tom Walker."

2   KIME, WAYNE R. "The Completeness of Washington Irving's A
Tour on the Prairies." Western American Literature, VIII
(Spring and Summer 1973), 55-66.
Far from being a simplistic, conventionalized account,
A Tour is "a carefully articulated narrative" of the au-
thor's development from a naïve romanticism to a realistic
appreciation and understanding of the West.

3   REICHART, WALTER A. "Washington Irving in der Dresdener und
     der Pariser Gesellschaft 1822-1825." Jahrbuch des Wiener
     Goethe-Vereins, LXXVII (1973), 134-146.

4   STOCKER, M. H. "Salmagundi: Problems in Editing the So-
     Called First Edition (1807-08)." Papers of the Biblio-
     graphical Society of America, LXVII (Second Quarter 1973),
     141-58.
         The publication history and textual revisions of the
     first American edition.

1974 A   BOOKS - NONE

1974 B   SHORTER WRITINGS

1   HARBERT, EARL N. "Washington Irving's Conquest of Granada:
     A Spanish Experiment that Failed." Clio, III (June 1974),
     305-13.
         Irving attempted to blend history and fiction in Con-
     quest of Granada. The public was confused by his experi-
     ment, and in his revisions Irving made the book more
     strictly historical.

2   SPRINGER, HASKELL. "Introduction." Rip Van Winkle and The
     Legend of Sleepy Hollow. Tarrytown: Sleepy Hollow Resto-
     rations, 1974, pp. 7-15.
         These stories reveal "Irving's special ability to enter-
     tain and delight by means of his remarkable control of the
     English language, combined with his witty, perceptive in-
     sight into human nature and the American scene."

Author/Title Index

A., 1836.B1

Abbotsford and Newstead Abbey,
    1835.B8, B9, B10, B13, B14, B17
    1836.B8
    1837.B9
    1947.B3
    1962.B4

Abel, Darrel, 1963.B1

"Abendunterhaltungen," 1823.B5

Abu Hassan, 1959.B8

Adams, Charles, 1870.A1

Adams, G. F., 1894.B1

Adams, Thomas R., 1953.B1

Addison, Joseph, 1859.B5

Aderman, Ralph M.,
    1969.B1
    1970.B1

Adkins, Nelson F.,
    1930.B1
    1933.B1, B2
    1934.B1

Addressed to 50, Albemarle Street, 1966.A2

Advance of the American Short Story, The, 1923.B2

"Adventure of the German Student,"
    1856.B5
    1936.B5
    1938.B2
    1955.B4
    1964.B4

Adventures of Captain Bonneville,
    1837.B5, B6, B7
    1849.B4
    1902.B3
    1931.B6
    1933.B5
    1956.B6
    1957.B8
    1961.B7
    1966.B4
    1967.B3
    1968.B5
    1970.A1
    1971.B5

"Aeolism in Knickerbocker's A History of New York," 1970.B4

Albert, Burton, Jr., 1971.B1

"Alexander Robertson: Irving's Drawing Teacher," 1971.B1

Alexis, Willibald,
    1822.B1
    1824.B1
    1830.B1
    1832.B1
    1844.B1

"Alfred Seton's Journal: A Source for Irving's Tonquin Disaster Account," 1970.B6

"Alhambra, Die--Das--," 1832.B1

Alhambra, The,
    1832.B1, B4, B5, B6, B7, B8, B9, B11, B12, B13, B14, B15, B16,
      B17, B18,
    1833.B1
    1834.B1
    1850.B8
    1851.B1
    1892.B1
    1925.B1
    1937.B5
    1955.B2
    1959.B11
    1961.B4
    1965.A1
    1971.A1

"Alhambra, The," 1833.B1

Allyn, R., 1856.B1

Author / Title Index

"Alma Mater to 'Geoffrey Crayon,'" 1960.B5

Along the Hudson with Washington Irving, 1913.B1

Alvarez Aguilar, M., 1930.B2

"America and American Writers," 1829.B12

"American Authors. No. I. Washington Irving," 1838.B3

"American Authorship. No. I--Washington Irving," 1853.B2, B3

"American Bookmen: Washington Irving," 1897.B4

"American Classic, An," 1894.B2

American Cultural History 1607-1829, 1829.B15

"American First Editions at Tx U: XII," 1959.B2

American Humorists, 1882.B1

American in England During the First Half Century of Independence, The, 1926.B8

American Lands and Letters: the Mayflower to Rip-Van-Winkle, 1897.B5

"American Lions," 1838.B2

American Literary Masters, 1906.B3

American Literature: An Historical Sketch, 1882.B2

American Literature and Culture, 1932.B3

American Literature and Other Papers, 1887.B4

American Literature as Viewed in Germany, 1818-1861, 1958.B3

American Literature in Nineteenth-Century England, 1944.B3

American Literature in Poland: A Preliminary Check List, 1790-1940, 1965.B3

American Literature in Spain, 1916.B1

American Literature, 1607-1885, 1889.B2

American Literature. Volume I: Colonial and Early National Writing, 1963.B1

American Novelists in Italy, 1965.B8

American Short Story, The,   1961.B6

American West of Washington Irving, The,   1970.A1

American Writer and the European Tradition, The,   1950.B4

"American Writers,"   1825.B13

American Writers on American Literature,   1931.B1

"Americans in Britain,"   1957.B9

"Americans in London,"   1831.B10

"America's First Man of Letters,"   1945.B1

"Amerika, du hast es besser,"   1932.B8

"Amerikans'ka novela epoxy romantyzmu,"   1967.B6

"Amérique du Nord. Littérature des États-Unis,"   1827.B2

Among My Books,   1870.B1

Anderson, Hilton,   1969.B2

Anglo-American Literature and Manners,   1852.B1

"Another Reprint of Irving's Biography of James Lawrence,"   1963.B7

Apetz, P.,   1914.B3

Arens, E.,   1927.B1

"Artist of the Past, An,"   1907.B1

Aspinwall, Thomas,   1859.B3

Astoria,
      1836.B9, B10
      1837.B1, B2, B3, B4, B8, B10, B11, B12
      1845.B1
      1849.B9
      1897.B1
      1902.B3
      1910.B3
      1927.B2
      1931.B6
      1933.B5

    1950.B3
    1957.B8
    1964.B3, B9
    1965.A2
    1967.B3
    1968.A1, B5, B6
    1969.B11
    1970.A1, B6
    1971.B5

"Astoria," 1837.B11

"Astoria, or, Enterprise beyond the Rocky Mountains," 1837.B2

"Authorship and Date of 'The Haunted Ship,' The," 1939.B2

"Authorship in Irving's Day," 1934.B11

"Authorship of 'Salmagundi,' The," 1936.B2

Autobiographical Recollections, 1860.B15

Avenel, M., 1822.B23

Axson, Stockton, 1933.B3

B., W., 1911.B3

Bainbrigge, William, 1821.B6

Baiocco, C. N., 1972.B1

Ballew, Hal L., 1967.B1

Balston, T., 1911.B1

Bancroft, George, 1860 A1, B5, B10

Barnes, Daniel R., 1967.B2

Barnes, H. F., 1930.B3

"Baron Von Gumppenberg, Emily Foster, and Washington Irving," 1945.B6

Barry, J. N., 1927.B2

Beach, Leonard B.,
    1934.B10
    1938.B3
    1948.B1

Beebe, Richard T., 1970.B2

Beers, Henry A., 1886.B1

Benét, Laura, 1944.A1

Bennett, S. S., 1934.B2

Bensly, Edward, 1911.B2

Benson, Adolph B., 1927.B3

Benson, Egbert, 1819.B3

Bergholz, Harry, 1953.B2

"Bibliographical Problems in Washington Irving's Early Works,"
    1968.B1

Bibliography and Bibliographical Contributions,
    1833.B2
    1883.B1, B4
    1898.B1
    1914.B1, B2
    1920.B1
    1929.B1, B6
    1930.B6, B12
    1932.B1, B2, B4
    1933.A1, B1, B2, B7
    1934.B1, B6, B11, B13
    1935.B5, B6
    1936.A1, B2
    1937.B3
    1939.B2
    1942.B1
    1947.B1
    1948.B2
    1952.B1
    1953.B2, B5
    1955.B1
    1957.B3
    1958.B5, B7
    1959.B1, B2
    1963.B7
    1964.B6, B8
    1965.B3
    1966.B11, B12
    1967.B2
    1968.B1, B15
    1969.B13, B23
    1971.B9
    1972.A1, B11

"Bibliography of Irving, A," 1883.B1

Bibliography of the Writings of Washington Irving: A Check List, A, 1936.A1

Binder, Sister M. Claudia, 1950.B1

Biographical and Critical Miscellanies, 1845.B3

Biographical Contributions,
    1831.B10
    1832.B10
    1836.B11
    1837.B9
    1854.B1
    1855.B5
    1856.B5
    1857.B5, B6
    1859.B3, B4, B6, B8, B9, B11, B12, B13
    1860.A1, B6, B7, B8, B9, B10, B11, B12, B13, B15, B16, B17, B20
    1862.B1, B3, B4, B5
    1863.B3
    1864.B1, B3
    1865.B1, B2, B3
    1869.B1
    1871.B1
    1873.B1
    1883.B7, B8
    1884.B2
    1885.B1
    1886.B4
    1890.B1
    1891.B4
    1896.B1
    1900.B1
    1902.B1, B2, B6
    1904.B2
    1909.B4
    1912.B2
    1916.B4
    1921.B1
    1926.B1, B3, B6, B7, B8, B9
    1927.B8, B9
    1930.B3, B5, B7, B13, B14, B15
    1933.B6, B9
    1934.B12
    1935.B1, B4
    1936.B6
    1937.B3, B4, B5
    1938.B3
    1940.B2
    1941.B1, B2

(Biographical Contributions)
    1943.B1
    1945.B5, B6
    1947.B2
    1948.B3
    1949.B3
    1950.B2
    1951.B1
    1955.B6
    1956.B12
    1957.A1, B1
    1958.B4
    1959.B6
    1960.B5
    1962.B5
    1963.B4
    1965.B7
    1966.A1, B6, B7, B9
    1967.B5
    1968.B9, B12, B14, B16
    1969.A1, B1, B5, B15, B16, B17, B25, B30
    1970.B3, B15
    1971.B1, B4, B7
    1972.A1, B7, B9
    1973.B3

Biographical Studies, 1859.B7

Biography and Poetical Remains of the Late Margaret Miller Davidson,
    1841.B2, B5, B7
    1844.B1

Biography, brief (See also Biographical Contributions),
    1825.B1, B2
    1832.B12
    1848.B4
    1853.B4
    1858.B1
    1859.B5
    1860.B14
    1862.B2
    1867.B3
    1870.A1
    1880.B1
    1883.B9, B11, B14
    1890.B2
    1891.A1
    1892.B1, B2
    1893.B2, B3
    1894.B3, B4
    1897.B3, B4, B5
    1903.A1
    1906.B3

(Biography, brief)
    1910.B2
    1922.B2
    1931.B1
    1932.B10
    1944.B5
    1945.B1
    1959.B3
    1961.B2

Biography, full length (See also Biographical Contributions and
    Biography, brief),
    1862.A1
    1879.A1
    1881.A1
    1901.A1
    1925.A1
    1935.A1
    1940.A1
    1944.A1
    1962.A1
    1971.A2

Birss, J. H.,   1932.B1

Black, Michael L.,
    1967.A1
    1968.B1
    1969.B3

Blackburn, Philip C.,
    1932.B2
    1933.A1

Blanck, Jacob,
    1936.B2
    1947.B1
    1959.B1

Bolingbroke, Viscount,   1959.B7

Boll, Ernest,   1944.B1

Bone, Robert A.,   1963.B2

Book of the Hudson, A,   1849.B2, B3

Borel, Pétrus,
    1936.B5
    1938.B2

Bound Together: A Sheaf of Papers,   1884.B2

Bowden, Edwin T.,
    1959.B2
    1964.B1

Bowen, E. W.,   1906.B1

Bowen, F.,   1849.B9

Bowers, Claude G.,   1940.A1

Boynton, H. W.,
    1901.A1
    1931.B1

Bracebridge Hall,
    1822.B1, B2, B4, B5, B6, B7, B8, B9, B10, B11, B12, B13, B14,
        B16, B17, B18, B19, B20, B21, B24, B25, B27
    1823.B2, B3, B4, B5, B9
    1824.B31
    1825.B6, B10, B11, B13
    1845.B2
    1850.B8
    1887.B1
    1914.B1
    1925.B1
    1949.B1
    1964.B11
    1965.A1
    1970.B7
    1971.A1

"Bracebridge-Hall Christmas for Van Buren, A,"   1970.B7

Brainard, C. H.,   1885.B1

Brevoort, Henry,   1915.B1

Brief Remarks on The Wife of Washington Irving,   1819.B3

Brightwell, D. B.,   1879.B1

British Criticisms of American Writings, 1815-1833,   1922.B1

British Criticisms of American Writings, 1783-1815,   1918.B1

Brooks, Elmer L.,
    1953.B3
    1954.B1

Brooks, Nathan C.,   1838.B3

Brooks, Van Wyck,
    1929.B2
    1944.B2
    1958.B1

Bruce, Wallace, 1913.B1

Bruner, Marjorie W., 1964.B2

Bryant and His Friends: Some Reminiscences of the Knickerbocker
    Writers, 1886.B4   .

Bryant, William Cullen,
    1855.B2
    1860.B6, B7
    1880.A1
    1886.B4

Bucco, Martin, 1964.B3

Buchanan, W. W., 1860.B8, B9

Buckingham, J. T., 1835.B18

Buell, Thomas Cochran, 1966.A1

Burton, Richard,
    1897.B2
    1903.B1

Butler, Joseph T., 1972.A1

"By the Fireside in the Frost," 1855.B1

Byron, George Gordon, Lord (See also Abbotsford and Newstead Abbey),
    1927.B5

"By-ways of Europe: The Kyffhauser and Its Legends," 1868.B1

Caballero, Fernán,
    1930.B13
    1934.B3, B4, B5

Cabell, Joseph C., 1951.B1

Cabot, James E., 1887.B1

Cairns, William B.,
    1918.B1
    1922.B1

Cameron, Kenneth W.,
    1960.B1
    1965.B1
    1968.B2

Campbell, Killis, 1917.B1

Campbell, Thomas. See Life of Thomas Campbell.

Canby, Henry S.,
    1909.B1
    1926.B2
    1931.B2

Carlyle, Thomas, 1850.B4

"Catalogue of the Hellman Collection of Irvingiana," 1929.B1

Cater, Harold Dean, 1957.B1

"Census of Washington Irving Manuscripts, A," 1964.B6

"Centennial of the Tour of the Prairies by Washington Irving
    (1832-1932)," 1932.B7

"Century of American Humor, A," 1901.B1

"Century of Washington Irving, A," 1913.B2

"Certain Nicholas of Patara, A," 1960.B2

"Chapter on Autography, A," 1841.B6

Character Studies, With Some Personal Recollections, 1894.B4

"Characterization in 'Rip Van Winkle,'" 1964.B7

"Charles Dickens and Washington Irving,"
    1916.B4
    1944.B1

Charles Fenno Hoffman, 1930.B3

Chasles, Philarète,
    1835.B19
    1851.B3
    1852.B1

"Cheves Family of South Carolina, The," 1934.B2

Christopher Columbus and How He Received and Imparted the Spirit of
    Discovery, 1891.B5

Chronicle of the Conquest of Granada, A,
    1829.B1, B2, B3, B4, B5, B6, B7, B8, B9, B10, B11, B16, B18
    1830.B1, B8, B11, B12
    1831.B11
    1832.B9
    1838.B1
    1845.B2, B3
    1850.B7
    1895.B1
    1897.B2
    1906.B3
    1937.B5
    1945.B2
    1969.B1, B6, B7
    1974.B1

Clark, James W., Jr., 1973.B1

Clark, Louis Gaylord,
    1844.B2
    1859.B4
    1860.B10, B11, B12, B13
    1869.B1

Clark, Willis Gaylord,
    1836.B11
    1844.B2

Clarke, Edward P., 1851.B4

Classic Americans, A Study of Eminent American Writers from Irving to
    Whitman, 1931.B2

Clemens, Samuel L., 1956.B1, 1959.B9

Clendenning, John, 1964.B4

"Clue Patterns in 'Rip Van Winkle,'" 1966.B2

Coad, O. S., 1925.B1

Cobb, J. B., 1850.B8

Cohen, Hennig, 1965.B2

Cohn, Jill Wilson, 1971.A1

Coleccion de los Viages y Descubrimientos, 1829.B17

Colombo, Rosa Maria, 1966.B1

Colon en España, 1884.B3

Columbus. See Life and Voyages of Christopher Columbus.

"Comments of a Reader—No. 2," 1830.B10

Commins, Saxe, 1945.B1

Companions of Columbus. See Voyages and Discoveries of the Companions
    of Columbus.

"Completeness of Washington Irving's A Tour on the Prairies, The,"
    1973.B2

Concept of European American Fiction from Irving to Hawthorne, The,
    1947.B7

"Concerning the Source of Irving's 'Rip Van Winkle,'" 1956.B7

Condon, Thomas J., 1961.B1

Condon, Vesta, 1970.B3

Conley, Patrick T., 1968.B3

Conquest of Granada. See Chronicle of the Conquest of Granada, A.

"Construction of The Devil and Tom Walker, The," 1968.B17

"Conte Fantastique Chez Irving, Borel et Dumas Père, Un," 1938.B2

Cooke, John Esten,
    1865.B3
    1873.B1

"Cooper and Irving," 1828.B17

Cooper, James Fenimore,
    1828.B17
    1937.B4

"Copy-Editing of Irving's Journals," 1969.B18

Corrector, The, 1968.B13

"Correspondence of Washington Irving and John Howard Payne," 1910.B1

"'corsivo vivente' di,Washington Irving, Il," 1970.B5

"Cosmopolitanism in American Literature Before 1880," 1950.B4

Cozzens, Frederick S., 1890.B1

Cracroft, Richard H., 1970.A1

Crayon Miscellany, The. See separate titles: Abbotsford and Newstead
    Abbey; Tour on the Prairies, A; Legends of the Conquest of Spain.

"Creative Contradictions in Irving," 1969.B21

Creighton, William, 1859.A1

"Cuentos de la Alhambra' y otros temas hispánicos de Washington
    Irving," 1959.B11

Curtis, George W.,
    1863.B2
    1883.B3
    1891.A1
    1894.B3

Cuyler, T. L., 1902.B1

D., E.,
    1827.B2
    1845.B2

Dahl, Curtis, 1961.B2

Dana, Richard H., 1819.B4

Dante, 1939.B3

"Dating the Action of 'Rip Van Winkle'," 1959.B14

"Davenant and Davenport," 1949.B1

Davenport, Walter, 1927.B4

Davidson, Margaret Miller. See Biography and Poetical Remains of the
    Late Margaret Miller Davidson.

Davis, Richard Beale,
    1829.B15
    1941.B1
    1951.B1

"Day With Washington Irving, A," 1859.B9

"De la littérature dans l'Amérique du nord," 1835.B19

De los historiadores de Colon. Estudios de critica literaria,
    segunda serie, 1895.B2

"Death of Washington Irving,"
    1859.B2
    1860.B1, B2

Dennett, J. R., 1866.B1

Depping, 1828.B18

Design of the Present: Essays on Time and Form in American
    Literature, The, 1969.B14

"Deux Adaptations Inconnues du Conte de Washington Irving: The
    Adventure of the German Student," 1955.B4

"Deux Emprunts de Gautier à Irving, 1964.B10

Development of the American Short Story, The, 1923.B3

Development of the Early American Short Story to Washington Irving,
    The, 1971.B3

"Devices of Repetition in Irving's 'The Wife,'" 1969.B4

"Devil and Tom Walker, The,"
    1931.B5
    1952.B3
    1956.B10
    1957.B6
    1968.B17
    1973.B1

Devil in Legend and Literature, The, 1931.B5

"Devil in the Writings of Irving, Hawthorne, and Poe, The,"
    1952.B3

DeVries, Tiemen, 1912.B1

"Dickens and Irving: The Problem of Influence," 1946.B4

Dickens, Charles,
    1916.B4
    1936.B4
    1944.B1, B3
    1945.B5
    1946.B4
    1971.B7

"Did Rip Van Winkle Ever Live?," 1937.B6

"Diedrich Knickerbocker's History of New York," 1820.B23

Dietrich, Rosalia Krystyna Tolczynska, 1965.B3

Discourse on the Life, Character and Genius of Washington Irving, A,
    1860.B6

Discourses and Addresses on Subjects of American History, Arts, and
    Literature, 1833.B3

"Dr. Buchanan's Reminiscences. Washington Irving," 1860.B8

"Dr. Holmes' Remarks," 1859.B8

Dolch, Martin, 1962.B2

"Dramatic View of Washington Irving, The," 1971.B12

Dramatized Narration in the Short Fiction of Irving, Poe, and
    Melville, 1971.B6

Dream Life: A Fable of the Seasons,
    1851.B5
    1863.B3

Dream of Arcadia: American Writers and Artists in Italy, 1760-1915,
    The, 1958.B1

Dumas, Alexandre,
    1936.B5
    1938.B2

Dunn, N. P., 1907.B1

Durant, David, 1970.B4

Dutch Founding of New York, The, 1903.B4

Dutch History, Art and Literature for Americans, 1912.B1

Duyckinck, E. A.,
    1860.A1
    1862.B2

"Earliest German Translations of Washington Irving's Writings: A
    Bibliography, The," 1957.B3

"Early American Books and Printing: Enter the Professional Author,"
    1934.B13

"Early Reception of Washington Irving's Works in Germany, The,"
    1956.B8

Eaton, V. L., 1948.B2

Eby, Cecil D., Jr., 1962.B1

Edge, Mary Allen, 1936.A1

"Editorial Narrative-History of the Knickerbocker Magazine: Number
    Seven," 1859.B4

"Editor's Easy Chair," 1883.B2

"Editors' Intentions in the Washington Irving Letters, The," 1970.B1

"Edward Everett on Washington Irving," 1860.B14

Edwards, Tudor, 1959.B3

"1815-1819: Prelude to Irving's Sketch Book," 1970.B15

Ellis, A. M., 1928.B1

Ellsworth, Henry L., 1937.B1

Emerson, Everett H., 1963.B3

Emerson, Katherine T., 1963.B3

Emerson, Ralph W., 1887.B1

"Empire of the West, The," 1971.B5

Emrich, Duncan, 1960.B2

"England and America," 1926.B4

"England of Washington Irving, The," 1935.B1

English Studies in Honor of James Southall Wilson, 1951.B1

"English Writers on America," 1926.B4

englische Erbe in der amerikanischen Literatur, Das, 1958.B9

Erskine, John, 1912.B4

Essays on American Literature in Honor of Jay B. Hubbell, 1967.B9

"Études de Littérature américaine. L'humour et les Humoristes," 1887.B2

Études sur la littérature et les moeurs des Anglo-Américains au XIXe siècle, 1851.B3

Everett, A. H.,
    1829.B14
    1832.B15

Everett, Edward,
    1822.B24
    1835.B20

(Everett, Edward)
    1837.B8
    1859.B5
    1860.A1, B14

"Example of Progressive Plate Deterioration, An," 1970.B10

"Experiment on the American Bookseller, An," 1957.B2

Expression in America, 1932.B5

Extracts from the Complete Works of Washington Irving, 1843.B2

Eyma, Xavier, 1864.B2

Fable for Critics, A, 1848.B8

"Fallen From Time: The Mythic Rip Van Winkle," 1960.B8

Fatout, Paul, 1956.B1

Faulkner, William, 1962.B1

Fay, T. S., 1832.B16

Felton, C. C., 1859.B6

Feltskog, E. N., 1970.B9

Ferguson, J. De L., 1916.B1

Fernán Caballero. See Caballero, Fernán.

Fetterolf, Adam H., 1897.B3

Fiction of History: Washington Irving Against a Romantic Transition, The, 1954.A1

Fiévet, P., 1891.B1

Fifteen American Authors Before 1900, 1971.B9

"Final Chapter of Knickerbocker's New York, The," 1969.B19

Finland. See "Some Printings of Irvings in Finland before 1900."

Fink, Guido, 1970.B5

"First Books of Some American Authors: III.--Irving, Poe and Whitman, The," 1898.B1

"First Version of the Writings of Washington Irving in Spanish, The," 1930.B12

Fiske, John C., 1955.B2

Fitz-Greene Halleck, 1930.B1

Folklore,
    1884.B1
    1937.B6
    1945.B7
    1946.B1
    1948.B1
    1951.B2
    1952.B3
    1953.B4
    1956.B10
    1957.B5, B6
    1959.B15
    1960.B8
    1961.B3
    1964.B11
    1968.B17
    1973.B1

Fontaney, A., 1832.B17

"Footnote to Washington Irving, A," 1966.B11

Ford, James L., 1901.B1

Form and Fable in American Fiction, 1961.B3

Forrest, Rex, 1940.B1

Foster, Emily,
    1933.B9
    1938.B3
    1945.B6
    1959.B8

Foster, W. E., 1883.B4

"Four American Authors," 1858.B1

Francis, F. C., 1942.B1

Francis, John W., 1860.B10

"Fray Antonio Agapida and Washington Irving's Romance with History,"
    1969.B6

Freeman, John F., 1959.B4

French Criticism of American Literature Before 1850, 1917.B2

From Irving to Steinbeck: Studies in American Literature in Honor of
    Harry R. Warfel, 1972.B6

From West to East: Studies in the Literature of the American West,
    1966.B3

Furst, Clyde, 1913.B2

G., W. E., 1883.B7

Gaedertz, Karl T., 1888.B1

Gallagher, William Davis, 1839.B2

"Gallery of Literary Characters: Washington Irving," 1831.B1

Gardner, James H., 1933.B4

Gates, William B.,
    1943.B1
    1959.B5

Gay, S. H., 1883.B5

"General James Wilkinson in the Knickerbocker History of New York,"
    1926.B5

"Genesis of La Familia de Alvareda, The," 1934.B3

"Genesis of the Rip Van Winkle Legend, The," 1883.B12

"Genius and Writings of Washington Irving, The," 1850.B8

Gentle Flute: Washington Irving as Biographer, 1966.A3

"Geoffrey Crayon,"
    1919.B1
    1954.B3

"George Bancroft on Washington Irving," 1860.B5

Gerdts, W. H., 1958.B2

"Geschichte," 1830.B2

Geschichte der nordamerikanischen Literatur, 1891.B3

"Ghost in Irving Place, A," 1909.B4

Gibson, William M., 1972.A1

Gil, Enrique, 1841.B4

Gilman, William H. 1971.B2

Gist, W. W., 1893.B2

Glowes, Katherine A., 1969.B4

Godwin, William, 1957.B2

Goethe, Johann Wolfgang von, 1932.B8

Goggio, Emilio,
    1930.B4
    1931.B3

Gohdes, Clarence, 1944.B3

"Goldsmith and Irving," 1851.B4

Goldsmith, Oliver (See also Life of Oliver Goldsmith),
    1851.B4
    1962.B6

Gosse, Edmund W., 1883.B6

"Gossip With Readers and Correspondents," 1860.B3

"Gothic Element in American Literature Before 1835, The," 1925.B1

Gothicism,
    1925.B1
    1964.B4

Gourmont, Remy de, 1887.B2

Granada. See Chronicle of the Conquest of Granada, A.

Granger, Bruce, 1972.B2

Gratz, Rebecca, 1935.B2

Gray, James L., 1971.B3

Great American Writers, 1912.B4

Green, David Bonnell, 1959.B6

Greene, George Washington,
    1858.B2
    1859.B7

Greenlaw, Edwin, 1916.B2

Griffith, Ben W., 1957.B2

Griswold, Rufus W., 1847.B2

Grosskunz, R., 1902.A1

Guerra, Angel, 1903.B2

Guide to the Study of Nineteenth Century Authors, A, 1889.B1

Guttmann, Allen, 1964.B5

Gwathmey, E. M., 1931.B4

H.,
    1824.B35
    1857.B3

Hagensick, Donna, 1969.B5

Hagopian, John V., 1962.B2

Hale, Edward Everett, 1902.B2

"Half an Hour at Sunnyside," 1859.B12

Halleck, Fitz-Greene, 1930.B1

Hamilton, Alexander, 1963.B3

Handbuch der nordamericanischen National-literatur, 1854.B2

Haphazard Personalities; Chiefly of Noted Americans, 1886.B2

Harbert, Earl N.,
    1969.B6, B7
    1974.B1

Hastings, G. E., 1929.B3

Haussaire, E., 1888.B2

Haweis, H. R., 1882.B1

Hawthorne, Nathaniel,
    1842.B5
    1876.B2
    1969.B8

Hazlitt, William, 1825.B10

Heart That Would Not Hold, The, 1971.A2

Hedges, William L.,
    1954.A1
    1956.B2
    1959.B7
    1965.A1
    1969.B8, B9
    1972.A1

Heine, Heinrich, 1957.B4

"Hellman Collection of Irvingiana, The," 1929.B6

Hellman, George S.,
    1915.B1
    1920.B1
    1925.A1
    1929.B1, B6
    1930.B5

Hemstreet, Charles, 1903.B3

Herold, A. L., 1926.B3

Herrig, L., 1854.B2

Hespelt, E. Herman,
    1927.B5
    1934.B3, B4, B5

Hewett-Thayer, Harvey, 1958.B3

Hill, David J., 1879.A1

Hillard, A. S., 1841.B5

"Hispanismo y romanticismo en Washington Irving (1859-1959),"
    1956.B11

"Historic Homes: Washington Irving and Sunnyside," 1884.B1

"Historiens de L'École américaine. IV, Washington Irving, Les,"
    1864.B2

History of Historical Writing in America, The, 1891.B2

History of New York, A,
    1810.B1
    1812.B1
    1819.B4
    1820.B6, B11, B12, B16, B17, B18, B19, B23
    1821.B1, B2, B3, B4
    1822.B24

(History of New York, A)
    1824.B3, B35, B37
    1825.B6, B11, B13
    1827.B1
    1829.B12, B14
    1833.B3
    1836.B3
    1845.B2
    1848.B4
    1850.B8
    1856.B1
    1857.B4
    1870.B1
    1876.B2
    1882.B2
    1883.B3, B10
    1887.B1
    1891.A1, B2
    1893.B3
    1894.B2
    1897.B2
    1903.B4
    1906.B3
    1912.B1, B2
    1913.B1
    1916.B2
    1926.B5
    1927.B3, B12
    1930.D1, B11
    1932.B9
    1934.B8
    1940.B2
    1952.B2
    1954.B2, B3
    1959.B7, B15
    1960.B2
    1961.B1
    1964.B1
    1965.A1
    1966.B10
    1967.A1, B10
    1968.B1, B7, B15
    1969.B3, B19
    1970.B4, B8
    1971.A3, A4
    1972.B6
    1973.B1

"History of New York: Significant Revisions in 1848, A," 1696.B3

Hodgkins, Louise M., 1889.B1

Hoffman, Charles Fenno, 1930.B3

Hoffman, Daniel G.,
    1953.B4
    1961.B3

Hoffman, Louise M.,   1945.B2

Hoffman, Matilda,
    1862.B1, B3, B4
    1902.B4
    1926.B9
    1927.B8
    1933.B9
    1959.B8

Holmes, Oliver Wendell,
    1859.B8
    1883.B8

Holt, Charles C.,   1968.B4

Homes of American Authors,   1853.B4

Höring, Wilhelm. See Alexis, Willibald

Horsford, Howard C.,   1952.B1

Hough, Robert L.,   1968.B5

"House of the Four Chimneys,"   1902.B6

Howard, Leon,   1960.B4

"How Irving Kept Warm,"   1926.B1

"How Should Journals Be Edited?,"   1971.B2

Howe, M. A. D.,   1897.B4

Howells, William Dean,   1895.B1

H-S,   1820.B21

Hubbell, J. B.,
    1929.B4
    1972.B3

Huddleston, Eugene L.,   1965.B4

Hudson, Ruth,   1959.B9

Hughes, T. S.,   1825.B11

Hulbert, H. W., 1884.B1

Humor,
    1882.B1
    1883.B13
    1887.B2
    1901.B1, B2
    1964.B1
    1965.A3

"Hunter's Syndrome: Gargoyles--Washington Irving--'Rip Van Winkle,'"
    1970.B2

"Ichabod Crane and Washington Irving," 1963.B4

"Ichabod Crane in Yoknapatawpha," 1962.B1

"Ichabod Crane's Scottish Origin," 1968.B8

"Illustration to the Legend of Prince Ahmed: An Unpublished Sketch
    by Washington Irving," 1952.B1

"Illustrations of the Works of Washington Irving, Esq.," 1824.B5

Image and Use of the Dutch in the Literary Works of Washington
    Irving, The, 1971.A4

"Impromptu by Washington Irving," 1953.B5

Ince., H., 1830.B10

Indian in American Literature, The, 1933.B5

Indians, Irving's treatment of,
    1931.B6
    1933.B5
    1966.B4
    1967.B12
    1968.B5

"inedito di Washington Irving, Un," 1966.B1

"Influence of Geography and History on Washington Irving's Writings,
    The," 1930.B8

Influence of Irving,
    1833.B3
    1834.B1
    1859.B10
    1863.B2
    1879.B1
    1883.B10

(Influence of Irving)
    1894.B5
    1912.B4
    1913.B3, B4
    1923.B2
    1925.B2
    1929.B3, B4
    1930.B1
    1931.B4
    1934.B3
    1936.B3, B4, B5
    1938.B2
    1940.B1
    1944.B1, B3
    1946.B3, B4
    1947.B6
    1948.B1
    1954.B2
    1955.B2, B4
    1956.B1, B8
    1957.A1, B4, B10
    1958.B2
    1959.B9, B15, B16
    1960.B2
    1962.B1
    1966.B10
    1967.B4, B11
    1968.B4, B5, B6, B13
    1969.B2, B8, B10
    1970.A2
    1971.B8
    1972.B12

Influence of the German Tale on the Short Stories of Washington
    Irving, Hawthorne, and Poe, The,   1928.B2

Ingraham, Charles A.,   1922.B2

Ingram, Frank L.,   1969.B10

"Inman and Irving: Derivations from Sleepy Hollow," 1958.B2

Inman, Henry,   1958.B2

"Inn-Window Poetry," 1964.B11

Insight I: Analyses of American Literature,   1962.B2

"Instinct for Misanthropy," 1965.B2

Interpretation en zu Irving, Melville und Poe,   1971.B11

"Irving," 1931.B1

"Irving--A Litterateur in Politics," 1969.B5

"Irving and His 'Favorite Author,'" 1962.B6

"Irving and Moore: A Note on Anglo-American Literary Relations,"
    1947.B2

"Irving and Moore Again," 1959.B6

"Irving and 'The Almighty Dollar,'" 1940.B1

"Irving and the Genteel Tradition," 1936.B3

"Irving and the Gothic Tradition," 1964.B4

"Irving and Ticknor in Spain: Some Parallels and Contrasts,"
    1967.B1

"Irving as a Journal Writer," 1969.B12

"Irving at Sunnyside," 1864.B1

"Irving at Sunnyside in 1858." 1865.B3

"Irving Dinner, The," 1832.B10

"Irving, Hawthorne, and the Image of the Wife," 1969.B8

Irving, Pierre M.,
    1862.A1, B3
    1927.B2
    1971.B4

"Irving: Recorder of Indian Life," 1931.B6

"Irving the Federalist," 1926.B2

"Irving the Historian," 1883.B5

Irving, Washington, Diaries,
    1926.B6
    1934.B5

Irving, Washington, Journals and Notebooks,
    1921.B1
    1927.B8, B9
    1930.B14
    1931.B7
    1934.B12
    1937.B5
    1944.B4
    1949.B2

(Irving, Washington, Journals and Notebooks)
    1958.B6
    1963.B5
    1966.B3
    1969.B12, B18, B28, B29
    1970.B13
    1971.B2

Irving, Washington, Letters,
    1859.B6
    1860.B12, B13, B15
    1862.A1
    1863.B3
    1891.B4
    1897.B5
    1907.B1
    1910.B1, B3
    1915.B1, B2
    1916.B4
    1917.B1
    1923.B1
    1926.B10
    1927.B2, B10, B11
    1928.B3
    1930.B13
    1932.B6
    1933.B8
    1934.B2, B4, B10
    1935.B3
    1945.B3, B8
    1947.B5
    1953.B1
    1956.B6
    1957.B2
    1958.B6, B8
    1959.B4
    1960.B5
    1963.B3
    1965.B1, B5
    1966.A2, B7
    1967.B4, B7
    1968.B2
    1969.A1, B15
    1970.B7
    1971.B14
    1972.A1, B9

Irving, Washington, Poetry,
    1930.B6
    1932.B1
    1937.B3
    1938.B1
    1953.B5

(Irving, Washington, Poetry)
    1965.B4
    1967.B8

Irving, Washington, Uncollected Writings,
    1830.B11, B12
    1915.B2
    1925.B2
    1931.B7
    1934.B1, B9
    1935.B5, B6
    1952.B1
    1953.B2
    1958.B7
    1964.B8
    1965.B6
    1966.B1, B11
    1967.B2
    1968.B15
    1971.B5
    1972.B4, B5, B8, B10, B11

Irving, Washington, Works. See individual titles.

"Irving--Writer and Patriot," 1932.B10

Irvingesque Story in the United States: 1820-1860, The, 1970.A2

"Irvingiana," 1955.B1

Irvingiana: A Memorial of Washington Irving, 1860.A1

"Irving's Alhambra," 1832.B15

"Irving's Astoria," 1897.B1

"Irving's Biography of James Lawrence--and a New Discovery," 1932.B2

"Irving's Columbus: The Problem of Romantic Biography," 1956.B2

"Irving's Conquest of Granada," 1845.B3

"Irving's Conquest of Granada: Authorial Intention and Untoward
    Accident," 1969.B7

"Irving's Eden: Oklahoma, 1832," 1971.B13

"Irving's Expurgation of the 1809 History of New York," 1932.B9

"Irving's German Sources in The Sketch Book," 1930.B9

"Irving's German Tour and Its Influence on His Tales," 1930.B10

"Irving's 'Haunted Ship,'" 1935.B6

"Irving's 'Haunted Ship'--A Correction," 1935.B5

"Irving's Headless Hessian: Prosperity and the Inner Life," 1963.B2

"Irving's Humor," 1883.B13

"Irving's 'Knickerbocker,'" 1883.B3

"Irving's Knickerbocker and Some of Its Sources," 1952.B2

"Irving's Last Volume," 1855.B7

"Irving's Literary Borrowing," 1969.B15

"Irving's Literary Midwifery: Five Unpublished Letters from British
    Repositories," 1967.B4

"Irving's Literary Pimpery," 1972.B9

"Irving's Miscellanies: Legends of the Conquest of Spain," 1836.B6

"Irving's Power of Idealization," 1883.B8

"Irving's Prayerbook--and a Letter," 1965.B1

"Irving's Rip Van Winkle,"
    1946.B2
    1952.B4

"Irving's 'Rip Van Winkle,'" 1947.B4

"Irving's 'Sketch-book,'" 1883.B6

"Irving's Stories in Quidor's Paintings," 1957.B10

"Irving's Sunnyside," 1951.B2

"Irving's Tour on the Prairies," 1835.B6

"Irving's Use of American Folklore in 'The Legend of Sleepy Hollow,'"
    1953.B4

"Irving's Use of His Italian Experiences in Tales of a Traveller:
    The Beginning of an American Tradition," 1959.B16

"Irving's Use of Spanish Sources in The Conquest of Granada,"
    1945.B2

"Irving's Version of Byron's The Isles of Greece," 1927.B5

"Irving's Washington and an Episode in Courtesy," 1930.B5

"Irving's 'Wolfert's Roost,'" 1933.B2, B7

"Irving's 'Wolfert's Roost': A Bibliographical Note," 1933.B1

"Irving's Works," 1856.B1

Isella Russell, Dora, 1962.B3

"Islamism," 1851.B7

"Italian Rip Van Winkle, An," 1945.B7

J., R. J., 1875.B1

Jackson, Andrew, 1945.B8

James, Henry, 1959.B16

"James Ogilvie and Washington Irving," 1941.B1

Jameson, J. F., 1891.B2

Janvier, Thomas A., 1903.B4

Jefferson, Joseph,
    1876.B1
    1927.B4
    1960.B3

Jeffrey, Francis,
    1820.B22
    1822.B25
    1823.B9
    1828.B19

Jenney, Adele G., 1970.A2

"John Bull and His American Descendants," 1929.B3

"John Bull versus Washington Irving: More on the Shakespeare
    Committee Controversy," 1972.B7

John Howard Payne, a Biographical Sketch of the Author of "Home
    Sweet Home," 1885.B1

"John Neal's Gleanings in Irvingiana," 1936.B6

John Pendleton Kennedy, 1931.B4

"John Quidor and the Literary Sources for his Paintings," 1972.B12

Johnson, H. Earle, 1958.B4

Johnston, Johanna, 1971.A2

Jones, Charles W., 1954.B2

Journal, 1803, 1934.B12

Journal of Emily Foster, The, 1938.B3

Journal of Washington Irving, 1828, and Miscellaneous Notes on
     Moorish Legend and History, 1937.B5

Journal of Washington Irving (1823-1824), The, 1931.B7

"Kanu and American Literature, Irving," 1963.B6

Keiser, Albert, 1933.B5

Kelley, Leon, 1926.B4

Kennedy, John Pendleton,
     1917.B1
     1929.B4
     1931.B4
     1967.B7

"Kennedy Papers: A Sheaf of Unpublished Letters from Washington
     Irving, The," 1917.B1

Khoursheed, Mariam, 1961.B4

Kime, Wayne R.,
     1967.B3
     1968.A1, B6, B7
     1969.B11
     1970.B6
     1971.B4, B5
     1972.B4, B5
     1973.B2

Kirby, P. R., 1950.B2

Kirby, Thomas, 1947.B2

Kirk, Clara, 1945.B3

Kirk, Rudolph, 1945.B3

Kirkland, Mrs. C. M.,
     1850.B9, B10
     1856.B4

Kleinfield, Herbert L.,
    1962.B4
    1964.B6
    1969.B12
    1972.A1

Knapp, Samuel Lorenzo, 1829.B15

"Knickerbocker," 1956.B4

"Knickerbocker, Bolingbroke, and the Fiction of History," 1959.B7

"Knickerbocker Era of American Letters," 1902.B7

"Knickerbocker Santa Claus," 1954.B2

Knickerbocker's History of New York. See A History of New York.

"Knickerbocker's History of New York," 1836.B7

"Knickerbocker's Newyork," 1812.B1

Knight, Grant C., 1932.B3

Knortz, Karl,
    1891.B3
    1909.B2

Krumpelmann, John T.,
    1955.B3
    1956.B3

Kunzig, Ferdinand, 1911.A1

Laird, Charlton G., 1940.B2

Lamb, G. F., 1947.B3

Lambert, John, 1811.B2

Lamberts, J. J., 1956.B4

Landmarks of American Writing, 1969.B9

Langfeld, William R.,
    1930.B6
    1932.B4
    1933.A1
    1938.B1

Lanman, Charles,
    1859.B9
    1886.B2

Larned, J. N., 1902.B3

Larrabee, Stephen A., 1958.B5

Lathrop, George P., 1876.B1, B2

Leading American Essayists, 1910.B2

Leary, Lewis,
    1961.B5
    1963.A1
    1972.B6

Lease, Benjamin, 1972.B7

"Leaves from the Journal of Frederick S. Cozzens," 1890.B1

Lee, Frank, 1939.B1

Lee, Helen, 1966.B2

Lee, Robert Edson, 1966.B3

Le Fevre, Louis, 1946.B1

"Legend of Sleepy Hollow, The,"
    1821.B5
    1856.B1
    1930.B9
    1953.B3, B4
    1956.B10
    1957.B5, B6
    1959.B10
    1961.B3, B6
    1962.B1
    1963.B2, B4
    1964.B2, B4, B5
    1966.B13
    1967.B10
    1968.B3, B8
    1969.B2, B20, B21
    1971.A1
    1973.B1
    1974.B2

"The Legend of Sleepy Hollow: A Mythological Parody," 1964.B2

Legends of the Conquest of Spain,
    1835.B21
    1836.B2, B3, B4, B5, B6, B7, B8, B12
    1914.B1
    1972.B6

Legis, Studens, 1824.B36

Leisy, Ernest E.,
  1934.B9
  1936.B3

"Leonard Kebler Gift of Washington Irving First Editions, The,"
  1948.B2

Leslie, C. R., 1860.B15

"Letter to the Editors, A," 1938.B1

Letters from Sunnyside and Spain, 1928.B3

"Letters of Cooper, Irving and Others Endorsing the Lyceum in Paris,
  France," 1968.B2

Letters of Jonathan Oldstyle,
  1824.B1, B7
  1941.B3
  1968.B1

"Letters of Timothy Tickler, Esq. to Eminent Literary Characters.
  No. XVIII," 1824.B12

"Letters of Washington Irving: Spanish Fetes and Ceremonies,"
  1927.B10

Letters of Washington Irving to Henry Brevoort, The, 1915.B1

Lewisohn, Ludwig, 1932.B5

Libman, Valentina A., 1969.B13

"Lieutenant Ichabod Crane, United States Marine Corps," 1966.B13

Life and Letters of Washington Irving, The, 1862.A1

Life and Voyages of Christopher Columbus, The,
  1828.B1, B2, B3, B4, B5, B6, B7, B8, B9, B10, B11, B12, B13, B14,
      B15, B16, B17, B18, B19
  1829.B11, B14, B15, B17
  1830.B2, B3, B4, B5, B6, B7, B9
  1841.B1, B4
  1842.B1, B2, B3, B4
  1843.B1
  1847.B1
  1860.B5
  1876.B3
  1883.B5
  1884.B3

(Life and Voyages of Christopher Columbus, The)
    1886.B3
    1891.B2, B5
    1895.B2
    1897.B2
    1902.B3
    1906.B3
    1916.B1
    1927.B3
    1956.B2
    1965.A1
    1966.A3
    1969.B1, B26

"Life and Voyages of Christopher Columbus," 1828.B6

"Life and Voyages of Columbus," 1828.B4

Life of Capt. James Lawrence,
    1932.B2
    1959.B1
    1963.B7

Life of George Washington, The,
    1855.B4
    1856.B2, B4
    1857.B1, B2, B3
    1858.B2
    1859.B1, B7, B9
    1860.B5
    1883.B5
    1902.B2, B3
    1906.B3
    1930.B5
    1966.A3
    1969.B26

Life of Mahomet. See Mahomet and His Successors.

Life of Margaret Miller Davidson. See Biography and Poetical Remains
    of Margaret Miller Davidson.

Life of Oliver Goldsmith, The,
    1848.B3
    1849.B5, B6, B7
    1850.B7, B9
    1859.B7
    1861.B1
    1913.B3
    1956.B1
    1962.B6
    1966.A3
    1969.B26

Life of Thomas Campbell,
    1825.B13
    1826.B1

Life of Washington. See Life of George Washington.

Life of Washington Irving, The,
    1883.B11
    1935.A1

"Life, Writings, and Genius of Washington Irving, The," 1860.B7

Literary and Social Essays, 1894.B3

"Literary 'Area of Freedom' Between Irving and Twain, A," 1959.B9

Literary Criticisms, and Other Papers, 1856.B7

Literary History of America, A, 1900.B2

Literary Leaders of America, 1903.B1

Literary New York, its Landmarks and Associations, 1903.B3

Literary, Political and Social Theories of Washington Irving, The,
    1940.A2

Literary Remains of the Late Willis Gaylord Clark, The, 1844.B2

Literatos extranjeros (impresiones criticas), 1903.B2

Literature and the American Tradition, 1960.B4

Literature of American History: a Bibliographical Guide, The,
    1902.B3

Literature of the Middle Western Frontier, The, 1925.B4

littérature américaine dans la "Revue des deux mondes" (1831-1900),
    1927.B6

"Littérature américaine. Washington Irving.--The Alhambra, La,"
    1832.B17

"Littérature aux États-Unis, La," 1882.B3

"Little About Washington Irving, A," 1944.B5

Little Journeys to the Homes of American Authors, 1896.B2

"Lives of Mahomet and His Successors," 1851.B2

Livingston, L. S., 1898.B1

Livingston, Serena, 1970.B15

Livius, Barham John, 1941.B2

Lloyd, F. V., Jr., 1946.B2

Lockhart, John Gibson,
   1820.B23, B24
   1837.B9
   1891.B4
   1966.B7

"Longfellow," 1863.B2

Longfellow, Henry Wadsworth,
   1834.B2
   1859.B10
   1860.A1
   1863.B2
   1902.B5
   1904.B1

"Long-Sleep-and-Changed-World Motif in 'Rip Van Winkle,' The,"
   1960.B1

Lopez Nuñez, Juan, 1929.B5

Loschky, Helen M. J., 1971.A3

"Lost New York," 1971.B7

Loughlin, Clara, 1902.B4

"Lover of Good Company, A," 1923.B1

Low, Mildred, 1923.B1

Lowell, James Russell,
   1848.B8
   1870.B1

Luquer, T. T. P., 1910.B1

Lydenberg, Harry Miller, 1952.B2

Lynch, James J., 1952.B3

Lynen, John F., 1969.B14

Lyon, T. J., 1966.B4

M., 1836.B12

M., A. G., 1837.B10

Mabbott, Thomas Ollive, 1925.B2

Mabie, Hamilton Wright,
    1902.B5
    1904.B1
    1912.B2

McBryde, J. M., 1906.B2

McCarter, Pete Kyle,
    1939.B2
    1940.A2

McClary, Ben Harris,
    1829.B15
    1965.B5
    1966.A2, B5, B6, B7
    1967.B4, B5
    1968.B8, B9
    1969.A1, B15, B16, B17
    1970.B7
    1972.B8, B9

McDermott, John F.,
    1944.B4
    1956.B5, B6
    1965.B6

McDougal, Edward D., 1971.B7

McDowell, George Tremaine,
    1926.B5
    1927.B12

McGee, S. L., 1927.B6

McLendon, Will, 1968.B10

Macy, John, 1913.B3

Mahomet and His Successors,
    1849.B8
    1850.B1, B2, B3, B5, B6, B10
    1851.B2, B7
    1966.A3
    1970.B9, B10

Main Currents in American Thought, 1927.B7

Mantz, H. E., 1917.B2

"Mark Twain's First Lecture: A Parallel," 1956.B1

Martin, Terence, 1959.B10

Martineau, Barbara J., 1971.B6

Marvel, Ik, 1851.B5

"Mary Shelley and John Howard Payne," 1930.B7

"Master of the Obsolete: Washington Irving in the Shadows, A," 1936.B1

Mathews, J. C., 1939.B3

Mayer, P. H., 1847.B3

"Meeting the West," 1937.B7

Melville, Gansevoort, 1966.B9

Melville, Herman, 1966.B10

"Melville's 'Ducking' Duyckinck," 1966.B10

Memoir of Ralph Waldo Emerson, A, 1887.B1

"Memoir of Washington Irving," 1825.B7

"Memoir of Washington Irving, Esq.," 1825.B5

Memoir of Washington Irving. With Selections from His Works, and Criticisms, 1870.A1

Memoirs, Journal, and Correspondence of Thomas Moore, 1856.B5

Memoirs of the Life of Sir Walter Scott, Bart., 1837.B9

"Memorial of Washington Irving," 1860.B10

"Memories of a Hundred Years," 1902.B2

"Memories of Distinguished Authors. Washington Irving," 1871.B1

"Memories of Famous Men," 1902.B1

Menendez y Pelayo, Marcelino, 1895.B2

Mengeling, Marvin E.,
    1964.B7
    1966.B8

Milne, R., 1886.B3

"Mr. Irving," 1823.B1

"Mr. Irving of the Shakespeare Committee: A Bit of Anglo-American Jealousy," 1969.B16

"Mr. Irving of the Shakespeare Committee: Anglo-American Jealousy," 1968.B9

"Mr. Warner on Washington Irving," 1893.B1

"Mr. Washington Irving, Mr. Navarrete, and the Knickerbocker," 1842.B4

Mitchell, D. G.,
    1851.B5
    1863.B3
    1864.B3
    1884.B2
    1897.B5

Mohammed. See Mahomet and His Successors.

Monteiro, George, 1968.B11

Montgolfier, Adélaïde, 1832.B18

Moore, Thomas,
    1856.B5
    1947.B2
    1959.B6
    1966.B5

"Moore-Irving Letter File, The," 1966.B5

"Moore's St. Nick: Model and Motif," 1959.B15

"Morning at Sunnyside with Washington Irving, A," 1873.B1

Morris, G. D., 1916.B3

Morris, John, 1896.B1

Morris, Muriel, 1930.B7

Morris, Robert L., 1945.B4

Morse, James H., 1883.B9

"morte e le maschera: Note sullo Sketch Book, La," 1970.B14

"'Most Negligent Man': Washington Irving's Opinion of John Murray, A," 1969.B1

Mowat, R. B., 1935.B1

Murray, John,
    1891.B4
    1966.A2
    1969.A1, B1

"My First Book. Treasure Island," 1894.B5

My Literary Passions, 1895.B1

Myers, Andrew Breen,
    1958.B6, B7
    1960.B5
    1965.A2, B7
    1966.B9
    1968.B12
    1972.A1, B10

N., C., 1825.B12

Narita, Narihisa, 1947.B4

"Narrative of the Knickerbocker Magazine: Number Twelve," 1860.B11

Natur in den Werken und Briefen des amerikanischen Schriftstellers
    Washington Irving, Die, 1902.A1

Navarrete, Martin Fernandez de,
    1829.B17
    1841.B1, B4
    1842.B1, B2, B3, B4
    1843.B1
    1918.B2

"Navarrete on Spain," 1841.B1

Neal, John,
    1823.B10
    1825.B13
    1936.B6

Negroes, Irving's treatment of, 1970.B12

"New in the Berg Collection: 1962-1964," 1969.B23

"New Verses by Washington Irving," 1932.B1

"New York and New England: Irving's Criticism of American Society,"
    1967.B10

"New York's Dutch Period: An Interpretive Problem," 1961.B1

Nichol, John, 1882.B2

Nichols, Robert H., 1893.B3

"Nil Nisi Bonum,"
    1860.B18, B19
    1863.B4

Noble, Donald R., 1970.B8

Nolan, Olive, 1930.B8

"Nor'wester," 1862.B4

"Note from Washington Irving to Elizabeth Gray Kennedy, A," 1967.B7

"Note on Astoria: Irving's Use of the Robert Stuart Manuscript, A,"
    1950.B3

"Note on Irving's Sources, A," 1953.B3

"Note on the Source of 'Rip Van Winkle,' A," 1954.B1

Notes and Journal of Travel in Europe 1804-1805, 1921.B1

Notes While Preparing Sketch Book &c., 1927.B8

"Notice biographique," 1891.B1

Noyes, James O., 1860.B10

O'Brien, Edward J., 1923.B2

Ogilvie, James, 1941.B1

"Oh These Women! These Women!: Irving's Shrews and Coquettes,"
    1970.B11

Olenjeva, B., 1967.B6

Olive, W. J., 1949.B1

"Ollapodiana," 1836.B11

Olliffe, Charles, 1843.B2

On the Western Tour With Washington Irving: The Journal and Letters
    of Count de Pourtalès, 1968.B16

"On the Writings of Charles Brockden Brown and Washington Irving,"
    1820.B24

"One Hundred Years Ago in the Region of Tulsa," 1933.B4

"One of Irving's Old Cronies," 1883.B7

O'Neill, E. H., 1936.B4

Osborne, Robert S., 1947.A1

Osborne, William S., 1967.B7

Osterweis, Rollin G., 1935.B2

"Our Incomparable Jefferson," 1960.B3

"Our Literary Diplomats, Part II: From the 'Era of Good Feeling' to
    the Ashburton Treaty. Washington Irving," 1900.B1

Outline Sketch of American Literature, An, 1886.B1

"Outre-Mer," 1834.B2

Pacey, W. C. Desmond, 1945.B5

Palm, Ada, 1914.B4

Paltsits, V. H., 1932.B6

Parrington, Vernon L., 1927.B7

Pattee, Fred Lewis, 1923.B3

"Paul Bunyan and Rip Van Winkle," 1946.B1

Paulding, James Kirke, 1926.B3

Pauly, Thomas H., 1971.B8

Payne, John Howard,
    1885.B1
    1910.B1
    1930.B7

Payne, W. M., 1910.B2

Peck, Richard E., 1967.B8

Pemberton, T. E., 1904.B2

Penney, Clara Louise,
    1926.B6
    1958.B8

Pensamiento, 1841.B4

Perrin, P. G., 1925.B3

"Personal Reminiscences of Washington Irving," 1896.B1

Pickering, James H., 1966.B10

Pictorial Mode: Space and Time in the Art of Bryant, Irving and
    Cooper, The, 1971.B10

"Pierre M. Irving's Account of Peter Irving, Washington Irving, and
    the Corrector," 1971.B4

"Pirated Editions of Schoolcraft's Oneóta," 1959.B4

Plath, Otto, 1913.B4

Pochmann, Henry A.,
    1928.B2
    1930.B9, B10
    1934.B6
    1967.B9
    1969.B18
    1970.B9, B10
    1971.B9

Poe, Edgar Allan,
    1835.B21
    1837.B11
    1841.B6, B7
    1842.B5
    1876.B2
    1925.B2
    1955.B6
    1956.B12
    1968.B6

"Poe, Irving and The Southern Literary Messenger," 1955.B6

"Poe, Irving, Hawthorne," 1876.B2

"Poems of Washington Irving, The," 1930.B6

"Poe's Use of Irving's Astoria in 'The Journal of Julius Rodman,'"
    1968.B6

Political Activities of Phillip Freneau and Washington Irving, The,
    1969.B25

Pollard, Matilda, 1911.B4

"Polly Holman's Wedding: Notes by Washington Irving," 1934.B9

"Possible Ancestor of Diedrich Knickerbocker, A," 1930.B11

Pourtalès, Count Albert-Alexandre de, 1968.B16

Prades, Juana de José, 1959.B11

premiers interprètes de la pensée americaine. Essai d'histoire et de
    littérature sur l'évolution du puritanisme aux États-Unis, Les,
    1909.B3

Prescott, W. H.,
    1822.B26
    1829.B18
    1845.B3
    1915.B2
    1930.B5

Preston, William C.,
    1930.B15
    1933.B6

Price, George R., 1948.B3

"Pride of the Village, The,"
    1879.B1
    1968.B11

"Problem in Plagiarism: Washington Irving and Cousen de Courchamps,
    A," 1968.B10

Professional Idler: Washington Irving's European Years: The Sketch
    Book and Its Sequels, 1966.A1

Proffer, Carl R., 1968.B13

Prose Writers of America, The, 1847.B2

Providence Public Library Monthly Reference Lists, 1883.B4

Publisher and His Friends: Memoir and Correspondence of the Late
    John Murray, A, 1891.B4

Pushkin, Alexander,
    1955.B2
    1968.B13
    1969.B10

"Puskin's Skazka o 'zolotom petuske' and Washington Irving's 'The
    Legend of the Arabian Astrologer,'" 1969.B10

Putnam, G. H.,
    1915.B1
    1926.B7

Putnam, G. P.,
    1860.B16
    1871.B1
    1880.A1

Quesnel, Leo, 1882.B3

Quest for Nationality, The, 1957.B7

Quidor, John,
    1957.B10
    1965.B2
    1972.B12

R., J. A., 1837.B12

Rabson, Barrie, 1951.B2

"Rambles with Washington Irving: Quotations From an Unpublished
    Autobiography of William C. Preston," 1930.B15

Randolph, A. D. F., 1890.B1

Randolph, a Novel, 1823.B10

Ratner, Lorman A., 1972.A1

"Real Ichabod Crane, The," 1968.B3

Rebecca Gratz: A Study in Charm, 1935.B2

Reception, British. See individual titles of Irving's works.

Reception, French,
    1820.B21
    1822.B23
    1825.B12
    1827.B1, B2
    1828.B18
    1829.B12

(Reception, French)
    1832.B18
    1835.B19
    1843.B2
    1851.B3
    1852.B1
    1855.B6
    1876.B3
    1916.B3
    1917.B2
    1960.B7

Reception, German,
    1822.B21
    1824.B1, B18, B34
    1825.B3, B4, B9, B14
    1829.B13
    1830.B1, B2, B8
    1831.B8, B11
    1832.B1
    1834.B1
    1835.B1, B5, B9, B13, B17
    1836.B1, B7, B8
    1837.B6
    1844.B1
    1845.B1
    1850.B6
    1857.B1
    1859.B1
    1932.B8
    1956.B8
    1957.A1, B3, B4
    1958.B3

Reception, Italian, 1931.B3

Reception, Polish, 1965.B3

Reception, Russian,
    1955.B2
    1968.B13
    1969.B13

Reception, Spanish, 1930.B12

"Recollections of Irving. By His Publisher," 1860.B16

"Recollections of Washington Irving,"
    1862.B1
    1869.B1

Redding, Cyrus, 1860.B17

Reed, Herbert B.,   1963.B4

Reed, Kenneth T.,   1970.B11, B12

Reichart, Walter A.,
    1935.B4
    1936.B5
    1941.B2
    1945.B6
    1953.B5
    1956.B7, B8, B9
    1957.A1, B3, B4, B5
    1959.B12, B13
    1962.B5
    1968.B14
    1970.B13
    1973.B3

"Remark on Knickerbocker, A,"   1824.B35

"Remarks of Col. Aspinwall,"   1859.B3

"Remarks of Mr. Everett,"   1859.B5

"Remarks of Mr. Longfellow,"   1859.B10

"Remarks of Professor Felton,"   1859.B6

"Reminiscences of Brooklyn,"   1857.B4

"Reminiscences of the Late Washington Irving,"   1860.B12

"Reminiscences of the Late Washington Irving: Number Two,"   1860.B13

Reminiscences of William C. Preston, The,   1933.B6

"Reparaciones de la historia de España: Fernandez de Navarrete y
    Washington Irving,"   1918.B2

"Retrospect of American Humor, A,"   1901.B2

"Revealing the Source of Irving's 'Rip Van Winkle,'"
    1955.B3
    1956.B3

Reviews, foreign. See Reception.

Richards, T. A.,   1856.B6

Richardson, Charles F.,   1889.B2

Riese, Teut,   1958.B9

Ringe, Donald A., 1971.B10

"Rip, Ichabod, and the American Imagination," 1959.B10

"Rip Van Winkle,"
    1820.B20, B22
    1821.B5, B6
    1822.B3
    1856.B1
    1868.B1
    1876.B1
    1883.B12
    1901.A2
    1903.B2
    1912.B1
    1923.B2
    1927.B4
    1928.B1
    1930.B9
    1934.B7
    1936.B1
    1937.B6
    1945.B7
    1946.B1, B2
    1947.B4
    1950.B5
    1952.B4
    1954.B1
    1955.B3
    1956.B3, B7, B9, B10
    1957.B5, B6
    1959.B8, B10, B14
    1960.B1, B3, B8
    1961.B6
    1962.B2
    1964.B4, B5, B7
    1966.B2, B8
    1967.B10
    1969.B14, B19, B20, B21
    1970.B2
    1971.A1, B11
    1972.B6
    1974.B2

"Rip Van Winkle: A Psychoanalytic Note on the Story and Its Author,"
    1959.B8

Ripley, George,
    1851.B6
    1855.B2

"Ripvanwinkle," 1821.B6

Rocky Mountains, The. See Adventures of Captain Bonneville.

Robert Stuart's Traveling Memoranda: A Source for Washington Irving's
    Astoria, 1951.B3

Rodes, Sara P.,
    1956.B10
    1957.B6

Rodriguez Pinilla, Tomas, 1884.B3

"Romantic Metamorphosis in Irving's Western Tour," 1969.B27

Romanticos y Bohemios. Un Hispanofilo Ilustre, 1929.B5

Rosenzweig, L. G., 1887.B3

Roth, Martin,
    1965.A3
    1968.B15

Rudwin, Maximilian, 1931.B5

Rusk, R. L., 1925.B4

Russell, Jason Almus, 1931.B6

Russian Studies of American Literature, A Bibliography, 1969.B13

S., W. S., 1912.B3

Sabbadini, Silvano, 1970.B14

Sachot, Octave, 1855.B6

Salmagundi,
    1807.B1, B2
    1811.B1, B2
    1819.B4
    1820.B6
    1823.B6, B7, B8
    1824.B5
    1825.B6, B11, B13, B14
    1829.B14
    1832.B3
    1835.B15
    1845.B2
    1891.A1
    1912.B2
    1925.B3
    1936.B2
    1947.B1

(Salmagundi)
    1954.B2
    1965.A1
    1968.B1, B15
    1971.A4
    1972.B2
    1973.B4

"Salmagundi," 1832.B3

"Salmagundi and Its Publisher," 1947.B1

"Salmagundi: Problems in Editing the So-Called First Edition
    (1807-08)," 1973.B4

Sampson, F. A., 1910.B3

Sandell, George W., 1903.A1

Satire, Humor, and Burlesque in the Early Works of Washington Irving,
    1965.A3

"Satiric Use of Names in Irving's History of New York, The," 1968.B7

Saunders, Frederick,
    1894.B4
    1932.B6

"Scandinavians in the Works of Washington Irving," 1927.B3

Schalck de la Faverie, A., 1909.B3

Scheick, William J., 1972.B11

Schik, Berthold, 1971.B11

Schiller, Friedrich, 1959.B13

Scott, Sir Walter. See also Abbotsford and Newstead Abbey,
    1837.B9
    1947.B3
    1949.B3
    1965.B5

"Scraps from the Book Kept at Stratford-upon-Avon," 1833.B2

"Second Footnote to Washington Irving, A," 1966.B12

Sedgwick, A. G., 1883.B10

Sedley, E., 1876.B3

Seigler, Milledge B., 1947.B5

<u>Sermons on the Occasion of the Death of the Late Washington Irving</u>,
    1859.A1

"Seven Letters of Washington Irving," 1945.B3

"'Seven Sons of Lara, The': A Washington Irving Manuscript,"
    1972.B11

Shakespeare, William,
    1932.B1
    1959.B5

"Shakespearean Elements in Irving's <u>Sketch Book</u>," 1959.B5

<u>Shapers of American Fiction, The</u>, 1947.B6

Shaw, Catherine M., 1971.B12

Shelley, Mary, 1930.B7

<u>Short Fiction in American Periodicals: 1775-1825</u>, 1968.B4

<u>Short Fiction of Washington Irving, The</u>, 1971.A1

Short, Julee, 1971.B13

<u>Short Sketch of W. Irving and His Writings, A</u>, 1903.A1

Short Story,
    1909.B1
    1923.B2, B3
    1928.B2
    1961.B6
    1967.B6
    1968.B4
    1970.A2
    1971.A1, B3, B6

<u>Short Story in English, The</u>, 1909.B1

Simison, Barbara D.,
    1937.B1
    1949.B2
    1963.B5
    1964.B8
    1966.B11, B12

"Simms and Irving," 1967.B11

Simms, William Gilmore, 1967.B11

Sir Nathaniel, 1853.B3

Six Classic American Writers: An Introduction, 1961.B5

Sketch Book, The (See also "English Writers on America";
    "Legend of Sleepy Hollow, The"; "Pride of the Village, The";
    "Rip Van Winkle"; "Spectre Bridegroom, The"; "Wife, The"),
    1819.B1, B2, B4, B5
    1820.B1, B2, B3, B4, B5, B6, B7, B8, B9, B10, B13, B14, B15, B20,
      B21, B22, B24
    1821.B4, B5
    1822.B3, B15, B22, B23, B26
    1824.B4, B5, B30, B34
    1825.B10, B13
    1830.B10
    1844.B2
    1845.B2
    1848.B6
    1850.B8
    1856.B1
    1859.B3
    1863.B1, B2
    1875.B1
    1876.B2
    1879.B2
    1883.B6
    1887.B3
    1888.B1, B2
    1891.A1, B1
    1906.B2, B3
    1911.B1, B2, B3, B4
    1912.B3, B4
    1913.B1, B2
    1914.B4
    1919.B1
    1923.B2, B3
    1925.B1
    1927.B8, B9
    1930.B10
    1931.B6
    1933.B5
    1935.B1
    1936.B1, B6
    1946.B3, B5
    1947.B6
    1954.B3
    1957.A1, B5
    1959.B3, B5
    1964.B5
    1965.A1
    1966.A1
    1969.B8, B9, B14, B22
    1970.B7, B11, B14, B15
    1971.A1, A4, B8
    1972.A1

"Sketch Book, The," 1820.B14

Sloane, David E. E., 1971.B14

Small, M. R., 1930.B11

Smiles, Samuel, 1891.B4

Smith, Francès P.,
    1937.B2, B3
    1938.A1, B2

Smith, Herbert F., 1969.B20

Snell, George,
    1946.B3
    1947.B6

Sokol, D. M., 1972.B12

"Some Anglo-American Literary Contacts," 1947.B3

"Some Autobiographical Notes of Washington Irving," 1963.B5

"Some Letters of Washington Irving: 1833-1843," 1963.B3

"Some Printings of Irving in Finland before 1900," 1958.B5

"Some Remarks on the Genius and Writings of Washington Irving, Esq.,"
    1820.B19

"Some Sources of Irving's 'Italian Banditti' Stories," 1959.B12

Somner, William S.,
    1835.B22
    1836.B13

Soria, Andrés, 1956.B11

Sources,
    1821.B6
    1822.B2
    1824.B22, B28
    1856.B5
    1868.B1
    1883.B12
    1901.A2
    1928.B2
    1929.B3
    1930.B4, B9, B10, B11
    1937.B5
    1938.B2

(Sources)
    1945.B2
    1950.B3
    1951.B3
    1952.B1, B2
    1953.B3
    1954.B1
    1955.B3, B7
    1956.B3, B4, B7, B9
    1957.A1
    1959.B12
    1963.B4
    1964.B1, B9
    1966.B13
    1968.B3, B10
    1969.B29
    1970.B2, B6
    1971.A4, B3, B8

Southam, Herbert, 1933.B7

"Southern Sleepy Hollow, A," 1969.B2

Southey, Robert,
    1891.B4
    1946.B5

"Soviet Controversy Over Pushkin and Washington Irving, The,"
    1955.B2

"Spain," 1842.B1

Spanish Adventures of Washington Irving, The, 1940.A1

Spanish Background of American Literature, The, 1955.B7

Spanish Papers,
    1839.B1
    1866.B1
    1867.B1, B2
    1958.B7

Spaulding, George F., 1968.B16

Spaulding, Kenneth A.,
    1950.B3
    1951.B3

"Spectre Bridegroom, The,"
    1821.B5
    1912.B4
    1930.B9

"Spell of Nature in Irving's Famous Stories, The," 1969.B20

Spencer, Benjamin T., 1957.B7

Spencer, J. Seldon, 1859.A1

Spiller, Robert E.,
    1926.B8
    1937.B4

Spirit of American Literature, The, 1913.B3

Spirit of the Age; or, Contemporary Portraits, The, 1825.B10

Sprenger, R., 1901.A2

Springer, Haskell S.,
    1969.B21, B22
    1972.A1
    1974.B2

Starke, Aubrey, 1935.B5

State Triumvirate, A Political Tale: and the Epistles of Brevet
    Major Pindar Puff, The, 1819.B5

Steegmuller, Francis, 1960.B6

Stevens, A., 1855.B7

Stevenson, Robert Louis, 1894.B5

Stocker, M. H., 1973.B4

Stoddard, R. H., 1883.B11

"Stout Gentleman, The," 1860.B15

Strobridge, Truman S., 1966.B13

"Structure and Tone in 'Rip Van Winkle': The Irony of Silence,"
    1966.B8

Stuart, Robert, 1951.B3

Studien zur Charakterisierungstechnik in Kurzgeschichten Washington
    Irvings, E. A. Poes, und Nathaniel Hawthornes, 1950.B1

Studies of Irving, 1880.A1

Study of Hawthorne, A, 1876.B1

Study of History, A, 1934.B7

"Study of Irving," 1894.B1

Study of Washington Irving's Development as a Man of Letters to 1825,
    A, 1947.A1

Sumner, George, 1859.B11

"Sunny Master of Sunnyside, The," 1961.B2

Sunnyside,
    1853.B4
    1856.B6
    1864.B1
    1865.B1, B2
    1884.B1
    1951.B2
    1957.B1
    1960.B6
    1972.A1

"Sunnyside, the Home of Washington Irving," 1856.B6

Swift, L., 1900.B1

Szladits, Lola L., 1969.B23

Takeda, Katsuhiko, 1963.B6

Tales of a Traveller. See also "Adventure of the German Student";
    "Devil and Tom Walker, The",
    1824.B3, B8, B9, B10, B11, B12, B13, B14, B15, B16, B17, B18, B19,
        B20, B21, B22, B23, B24, B25, B26, B27, B28, B29, B30, B32,
        B33, B34, B36, B37
    1825.B1, B2, B3, B4, B6, B8, B9, B11, B12, B13
    1842.B5
    1860.B15
    1894.B5
    1913.B4
    1925.B1
    1930.B10
    1931.B7
    1955.B4
    1957.A1
    1959.B12, B16
    1965.A1, B8
    1971.A1

Taylor, Bayard, 1868.B1

Taylor, J. F., 1915.B2

"Teaching of The Sketch Book, The," 1914.B4

Teichmann, Elizabeth, 1955.B4

Tennyson, Alfred, Lord, 1879.B1

"Tennyson and Washington Irving," 1879.B1

Terrell, Dahlia J.,
    1967.A2
    1969.B24

"Textual Errors in A Tour on the Prairies," 1969.B24

Textual Scholarship,
    1927.B12
    1937.B2
    1941.B3
    1967.A1, A2
    1968.B1
    1969.B3, B7, B22, B24
    1970.B1, B9, B10
    1971.B2
    1973.B4

Textual Study of Washington Irving's A Tour on the Prairies, A,
    1967.A2

Thackeray, William M.,
    1860.B18, B19
    1863.B4
    1890.B1

Thoburn, Joseph B.,
    1932.B7
    1955.B5

Thompson, J. B., 1883.B12

Thompson, Ralph, 1935.B6

"Three Arkansas Travelers," 1945.B4

Tieck, Ludwig, 1931.B8

Tillett, A. S., 1960.B7

Tilton, Theodore,
    1859.B12, B13
    1860.B10

Todd, Edgeley W.,
     1957.B8
     1961.B7
     1964.B9

Tour in Scotland 1817 and Other Manuscript Notes, 1927.B9

Tour on the Prairies, A,
     1835.B1, B2, B3, B4, B5, B6, B7, B11, B12, B16, B17, B18, B20
     1931.B6
     1932.B7
     1933.B4, B5
     1937.B1
     1944.B4
     1945.B4
     1955.B5
     1956.B5
     1957.B8
     1959.B9
     1966.B3
     1967.A2, B3, B12
     1968.B5, B16
     1969.B23, B24, B27
     1970.A1
     1971.B13
     1973.B2

Townsend, Walter, 1879.B2

Toynbee, Arnold J., 1934.B7

"Tragedy and Irony in Knickerbocker's History," 1940.B2

"Travel Books and Histories in Irving's European Journal, 1804-1805,"
     1969.B29

Travel Sketch Book and the American Author, The, 1971.B8

Trent, William P.,
     1901.B2
     1912.B4
     1921.B1

Trop, Sylvia, 1945.B7

Troughton, Marion, 1957.B9

Tuckerman, H. T.,
     1853.B4
     1860.B4
     1896.B2

Turnbladh, Edwin, 1966.B13

Twain, Mark. See Clemens, Samuel L.

"Two Famous Bachelors and Their Love Stories," 1902.B4

"Two of Washington Irving's Friends Identified," 1966.B6

"Two Unpublished Anecdotes by Fernán Caballero," 1934.B4

"Two Voices of Washington Irving, The," 1972.B6

U., 1831.B11

Über die Quelle von Washington Irvings Rip Van Winkle, 1901.A2

"Über Washington Irving," 1824.B34

"Uncollected Tale by Washington Irving, An," 1934.B1

Underwood, F. H., 1890.B2

"Unpublished Letters of Washington Irving: Sunnyside and New York
    Chronicles," 1927.B11

"Unpublished Poem by Washington Irving, An," 1967.B8

"Unpublished Washington Irving Manuscript, An," 1965.B6

"Unwritten Drama, An," 1925.B2

Vail, R. W. G., 1929.B6

Van Arkel, G, 1902.B6

Van Buren, Martin,
    1902.B6
    1970.B7

Van Wart, R. B., 1949.B3

"Vermischte Schriften," 1836.B1

Verplanck, Gulian C.,
    1819.B5
    1833.B3

Vincent, L. H., 1906.B3

"Visit to Sunniside on the Banks of the Hudson, A," 1865.B1

"Visit to Sunnyside, A," 1865.B2

"Visit to Washington Irving, A," 1859.B13

Von Faber, Cecilia Böhl. <u>See</u> Caballero, Fernán.

<u>Voyage to the Eastern Part of Terra Firma, A</u>, 1898.B1

<u>Voyages and Discoveries of the Companions of Columbus</u>,
    1831.B1, B2, B3, B4, B5, B6, B7, B8
    1929.B2

W., C. A., 1851.B7

W., J. V., 1883.B15

Wadepuhl, Walter, 1932.B8

Wagenknecht, Edward, 1962.A1

Wainstein, Lia, 1958.B10

Waldron, William Watson, 1867.B3

Walker, R. J., 1954.B3

Wallace, H. B., 1856.B7

"Want of a National Name," 1839.B1

"War with the Book Pirates," 1937.B4

Warner, Charles Dudley,
    1880.A1, B1
    1881.A1
    1883.B13
    1884.A1
    1893.B1

"Was There a Real Rip Van Winkle?," 1927.B4

"Was Washington Irving Stendhal's first American critic?," 1953.B2

"Washington and Hamilton," 1857.B3

<u>Washington Irving</u>,
    1879.A1
    1881.A1
    1883.B14
    1890.B2
    1901.A1
    1963.A1

"Washington Irving,"
    1824.B20
    1832.B2
    1835.B22
    1836.B4
    1841.B3
    1846.B1
    1847.B3
    1848.B2, B5, B7
    1849.B1
    1851.B6
    1853.B1
    1855.B2
    1856.B3
    1860.B17
    1862.B2, B5
    1864.B3
    1880.B1
    1883.B9, B10
    1892.B2, B3
    1893.B2, B3
    1926.B7
    1942.B1
    1959.B3

Washington Irving: A Bibliography, 1933.A1

"Washington Irving--A Bibliography," 1932.B4

Washington Irving á Bordeaux, 1947.A2

"Washington Irving: A Grace Note on 'The Pride of the Village,'"
    1968.B11

"Washington Irving: A Revaluation," 1946.B3

Washington Irving. A Sketch, 1891.A1

Washington Irving: A Tribute, 1972.A1

"Washington Irving alla ricerca del passato," 1958.B10

"Washington Irving: Amateur or Professional?," 1967.B9

Washington Irving: An American Study, 1802-1832, 1965.A1

"Washington Irving: An Unrecorded Periodical Publication," 1967.B2

"Washington Irving and Adet Kissam," 1860.B9

"Washington Irving and Andrew Jackson," 1945.B8

"Washington Irving and Astoria," 1927.B2

"Washington Irving and Charles Dickens," 1945.B5

Washington Irving and Cotemporaries, in Thirty Life Sketches,
     1867.B3

"Washington Irving and E. A. Poe," 1956.B12

"Washington Irving and Fernán Caballero," 1930.B13

Washington Irving and France, 1938.A1

"Washington Irving and Frederick Saunders," 1932.B6

"Washington Irving and Frontier Speech," 1967.B3

Washington Irving and Germany, 1957.A1

"Washington Irving and Gilbert Stuart Newton: A New-York Mirror
     Contribution Identified, 1972.B10

"Washington Irving and His Friends," 1883.B15

"Washington Irving and Italy," 1930.B4

"Washington Irving and Joseph C. Cabell," 1951.B1

"Washington Irving and Ludwig Tieck," 1931.B8

"Washington Irving and Matilda Hoffman," 1926.B9

"Washington Irving and New England Witchlore," 1973.B1

Washington Irving, and Other Essays, Biographical, Historical,
     and Philosophical, 1922.B2

"Washington Irving and Scotland," 1949.B3

"Washington Irving and Sunnyside," 1957.B1

"Washington Irving and the Astor Library," 1968.B12

"Washington Irving and the Battle of Waterloo," 1939.B1

"Washington Irving and the Conservative Imagination," 1964.B5

"Washington Irving and The Empire of the West," 1971.B5

"Washington Irving and the 'Extension of the Empire of Freedom': An
     Unrecorded Contribution to the Evening Post, May 14, 1804,"
     1972.B5

Washington Irving and the House of Murray: Geoffrey Crayon Charms
the British, 1817-1856, 1969.A1

"Washington Irving and the Journal of Captain Bonneville," 1956.B6

"Washington Irving and the Knickerbocker Group," 1933.B3

"Washington Irving and the Negro," 1970.B12

Washington Irving and the Storrows: Letters from England and the
Continent, 1821-1828, 1933.B8

"Washington Irving and the Theatre," 1968.B14

"Washington Irving--Another Letter from Spain," 1953.B1

Washington Irving. Apuntes literarios. Las Cien mejores obras de
la literatura universal, 1930.B2

"Washington Irving as a Source for Borel and Dumas," 1936.B5

"Washington Irving as a Writer," 1848.B1

"Washington Irving as Imitator of Swift," 1934.B8

Washington Irving as United States Minister to Spain: The Revolution
of 1843, 1969.B30

"Washington Irving at Newstead Abbey," 1962.B4

"Washington Irving, Barham Livius and Weber," 1950.B2

"Washington Irving, Biographer," 1969.B26

"Washington Irving Collection Formed by Isaac N. Seligman, The,"
1920.B1

Washington Irving: Commemoration of the 100th Anniversary of His
Birth by the Washington Irving Association, 1884.A1

"Washington Irving Country, The," 1902.B5

Washington Irving Diary: Spain, 1828-1829, 1926.B6

"Washington Irving Discovers the Frontier," 1957.B8

"Washington Irving, Esq.," 1821.B5

Washington Irving Esquire, Ambassador at Large from the New World to
the Old, 1925.A1

"Washington Irving Exhibition," 1914.B2

Washington Irving, Explorer of American Legend,   1944.A1

Washington Irving, Fur Trade Chronicler: An Analysis of Astoria
    With Notes For a Corrected Edition,   1965.A2

"Washington Irving; His Home and His Works," 1855.B3

"Washington Irving im Rheinland (1822). Ein Beitrag zur Geschichte
    der Rhein-Romantik," 1927.B1

"Washington Irving in der Dresdener und der Pariser Gesellschaft
    1822-1825," 1973.B3

"Washington Irving in England," 1904.B2

"Washington Irving in London in 1846," 1966.B9

"Washington Irving in Mississippi," 1943.B1

"Washington Irving in Russia: Pushkin, Gogol, Marlinsky," 1968.B13

"Washington Irving in Spain: Unpublished Letters Chiefly to Mrs.
    Henry O'Shea, 1844-1854," 1958.B8

"Washington Irving in Tarrytown," 1909.B2

"Washington Irving in the Revue Encyclopédique," 1960.B7

"Washington Irving, Indians, and the West," 1968.B5

"Washington Irving Manuscripts," 1914.B1

"Washington Irving, Matilda Hoffman, and Emily Foster," 1933.B9

Washington Irving: Moderation Displayed, 1962.A1

"Washington Irving on French Romanticism," 1937.B2

Washington Irving on the Prairie, or A Narrative of a Tour of the
    Southwest in the Year 1832, 1937.B1

"Washington Irving Once More," 1906.B2

"Washington Irving Postscript, A," 1967.B5

Washington Irving Reconsidered,
    1969.B3, B4, B5, B7, B8, B12, B20, B21, B26, B27, B29

Washington Irving: Representative Selections, 1934.B6

"Washington Irving: Rip Van Winkle," 1971.B11

"Washington Irving (1783-1859) und Friedrich Schiller (1759-1805)," 1959.B13

"Washington Irving: The Artist in a Changing World," 1948.B1

"Washington Irving, the Fosters, and Some Poetry," 1937.B3

"Washington Irving, the Fosters, and the Forsters," 1935.B4

"Washington Irving: The Sketch Book of Geoffrey Crayon, Gent.," 1969.B9

"Washington Irving to Walter Scott: Two Unpublished Letters," 1965.B5

"Washington Irving to William C. Preston: An Unpublished Letter," 1947.B5

Washington Irving: Traveller, Diplomat, Author, 1897.B3

"Washington Irving. Travels in Missouri and the South," 1910.B3

Washington Irving und seine Beziehungen zur englischen Literatur des 18. Jahrunderts, 1911.A1

"Washington Irving Writes from Granada," 1935.B3

"Washington Irving y el alma espanola," 1962.B3

Washington Irving's A History of New York with Emphasis on the 1848 Revision, 1967.A1

"Washington Irving's Alhambra," 1961.B4

"Washington Irving's Alhambra," 1832.B13

"Washington Irving's 'Alhambra,'" 1892.B1

"Washington Irving's Amiable Scotch Friends," 1966.B7

"Washington Irving's Andalusia," 1970.B3

Washington Irving's Astoria: A Critical Study, 1968.A1

"Washington Irving's Aufenthalt in Dresden," 1914.B3

"Washington Irving's Biographie Georg Washingtons," 1857.B1

"Washington Irving's British Edition of Slidell's A Year in Spain," 1969.B17

"Washington Irving's 'Celebrated English Poet,'" 1946.B5

"Washington Irving's Comedy of Politics," 1916.B2

"Washington Irving's Conquest of Granada," 1829.B7

"Washington Irving's Conquest of Granada: A Spanish Experiment that Failed," 1974.B1

Washington Irving's Contribution to The Corrector, 1968.B15

"Washington Irving's Einfluss auf Wilhelm Hauff," 1913.B4

Washington Irving's Fiction in the Light of French Criticism, 1916.B3

"Washington Irving's First Academic Laurels," 1965.B7

"Washington Irving's First Stay in Paris," 1930.B14

"Washington Irving's Friend and Collaborator: Barham John Livius, Esq.," 1941.B2

"Washington Irving's Hispanic Literature," 1972.B1

"Washington Irving's Influence on German Literature," 1957.B4

"Washington Irving's 'Insuperable Diffidence,'" 1971.B14

"Washington Irving's Interest in German Folklore," 1957.B5

Washington Irving's Knickerbocker's History of New York: Folk History as a Literary Form, 1971.A3

"Washington Irving's Knowledge of Dante," 1939.B3

"Washington Irving's Leben Muhammed's und seiner Nachfolger," 1850.B6

"Washington Irving's Letters to Mary Kennedy," 1934.B10

"Washington Irving's Librettos," 1948.B3

"Washington Irving's 'Life of Capt. James Lawrence,'" 1959.B1

"Washington Irving's Life of Columbus," 1828.B3

"Washington Irving's Madrid Journal 1827-1828," 1958.B6

"Washington Irving's Mexico: A Lost Fragment," 1915.B2

"Washington Irving's Miscellanies," 1835.B15

"Washington Irving's Moorish Manuscript," 1958.B7

"Washington Irving's 'My Uncle,'" 1964.B8

"Washington Irving's neuestes Gemälde: 'A tour on the Prairies,'" 1835.B5

"Washington Irving's neuestes Werk," 1835.B13

"Washington Irving's New 'Sketch Book,'" 1832.B16

"Washington Irving's New Work," 1824.B26

"Washington Irving's Notes on Fernán Caballero's Stories," 1934.B5

"Washington Irving's Old Christmas," 1879.B2

"Washington Irving's 'On Passaic Falls,'" 1965.B4

"Washington Irving's 'Peter' Pun," 1970.B8

"Washington Irving's Place in American Literature," 1906.B1

"Washington Irving's Quelle für seinen 'Rip Van Winkle,'" 1956.B9

"Washington Irving's Reise durch Österreich," 1962.B5

"Washington Irving's Reisen der Gefährten des Colombo," 1831.B9

"Washington Irving's Religion," 1926.B10

"Washington Irving's Revision of the Tonquin Episode in Astoria," 1969.B11

"Washington Irving's Services to American History," 1897.B2

"Washington Irving's 'Sketch Book, "
    1911.B1, B2, B3, B4
    1912.B3

Washington Irving's Sketch Book: A Critical Edition, 1969.B22

"Washington Irving's 'Snuggery,'" 1960.B6

"Washington Irving's Use of Traditional Folklore,"
    1956.B10
    1957.B6

"Washington Irving's Wilderness," 1966.B4

"Washington Irving's Works," 1850.B4

"Washington Irving's Works in Italy," 1931.B3

Watts, Charles H., II,
    1955.B6
    1956.B12

Weatherspoon, Mary A.,
    1969.B25
    1970.B15

Webb, James W., 1962.B6

Weber, Carl Maria von, 1948.B3

Webster, Clarence M.,
    1932.B9
    1934.B8

Wegelin, Christof A.,
    1946.B4
    1947.B7

Weller, Arthur, 1932.B10

Wells, George C., 1955.B5

Wendell, Barrett, 1900.B2

Wess, Robert C., 1971.A4

West, Elsie Lee,
    1963.B7
    1969.B26

Wetzel, George, 1952.B4

"What Does Irving Say?," 1928.B1

"Whim-Whamsical Bachelors in Salmagundi, The," 1972.B2

Whipple, Edwin P., 1887.B4

White, T. W., 1918.B2

Whitford, Kathryn, 1969.B27

Whitman, Walt, 1857.B4

Who Are the Major American Writers?, 1972.B3

"Why Irving Was Never Married," 1862.B3, B4

Whyte, Peter, 1964.B10

"Wife, The,"
    1819.B3
    1906.B2
    1927.B8
    1969.B4, B8

Wilkins, W. G., 1916.B4

Williams, Lawrence, 1909.B4

Williams, Ruth S., 1957.B10

Williams, Stanley T.,
    1926.B9, B10
    1927.B8, B9, B10, B11, B12
    1928.B3
    1930.B13, B14
    1931.B7
    1933.B8, B9
    1934.B4, B5, B9, B10, B11, B12
    1935.A1
    1936.A1
    1937.B1, B5
    1938.B3
    1941.B3
    1945.B8
    1950.B4, B5
    1955.B7

"Willis at Sunnyside," 1857.B5

"Willis at Sunnyside. No. II," 1857.B6

Willis, N. P.,
    1857.B5, B6
    1860.B10

Wilson, James Grant, 1886.B4

Wilson, James L., 1946.B5

Wimsatt, Mary A., 1967.B11

Winsor, Justin, 1891.B5

Winterich, J. T., 1934.B13

Winthrop, R. C., 1860.B20

Wise, Daniel, 1883.B14

Wolfe, J. W., 1937.B6

Wolfert's Roost,
    1855.B1, B5, B6, B7
    1933.B1, B2, B7
    1968.B10

Women, Irving's treatment of, 1970.B11

Wood, James Playsted, 1967.B12

Woodberry, G. E., 1902.B7

Woodring, Carl H., 1972.A1

Woodward, Robert H.,
    1959.B14, B15
    1964.B11

World of Washington Irving, The, 1944.B2

Wright, Nathalia,
    1959.B16
    1965.B8
    1969.B28, B29

Writers of Knickerbocker New York, The, 1912.B2

"Writings of Washington Irving, The," 1836.B13

Wynne, J., 1862.B5

X., 1825.B14

Yanow, Lilli Anne, 1969.B30

Yarborough, M. C.,
    1930.B15
    1933.B6

"Young American Abroad," 1958.B4

Young, John P., 1947.A2

Young, Philip, 1960.B8

Zabriskie, G. A., 1944.B5

Zeydel, E. H., 1931.B8

Zirkle, Mary, 1937.B7

"Zu Washington Irvings Skizzenbuch (Stratford am Avon)," 1888.B1

Zug, Charles G., III, 1968.B17

<u>Zur Kenntnis der altenglischen Buhne</u>, 1888.B1